Dreams of a Lifetime

Dreams of a Lifetime

HOW WHO WE ARE SHAPES
HOW WE IMAGINE OUR FUTURE

Karen A. Cerulo

Janet M. Ruane

PRINCETON UNIVERSITY PRESS

PRINCETON AND OXFORD

Published by Princeton University Press
41 William Street, Princeton, New Jersey 08540
6 Oxford Street, Woodstock, Oxfordshire OX20 1TR

press.princeton.edu

Library of Congress Cataloging-in-Publication Data

Names: Cerulo, Karen A., author. | Ruane, Janet M., author.
Title: Dreams of a lifetime : how who we are shapes how we imagine our
    future / Karen A. Cerulo, Janet M. Ruane.
Description: Princeton, New Jersey : Princeton University Press, [2022] |
    Includes bibliographical references and index.
Identifiers: LCCN 2021040790 (print) | LCCN 2021040791 (ebook) | ISBN
    9780691229096 (hardback ; alk. paper) | ISBN 9780691229089 (ebook)
Subjects: LCSH: Desire. | Dreams. | Ambition. | Fantasy. | Self-actualization
    (Psychology) | Identity (Psychology) | BISAC: SOCIAL SCIENCE /
    Sociology / General | PSYCHOLOGY / General
Classification: LCC BF575.D4 C44 2022 (print) | LCC BF575.D4 (ebook) |
    DDC 135/.3—dc23
LC record available at https://lccn.loc.gov/2021040790
LC ebook record available at https://lccn.loc.gov/2021040791

British Library Cataloging-in-Publication Data is available

Editorial: Meagan Levinson and Jacqueline Delaney
Production Editorial: Ellen Foos and Jaden Young
Text Design: Karl Spurzem
Jacket Design: Lauren Smith
Production: Erin Suydam
Publicity: Maria Whelan and Kathryn Stevens
Copyeditor: Hank Southgate

Jacket image: Devonyu / iStock

This book has been composed in Arno Pro

Printed on acid-free paper. ∞

Printed in Canada

10 9 8 7 6 5 4 3 2 1

Contents

Illustrations

Figures

Tables

Acknowledgments

So many people support the writing of a book. First and fore-most, we are grateful to all the study participants who told us about their dreams for the future. We loved hearing what they had to say and appreciated people taking the time to share their thoughts with us. Our thanks also go to our many family members who let us test out the idea for this book and an-swered some questions on dreaming. Their responses made us more confident that we were onto something interesting. We are grateful to Paul DiMaggio, Iddo Tavory, and the mem-bers of the New York University Culture Workshop for giving us feedback on the early stages of the project, to those who attended the Rutgers University colloquium for their com-ments on early versions of this work, and to Anne Glassman for helping us negotiate some of the more difficult data col-lection tasks. Warm appreciation to Sangeeta Parashar, Giri Nandikotkur, Yong Wang, Vikash Singh, Peter Stein, and Sha-ron Bzostek, who discussed the project over our dinner table and gave us much valued feedback, to Arlene Stein and Vanina Leschziner, who provided thoughtful and constructive com-ments on portions of the manuscript, and to Olivia Dolly for her constant support throughout this project. Finally, we are grateful to Meagan Levinson for her enthusiastic encourage-ment of this book and her valuable feedback on our work, and to the wonderful production team at Princeton University Press: Jacqueline Delaney, Ellen Foos, Lauren Smith, Hank Southgate, Karl Spurzem, Kathryn Stevens, Erin Suydam, Tobiah Waldron, Maria Whelan, and Jaden Young.

Dreams of a Lifetime

Chapter 1

If You Knew You Couldn't Fail . . .

I was in the car, running last-minute errands for the Christmas holiday, when I heard a radio talk show host pose this question: *If you knew you could not fail, what would you do?* The host encouraged listeners to call in with their answers and, almost immediately, the station's phone lines lit up. Everyone had ideas to share: visions of fame and fortune, dreams about romance or happiness, healthy families, yearnings for exciting futures filled with adventure. People started sharing and I couldn't stop listening.

Before long, I began to quiz myself: *If you knew you couldn't fail, what would you do?* My mind raced a bit. I'd write a best-selling novel or a hit Broadway musical—maybe I'd even appear in it! I'd be a prize-winning photographer or hard-hitting journalist—the kind who wins a Pulitzer Prize. Maybe I would start my own business—a chic restaurant, a designer floral shop, or perhaps I would train dogs; I always loved them. I could start a think tank and research issues impacting social justice policy. I was amazed. There seemed no shortage of possibilities. The list went on and on, all imaginings of things I had dreamed about at one time or another, though none matched the path my life had taken.

FIG. 1.1. Mom the Lounge Singer
(Copyright Karen A. Cerulo)

I found myself asking the question of more and more people. *If you knew you couldn't fail, what would you do?* My coauthor responded, "I'd be the next Oprah . . . or maybe I'd become a lawyer, one internationally known for fighting social injustice. And, for sure, I would live in Cape May—right on the ocean!" A few days later, we posed the question to friends and relatives at the Christmas dinner table. Mom, still dreaming in her nineties, said, "I would become a lounge singer. I've always wanted to sing. I would just love doing that every night of the week." Never too young to dream, our nephew, then ten years old, said, "I'd either be a soccer star or a famous computer game designer," seeing both with equal appeal. More answers soon flowed from family and friends: "I'd have my own exclusive bed and breakfast," "I would paint," "be an inspirational speaker," "run a PAC," "be a major-league pitcher," "I'd live at the shore," "travel the world over and over," "I'd be president of the United States."

The dreams shared with us were often surprising, but one thing was certain. Everyone at the table had dreams, and they shared them easily and without hesitation. Even more striking was this: no one at the table was horribly sad or unhappy; they were not living a life of regret. In fact, many people said that, while they had dreams, they were also quite happy with their lives. Yet young or old, happy or sad, rich or just getting by, everyone was willing to consider a different, perhaps a loftier possibility. For those radio callers . . . for us . . . for our friends and relatives, dreaming seemed easy—in fact, it seemed to come naturally.

This experience got us thinking more and more about dreams. What does it mean to dream—to imagine your future possibilities? Does everyone do it no matter what their reality? And what do our dreams look like? Do they unfold in uniquely personal ways, or are they patterned, following some sort of cultural scripts or "lessons"? We wondered too: how do people's dreams differ from age to age, from group to group, from context to context? Finally, do people ever fail to dream or simply stop dreaming? If so, why?

If we thought about dreams from a psychoanalytic perspective, the idea of patterned dreams would likely be discarded. For the psychoanalyst, such daydreams and imaginings are a way of revealing every individual's particular repressed desires. Thus, identical dreams can often mean vastly different things based on a person's biography and emotional development. On the other hand, historians, anthropologists, and even some sociologists would say that dreams are highly patterned. In fact, among Americans, many would contend that dreams can be largely reduced to one thing: the "American Dream"—a singular focus on prosperity and success.

In *Dreams of a Lifetime*, we would like to propose a middle ground. While dreams are generally treated as personal and unique, we argue that people's dreams are quite clearly patterned in very predictable ways. However, people's dreams are not homogenous recreations of the American Dream. Rather, people's dreams differ from age to age, from group to group, from context to context. More specifically, one's "social location"—that is, where class, race, gender, stage of life, or unexpected disruptions to one's life narrative place a person in the broader society—shapes what, when, how, and if we dream.

Most people understand that class, race, gender, age, and tragedy can create inequities in life's opportunities. But we are told that, in dreaming, anything is possible. Can social location really invade our private imaginings of the future? We argue that it can, and in this book, we will show how one's social location shapes the seemingly private life of our minds. We are all free to dream. Yet, we will show that our dreams are restricted in ways of which we are not fully aware. Our social location seeps into our mind's eye, quietly influencing what and how we dream, whether we embrace dreaming or simply give up on it, whether we believe our dreams—whether realistic or fantastical—can come true, and whether we try to make them come true. So Jiminy Cricket's promise, "When you wish upon a star, makes no difference who you are. Anything your heart desires will come to you," may be true for some. But for others, it is a false promise. Given this, studying dreams provides a new avenue for a better understanding of inequality—inequality that is deep-seated in the mind and often precedes action or outcome.[1]

What Do We Mean by "Dreams"?

In the social sciences, there has been an enormous amount of work on concepts we might call the "cousins" of dreams. For example, psychologists, social psychologists, and economists have written reams about what they call "aspirations" and "achievement motivation." Most of this work examines people's educational and career goals, and such studies accomplish three major tasks: they explore how people develop plans or road-maps for the future; they detail the concrete, often patterned actions people take to achieve their schooling or job-related goals; and they illustrate the social foundations of aspirations, showing how aspirations vary by gender, race, and socioeconomic status.[2] Some sociologists study a similar concept, writing about "projects." According to Iddo Tavory and Nina Eliasoph, projects involve rational, willed actions and plans made in relation to others and aimed at a specific end. As Ann Mische and Pippa Pattison note, these projects do not necessarily emerge from a single individual. Rather, projects are likely collectively planned interventions that are designed to organize the concrete relationships one finds in changing political or social arenas.[3] What is important here is this: aspirations, achievement motivations, and projects involve planning. Once you set a goal or objective, you must develop a strategy for achieving it.

"Hope," another cousin of dreams, has attracted social scientists' attentions as well.[4] Hope involves a wish for something—something considered truly possible to achieve.[5] Thus, like aspirations and projects, hope has a footing in concrete experience. In fact, hope often develops as a response to a situation, a particular event, a problem, or some developmental standard or benchmark.[6] You discover you are ill and you hope to be cured; you discover your job is in jeopardy and you hope you'll retain your position; you fall in love and hope for a successful relationship or become pregnant and hope for a healthy child; you face crippling debt and hope you purchased a winning lottery ticket; in the face of terror or political strife, you hope for peace, safety, and unity. As Jerome Groopman writes in *The Anatomy of Hope*, "Hope can arrive only when you recognize that there are real options and that you have genuine choices. Hope can flourish only when you believe that what you do can make a difference, that your actions can bring a future different from the present."[7] Groopman's definition perhaps explains why hope has become part of our political lexicon. Politicians promote it as a concrete strategy for meaningful change. Remember the "Man from Hope," Bill Clinton, or Barack Obama's mantra of "Hope and Change?" Moreover, hope is compatible with the culture of optimism that so characterizes American culture in particular.[8] People generally hope for positive things or things that will directly benefit them.

Aspirations, projects, and hopes are related to dreams, yet they are not quite the same. Dreams are their own unique "beast." Unlike these other phenomena, dreams are imaginings that are not necessarily rational, observable, or linked to planned patterns of action or concrete outcomes. Dreams do not articulate a roadmap for achievement or the path to a specific end. In some ways, dreams are akin to what Jens Beckert calls "fictional expectations"— unobservable states that may or may not materialize.[9] In fact, as we will see, many dreams present unlikely scenarios. Nonetheless, we envision these futures for ourselves. Thus, dreams are mental exercises that provide a vision of a person's inner self; they are a way by which people get to know themselves. Dreams tell us where a person's bliss lies—their ambitions, ideals, and desires— all expressed in the seeming freedom of an imagined world. As one of our study participants told us, "Dreaming is a healthy way of just thinking about what matters to you and kind of keeping hold of who you are and what's important."[10]

It is easy to illustrate the difference between aspirations, projects, or hopes and what we call dreams. Suppose you aspire to be a lounge singer. Chances are you will develop a concrete plan or project designed to help you achieve that goal. You may set up a practice schedule to hone your craft. You may try to make contacts, apply for jobs in various establishments, perhaps frequent "open mic" nights, and so on. In contrast, dreams of lounge singing are a fait accompli: they are about desired outcomes, not processes. The person who dreams of being a lounge singer occupies a different "space." The dream presents someone as the focal point of a small community, as a person enjoying the spotlight of that community's attention and praise, as someone living in a world where their work is a "labor of love." Dreams of lounge singing likely do not include plans and schedules or the struggle of minimal income; they do not include thoughts of working in potentially dangerous or unseemly environments, heavy exposure to alcohol and second-hand smoke, repetition and boredom, or even a true assessment of one's actual talent. Rather, in dreams of lounge singing, one has "arrived" at a desired end. The dream is a vehicle that articulates one's essence, one's desire to be creative, giving, independent, to be someone existing in a context where they matter, where they are sought after and appreciated.

Now consider someone who hopes to be president of the United States. Such a person likely grounds this hope in some sort of experience. The presidential hopeful may have been inspired by a political role model; she or he may have worked on a political campaign or had a taste of politics in a school or local election. Once hope is kindled, the person takes steps to move forward and keep the hope alive. In this way, a presidential hopeful might begin by seeking elected office in her or his local town, county, or state; she or he might become involved in party politics, assemble a cadre of advisors to help with image and public relations, and create a network of potential donors.

Dreams of becoming president of the United States are something quite different. Such dreams are likely filled with the satisfaction and the intoxication of power, with musings about the ability to control an era's problems and challenges, to establish order in the face of chaos or comfort in the face of disturbance, to be the most important person in the world. Dreams of a presidency likely ignore elements such as personal danger, onerous burden, continuous criticism, and highly consequential failures. Rather, the dream provides a safe haven in which to articulate one's desire to be a strong, confident, wise, even a worshipped leader who has power and centrality.

If dreams are not directly linked to action or actual outcomes, why should we study them? We argue that dreams about who we wish to be or what our perfect world would look like can tell us something important about a person's essence, their identity and sense of self, about the things they value and why they value them, about how they communicate with themselves. But there is something more. Dreams represent the starting point of our perception of "fit." Where do we want to belong? Where do we wish we could land? What life paths would we take if no obstacles existed? What do we feel we deserve? Dreams tell this story—even before the story is lived. And it is a story built from the cultural lessons to which we are exposed in our daily social interactions and the cultural contexts in which we live and learn.

How Did We Examine Dreams?

To pursue our analysis of dreams, we tapped a variety of data sources. Primarily, we used interviews and focus groups to talk about dreams with people of different social backgrounds—people with different pasts, presents, and futures. Economically speaking, we talked to people who were just getting by, who were up and coming, and those who were affluent and comfortable. We tapped different racial and gender groups—Asians, Blacks, Latinx, Multiracials, and Whites; men and women. We spoke to people at very different stages of life: people at the "starting line" (for us, third and fourth graders); people crossing thresholds that lead to adulthood—high-school seniors, and college juniors and seniors. We also talked to people who were closer to the "finish line"—retirees and other senior citizens. We talked to people at special turning points in life: newlyweds, new parents, and recent immigrants. We also talked to people facing serious hardships—poverty, homelessness, serious medical diagnoses, or unemployment.

In addition to talking to people, we looked at how dreams are represented in American popular culture. We combed through American public culture to identify the extensive storehouse of both positive and negative lessons, stories and images on dreaming. We also made use of surveys, polls, and other secondary data that report on people's dreams at various moments in time. At times, such data became touchstones for a comparison of our respondents and those located in other places and times.

Dreams of a Lifetime focuses predominantly on the experience of people living in the United States, though we hope to do a follow-up study comparing our U.S. findings with those collected from other nations. We chose the United States as a starting point because, as two sociologists who have devoted their careers to the study of American culture, we know that dreams are at the core of the American experience. There is something distinctive about dreaming in America. The practice is central to the national narrative. Indeed, there is a popular worldwide view that America is where dreams are fulfilled.

Anyone born in the United States after 1931 grew up in a world where John Trunslow Adams's concept of the "American Dream" was a pivotal part of our cultural lessons. Cultural planner Lawrence Samuel argues that the American Dream "plays a vital, active role in who we are, what we do, and why we do it. No other idea or mythology—even religion—has as much influence on our individual and collective lives."[11] Of course, this sentiment existed well before Adams's label. As Jim Cullen so eloquently recounts,

> The Pilgrims may not have actually talked about the American Dream, but they would have understood the idea; after all, they lived it as people who imagined a destiny for themselves. So did the Founding Fathers. So did illiterate immigrants who could not speak English but intuitively expressed rhythms of the Dream with their hands and their hearts. What Alexis de Toqueville called "the charm of anticipated success" in his classic *Democracy in America* seemed palpable to him not only in the 1830s but in his understanding of American history for two hundred years before that. And it still seems so almost two hundred years later.[12]

There have been several impressive histories of the American Dream, as well as books that explore its pitfalls and failings.[13] While we acknowledge the pivotal role of the American Dream, we do not seek to retell its story, for it has been fully explored. We mention the American Dream simply because the concept encourages dreaming and optimism as a viable— indeed, an expected—activity among those living in the United States. The American Dream is a cultural lesson that creates a context or a space for such imaginings, making it important to · acknowledge.

Where Will This Book Take You?

Dreams of a Lifetime will cover lots of ground. In chapter 2, we deal with the dreams themselves—those future imaginings that people shared with us in focus groups and interviews. Using the voices of our 272 respondents, we recount the content of people's dreams—the breadth of dream *themes* addressed by our participants and the *feasibility* of their dreams. We then move on to explore several additional facets of what and how people dream, including their *reach* (are they long- or short-terms images?), their *clarity* (are people's dreams highly detailed and easily understood or more abstract in nature?), their *social scope* (who and what is included in them?), their *flexibility* (are dream themes fixed and consistent or do they exhibit variety or change over time?), their *longevity* (how long do people hold on to their dreams?), their *transportability* (do people intend to pass on their dreams?), their *grounding* (do people's dreams realistically reflect their talents and abilities; are they likely to occur?), and the level of *control* people attach to their dreams (can people affect a dream's fruition?).[14] Finally, we explore the level of *importance* people attribute to the act of dreaming. Does everyone dream . . . should they . . . and when, if ever, should one relinquish one's dreams?

In chapter 3, we try to better understand where the substance of dreams come from. If, as we have argued, dreams do not simply reflect the tenets of the American Dream nor an individual's unique fantasies, then there must be a middle ground. Here, we try to better describe that middle ground of dreaming. We begin by identifying publicly accessible cultural lessons on dreaming. We then examine how those lessons become ingrained in people's bodies and minds. The public culture of dreaming includes many lessons—narratives, stories, and scripts that are both positive and negative. Again, using the voices of our respondents, we focus on which of those lessons drive people's dreams and how they use those lessons to build and articulate their dreams.[15] We also ask, Are people's dreams something about which they consciously deliberate and can easily articulate? Or are they somewhat unconscious, seemingly automatic responses that people make without being able to fully explain where the dreams come from or what they truly mean? Both cognitive scientists and cognitive sociologists are asking exciting questions about our thoughts and desires, wondering how conscious and deliberative we are in defining our values, attitudes, wants, and perceptions of the world. Our respondents help us explore such ongoing debates.[16]

In the remaining chapters of *Dreams of a Lifetime*, we concentrate on subsets of our study participants. Social class, race, gender, life course position, and ruptures to life narratives influenced our respondents' dreams in many, many ways. Here we give a few highlights of what each chapter reveals. Chapter 4 groups our respondents by social class, race, and gender, presenting important differences in how members of these groups dream. We found, for example, that people from different social classes favored different dream themes. In addition, different cultural lessons drove the dreams of those in different social classes. As we moved from lower- to upper-class respondents, we found that people reported increasingly more diverse and short-term dreaming, a greater reluctance to give up on dreams, and a greater belief that one's dreams would come true. We will present these findings and more via the voices of our participants.

When it came to race, we found important differences as well. For example, Asian, Latinx, and Multiracial respondents were concentrated dreamers; their future imaginings were often fixed in one specific area. In contrast, Black and White respondents dreamed in more diverse ways. We also found that people of color report holding on to their dreams longer than Whites, while at the same time expressing impatience with regard to finally achieving them. Our Latinx respondents stood out as least confident about achieving their dreams and most likely to embrace negative cultural lessons on dreaming. The voices of our study participants will elaborate these and other racial differences in dreaming.

Chapter 4 ends by exploring gender and its relationship to dreaming. Among many interesting findings, we saw that twenty-first-century men and women often clung to several gender-stereotypical aspects regarding what, when, and how much they should dream. For example, women often dreamed of family and self-improvement themes, while men's dream themes often tapped adventure and fame, wealth, and power. Our study participants also showed us that women were more diverse, committed, and optimistic in dreaming than men—something surprising that we explore further in the chapter.

In chapter 5, we analyzed how dreams differ among those at various stages of life. We mention here just some of the many differences that emerged from our discussions. For example, fourth graders were the first to express dreams that were more feasible than fantastical, although most people's dreams, no matter their age, had an element of fantasy. We also found that the dreams of people at early life's socially defined transitional moments—e.g., moving to junior high or graduating from high school or college—appeared more similar to one another than to those in later stages of life. And as we moved from respondents in young adulthood to midlife to those in their senior years, we found more diversity in the dream themes people expressed. These differences represent just some of the ways in which life course position influences future imaginings.

In chapter 6, we look at people facing "ruptures" in their life narratives: those displaced by economic or natural disasters, those victimized by serious medical disease, or those who found themselves suddenly unemployed. As you will see, these conditions had many varying effects on what and how people dream. To mention just a few, we found that displaced and health-challenged respondents favored self-improvement and philanthropic dreams, while the unemployed were focused on dreams related to recovered careers. The dreams of the displaced and health challenged were most often driven by positive cultural lessons. We also found that the health challenged showed the most diversity in dreaming and that they were the most confident about achieving their dreams. Illness seemed to give these respondents a "second life" when it came to dreaming. Unemployment, in contrast, was a major obstacle to dreaming, resulting in future imaginings that were vague at best and often fueled by negative cultural lessons and a lack of control.

Chapter 7 brings our book to a close. In it, we look at some of the broader conclusions of our work. Have we proven the case for the middle ground of dreaming? Have we adequately explored how an uneven playing field with regard to future imaginings really sets the stage for the more tangible inequities in life chances and opportunities that plague those of certain social classes, races, genders, and the like? We also revisit the importance of dreaming in American culture. In so doing, we explore one last critical question. Is dreaming a positive or negative thing? The answer may surprise you.

Final Reflections

Langston Hughes once wrote of the importance of dreams, saying that without them "life is a broken-winged bird that cannot fly."[17] If this sentiment is true, then learning something about dreaming may be the most important study we can undertake. Knowing this, *Dreams of a Lifetime* will dig deep into the world of future imaginings—not simply what we dream about, how we articulate those dreams, and from where our dreams emerge, but the systematic ways in which people's dreams can differ by one's social location. Moreover, as the very foundation of who we are, or perhaps, who we "should" want to be, dreams help us explain just where the uneven social playing field begins. Exploring the culture *of* dreams and the culture *in* dreams helps us understand the role of future imaginings in social life—both for the good and the bad.

Chapter 2

What Do Dreamers Sound Like?

It's always exciting to start a new project . . . and always a little scary as well. On the way to our first focus group, we wondered, Will people be open to sharing their dreams with us? Will they be talkative and reflective, or will they be self-conscious and quiet? Will they find our questions puzzling . . . confusing? We were about to find out.

It was an interesting time to be studying dreams. We began collecting data in the spring of 2017 and continued data collection through the early part of 2018. Lots of things were happening in the country at the time—things we knew could greatly influence our discussions. Donald Trump had just taken office after a contentious presidential campaign. Before long, the Russia investigation, with its cast of characters, began in earnest: Comey, Flynn, Mueller, Sessions, Cohen, Manafort, and of course, Trump and his family. The stock market boomed, with the Dow Jones Industrial average increasing by 25.1%! Unemployment rates dropped substantially and interest rates slowly began to climb. North Korea initiated open nuclear testing, heightening the tensions between leaders of North Korea and the United States, with tensions openly expressed via Twitter. Hurricanes Harvey, Irma, and Maria ravaged several U.S. states as well as Puerto Rico. At the same time, the United States expressed its intent to withdraw from the Paris Climate Agreement. A mass shooting in Las Vegas took the lives of fifty-eight people and resulted in the injury of hundreds more. Just six months later, a gunman at the Marjory Stoneman Douglas High School claimed the lives of seventeen teenage students. Following the Women's March of 2017, the MeToo movement kept issues of harassment and violence in the spotlight, with full exposure of many high-profile personalities: Bill Cosby, Louis C. K., Robert "R." Kelly, Matt Lauer, Charlie Rose, Kevin Spacey, and Harvey Weinstein among them. The Trump administration imposed travel bans on citizens from various Muslim-majority nations. White supremacists boldly marched as Confederate monuments fell in Charlottesville, Virginia. Many NFL players began to "take a knee" to raise awareness of social injustice toward racial minorities. Drug overdoses became the leading cause of death for Americans under the age of fifty. Tariffs, "fake news," and "Stormy Daniels" entered the daily lexicon. And Americans stood mesmerized by the solar eclipse. What would dreaming look like in such a context?

In this chapter, we provide an overview of what we heard from our respondents as we moved from group to group and interview to interview. For before we analyze the impact of social class, race, gender, stage of life, or life disruptions on dreaming, we thought it important to clarify the general parameters that guide what people dream, how they dream, and how persistently they cling to dreams, if at all.

Who Were Our Dreamers?

We talked to a broad array of people—272 in all—in order to hear people's dreams firsthand. We encountered most people in small focus groups averaging five to seven people per group.

TABLE 2.1: Demographic Breakdown of Our Sample

Age	
In Third and Fourth Grade	10%
In High School	9%
In College	10%
In Their Twenties	11%
In Their Thirties	13%
In Their Forties	14%
In Their Fifties	14%
In Their Sixties	12%
Seventy or Older	7%
Self-Identified Social Class	
Lower	9%
Working	21%
Middle	60%
Upper	10%
Self-Identified Race	
Asian	7%
Black	15%
Latinx	13%
Multiracial	10%
White	55%
Self-Identified Gender	
Female	56%
Male	44%

We also talked to thirty people via one-on-one interviews,[1] and we spoke with elementary school children right in their classrooms. We recruited these respondents from a variety of places: schools, religious groups, social clubs, recreational teams, workplace settings, support groups, social media sites, and so on. Our sampling strategy, while not suitable for generalization, was ideal for our purpose of exploration.

Our study participants spanned various age groups from those in third grade (seven to eight years of age) to those seventy and older. Participants self-identified their social class—lower, working, middle, or upper—relative to their annual income and assets.[2] They self-identified their race: Asian, Black, Latinx, Multiracial, or White. (We were unable to recruit any Native Americans to our study.) Study participants also self-identified their gender—female or male; we offered a "trans-gendered" choice, but no one self-identified as such. Table 2.1 gives a full demographic breakdown of our sample.[3]

The Protocol for Focus Groups and Interviews

For our focus groups, we arranged participants around a conference-type table and welcomed them to the group. We then described the purpose of the research as follows:

> We are conducting research on dreams—not the dreams we have when asleep, but rather the wishful, future imaginings of people living in the United States. We want to learn more about the content of such dreams, how they are constructed and expressed, how they make people feel, how they differ from age to age, group to group, context to context, and if people ever stop dreaming.

The same script was used in the one-on-one interviews, all of which were conducted in our offices or in public spaces, such as coffee shops or libraries. Focus group participants could see and hear one another. People wrote their first names on small placards so we could call one another by name. In interviews, we sat opposite respondents, also calling one another by name.

We asked every respondent, in groups or interviews, the following question in just this way: *If you knew you could not fail, what would you do ... or where would you go ... or what would you want to have ... or who would you want to be?* Why this question? We pretested other questions before formally beginning our work, including "What are your dreams for the future?" or

"What do you wish the future holds for you?" among others. We found that these alternatives delivered bucket lists of superficial aspirations and projects and not the kinds of things that, as you will see, our participants themselves defined as dreams.

Each participant received an "answer packet" where they identified their top-three "could not fail" dreams for the future and rank ordered them according to importance. Then, study participants answered some basic questions on their demographic background—age, gender, race, social class, and the like. While most of our interactions involved talking, we wanted people to commit their dreams to paper before the dialogue began. We did this to determine if people stuck by their answers or if their initial thoughts were swayed by the group. For the record, very few people—less than 2%—changed their written answers once asked to state them publicly.

Let the Data Collection Begin!

Our very first focus group involved college seniors—students just months away from graduation. We prepared the room for these students just as we would for the thirty-nine groups and thirty interviews to follow. And so we began.

> *If you knew you could not fail, what would you do . . . or where would you go . . . or what would you want to have . . . or who would you want to be?*

As we engaged this very first group, we heard a variety of answers—many, many of which would be repeated again and again in the dozens of focus groups and interviews we did during our time in the field: I would start a business; build a *Fortune* 500 company and become wealthy; travel to outer space; visit planets no one has seen; become the president of the United States.

(The presidency was a popular answer.) I would find a cure for a disease (type I diabetes, cancer, heart disease); end all violence; end all wars. I would be an angel investor; start a center that will help the sick, the homeless, the poor, or abandoned children. I would learn dozens of languages and travel around the world, maybe living anywhere I chose. (World travel was a common dream.) I would own and run an animal rescue farm—for horses, for dogs, for exotic animals; I would become invisible; levitate myself. I would publish a book of poems; compose a hit song; I would solo in a world-famous orchestra; be the star player on a sports team; I would gain more self-confidence; be more compassionate; be a world-famous motivational speaker; I would fall in love and live with one person for the rest of my life; I would have several healthy children; I would reconcile with my daughter or son. The faces changed as did the demographic profiles of the people to whom we spoke. But as the weeks moved on, we came to see that dreams, those imaginings we think of as individualized and personal, were patterned in very specific ways. Our participants were not sharing plans with us. Rather, they were telling us stories—often very similar stories—about things that had not yet happened, might never materialize; stories about things they felt appropriate to imagine and would likely "live out" only in the confines of their minds.

As we listened to these stories, we felt confident that our study participants were thinking about dreams in the same way we did. Recall that in chapter 1, we defined dreams as

unobservable states that may or may not materialize. In fact, as we will see, many dreams present unlikely scenarios. Nonetheless, we envision these futures for ourselves. Thus, dreams are mental exercises that provide a vision of a person's inner self. They tell us where a person's bliss lies—their ambitions, ideals, and desires—all expressed in the freedom of an imagined world.

When we asked people what dreaming meant to them, we heard ideas that resonated with our thinking. Arielle, a high-school student, said, "Dreams take you away from the mundane and really focus on what you might be capable of." Fred, in college, said, "Dreams make you less rigid, let you imagine possibilities and see who you are." Mike, a man in early midlife, told us, "If a dream is on your mind, it's telling you something about yourself and your desires. It keeps you moving on." Rhonda, unemployed in late midlife, said, "It's important to look at dreams and say, 'What is it? What's the heartbeat or kernel of it?' Because a lot of times that tells us who and where we want to be." Yolanda, a senior citizen, saw dreams as "something that create happiness you can pass on and hope to live another day." And Don, a man in early middle-age, summed up dreaming this way: "It's about what role dreams play in how we conceive of who we are. A lot of the way we think about ourselves is by dropping ourselves into dream situations." In our study, people were moving beyond plans, goals, or hopes. They were digging deep into their private visions of an imagined future.

Capturing the Patterns of Dreams

How did we zero in on the patterns and parameters important to studying dreams? Currently, a number of sociologists are studying the ways in which people imagine the future. For our purposes, the work of three individuals—the team of Iddo Tavory and Nina Eliasoph and that of Ann Mische—proved especially useful in guiding our work.[4]

Tavory, Eliasoph, and Mische all note that the study of future imaginings can take different forms. To distinguish these forms, we must place future imaginings in their cognitive context. For example, people may engage in short-term, moment-to-moment anticipations about what will happen next. (Consider the baseball outfielder who quickly positions himself for an oncoming fly ball.) Tavory and Eliasoph, building on the philosopher Edmund Husserl, discuss these moments as "protentions." They are taken for granted imaginings that are less conscious and much less encompassing than dreams. In contrast, people may imagine their long-term futures, what Tavory and Eliasoph call "trajectories." Dreams clearly fall into this category, functioning as overarching stories that carry us forward.[5] In considering dreams, the concept of "temporal landscapes" is important as well. Tavory and Eliasoph define these landscapes as established rhythms of social life. Consider, for example, some familiar cultural plans—one should attend school, get a degree, and get a job; one should date, marry, and have children. "Actors assume that the path is already laid, and all they need to do is take the expected or even required steps on it."[6] Thus temporal landscapes are rhythms with which people must coordinate their dreams.[7] As we begin to recount people's dreams and the stories they use to convey them, we will see these factors at work.

What are the building blocks that people use to construct their dreams? Of course, we cannot get into people's heads, but we can listen to the ways in which people reflect on, declare, and explain their dreams. We can also record the stories they use to unfold their dreams. Once doing so, we can begin searching for various patterns. For this task, we found the work of Mische especially helpful. She identifies a number of culturally informed factors that she believes drive future imaginings like dreams. We saw many of these factors in our data, and we attended to these elements in our discussions with study participants. We also discovered several additional factors that emerged from our discussions, and we made sure to attend to these in our analysis as well.[8] In the end, the following aspects of dreaming proved central to our work:

Dream Themes: What is the range of topics and possibilities that people consider in building their dreams?

Feasibility: Were the dreams people shared with us things that could be realistically achieved, or were they the stuff of fantasy?

Reach: Do people's dreams take them to a place far in the future, or rather, to a place that is merely a short-term excursion?

Clarity: Are people's dreams highly detailed and well-articulated, or are they vague and abstract in kind?

Social Scope: Who and what are included in people's dreams?

Flexibility: Are people's dreams concentrated and linked to a single theme, or are they diverse and wide-reaching?

Longevity: How long do people hold on to their dreams? Do they ever give them up, or are they forever images?

Transportability: Do people wish to pass on their dreams? If so, to whom?

Grounding: Do people's dreams realistically reflect their talents and abilities? Do people view their dreams as attainable even if they seem fantastical to others?

Control: Do people feel they have a high probability of achieving their dreams, or are their dreams squashed by circumstance?

Importance: Do people see a positive value to dreaming, or is it viewed as a foolish, even a destructive practice?

Here are the initial patterns we discovered as we talked with our study participants about dreaming.

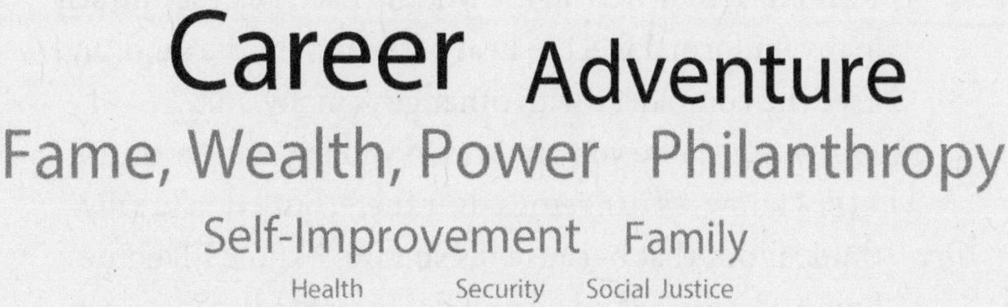

Career Adventure
Fame, Wealth, Power Philanthropy
Self-Improvement Family
Health   Security   Social Justice

FIG. 2.1. Word Cloud of Dream Themes

Dream Themes

We began by looking for identifiable themes driving people's dreams. These themes helped us fully understand the range of issues people envisioned when imagining future possibilities. Since dreams are typically described as highly personal and in-dividualized, one might reasonably expect to see a wide breadth of possibilities in the stories people tell. However, for our study participants, this was not the case. Indeed, 95% of participants' dreams could be categorized within six broad themes: these were, in order of frequency, career; adventure; fame, wealth, and power; philanthropy; self-improvement; and family.[9] Figure 2.1 gives a visual depiction of the distribution of dream themes. As we show by scaling the size of the words, some dreams were more common than others.

Career was the most common dream theme we encountered. Twenty-four percent of our participants dreamed either of working toward a career goal or expanding their current career horizons. For example, Alfie,[10] a college student, was preparing for military service and, upon his return from service, hoped to join a police force. But note that this was not a career project; Alfie had no concrete plans. Rather, his was a very idyllic dream of his future.

ALFIE: I'm somewhere in the Middle East. I can see myself in my uniform. I feel the heat of the desert, the sand, and I see the comradery with other guys in my unit.

RESEARCHER: Are you afraid? Do you feel danger or risk?

ALFIE: I know it's dangerous over there, but I don't really think about that because it's so rare. I know I'll come home. I know it. And when I do, I want to live in a town like Mayberry—do you know that show? I'll be the sheriff or something like that.

RESEARCHER: It's a happy, small-town life. Have you ever lived in a place like that?

ALFIE: No . . . but I feel like it exists somewhere.

Middle-aged Wanda, who is an active deacon at her church, dreamed of continuing that work. But in her dream, her career unfolded in a very different way:

WANDA: I want to start my own congregation. I want to start something new, a church unlike anything I know. I want to serve women in particular. Once I hone my craft, I want to write a book about my ministry and, eventually, have a radio show where I can reach many more people.

RESEARCHER: That's a big agenda!

WANDA: It's a big dream!

Others had career dreams that dramatically shifted their current career paths, or dreams that placed them on fantastical paths. Vera, a senior citizen, resurrected a career dream she had given up over thirty-five years ago: being a doctor. She thought aloud about how such a dream might still unfold:

I still think I could go back to school. I still think I could become a doctor. I took care of my mother till the day she died.

She had cancer. Now I take care of my father. My dad is ninety-three. I weaned him off of medicines that will harm him and, like, I'm there. I'm like his assistant. I have a close relationship with the doctor, and he commends me because I do watch and help him a lot by telling him what's wrong with my father. I did go to medical school for a short time, about a year, but my parents didn't have the money to support my needs. So I wanted to join the military and get training that way, but my dad wouldn't let me because I was a girl. I did get a job being a chemical technician. I kinda stayed in the area, but I wasn't where I wanted to be. I settled for something rather than being what I really wanted. I'm old now, but maybe . . . who knows?

Frank, a restauranteur in midlife, dreamed of making a huge change and becoming the head of operations for the New York Giants:

I've thought about it for a long time. You probably have to know someone to get a job like that. Obviously, I don't. But I can see myself in the front office. I really see it. I'm in a pair of shorts. Just sitting down in an operations meeting, going over rosters and making big decisions.

Even though these dreams are about careers, these individuals are not talking about concrete plans or projects. Instead, they are dreaming of things that are "bigger" or completely unrelated to their current paths, about things that are highly desirable, perhaps even magical for them.

About 20% of our dreamers, the next-largest group, hoped to embark on an exciting adventure. Sometimes, these adventures involved risk, and often they involved new terrain for the individual. For example, John, a retiree, dreamed of white-water rafting on the great rivers of the United States. He'd had some rafting experience, but nothing comparable to his high-risk dream:

> I have rafted before, but this would be different. I know the rapids I would want to try, the names of them. I see videos of the big eighteen-foot rafts being dumped upside down. I see myself working those rapids. I'm workin' them and I'm winning. I've seen my friends paddling them and how they did it. I see the line of the rapid. I have spent a lot of time scouting and have a good sense of what it would be like.

In contrast, some adventures were new to the dreamer and literally out of this world. Space exploration was a fairly common dream. Third-grader Mark wanted to be an astronaut and "touch the moon." College student Frank told us,

> I want to feel g-forces. I want to push the limits. I'm not necessarily trying to detach from the planet, although that would be cool. But I could also be a test pilot of some kind instead of an astronaut.

Juanita, a female college student, wanted to take to the skies as well, albeit in a more conventional vehicle. She had long dreamed of being a pilot:

> I see myself flying a two-level plane and traveling across the world. I'm taking the helm and flying that thing! I see skylines and feel in control of something that's so, so big.

For other participants, adventure came in the form of earthly travel. But here too, such dreams represented something new for the individuals. Some dreams involved living in a foreign country for an extended period of time. For example, Patrick, a senior citizen, dreamed of having a yacht, docking it in Amsterdam, and living there for at least a year. Other dreams involved frequent travel, as Judy, a small-business owner in midlife, told us:

> JUDY: I want to travel three to four times a year until I've visited every country on the planet. I've started that journey, visiting several countries in Europe.
> RESEARCHER: How many places have you visited so far?
> JUDY: About five or six, but they're familiar to me. Now I want to get more, well, adventuresome, hitting places in Asia and Africa. I want to expand my horizons in new ways, exciting ways. Do something I thought I would never do. Who knows?

Describing something for which there was no prior game plan and no blueprint for the future (as Judy says, "Who knows?") distinguishes these dreams from projects or aspirations. For our study respondents, dreams were something more "grandiose."

For a number of our participants (16%), dreams of fame, wealth, and power took precedence over all else. From angel investors, to politicians, to stars of stage and screen, from NFL receivers and major-league baseball players, to those winning prizes and accolades for breakthrough discoveries or some recognized skill, these participants saw themselves as "making it" in a way that differed significantly from their current lives. For example, Aaron, a college senior, told us he wanted to be the president of Nigeria:

> I was really inspired when I saw Obama become president, so I started looking into it. I wasn't born in this country, so I can't fulfill this dream here. I thought about it and I decided that, hey, I could become president of my homeland— Nigeria. I really think I can do it—maybe by the time I'm forty. My dad will help me. I will become a really famous and a really powerful man.

There was Mary, a writer in midlife, who dreamed of winning a national Scrabble competition held in a swanky Las Vegas hotel, or Haley, a woman in her twenties, who dreamed of being a Broadway star. Ian, a senior citizen, known as the best piano player in the senior center, wanted to turn that talent into stardom:

> I always looked at Liberace; you know he owned the only two crystal pianos in the world. I would like to be like that. I like music but when I saw Liberace on TV and all he could do, well wow! His father was classical, but he was bold and did other kinds of music. Everybody loved that guy. He changed the game.

While the dreams people shared with us were about outcomes, they assumed they had made a hard climb to the top. However, no path or plan for "arriving" was described by our participants. The dreams emphasized the fait accompli, not the process. Ed, a midlife male, made that clear as he dreamed of an Elon Musk sort of existence. He knew where he landed but was not exactly sure how he got there:

> I'm into building something, working hard to build a huge, huge business, my own building with my office all the way at the top. I work 24/7 although I'm not sure at what, but after all that work, I'm filthy rich. I can see myself, in a suit, a really slick one, feet on my desk. I'm living life! I own my own business. I am the boss of everybody. I'm in New York City for sure. An office with lots of windows.

And in dreams about fame, wealth, and power, power could take on some interesting forms. For example, James, a senior citizen, dreamed of being able to levitate himself.

> OK, this may sound crazy, but here goes. I want to be able to levitate myself. Sometimes I can feel myself as if I am levitating.

I'm just lifting off the ground through my willpower. This dream is really about power, the power to take control of yourself and do things yourself.

Fergie, a man in his twenties, wanted to create a utopian world using virtual-reality technology. For him, "the knowledge to create is power." And several of our grammar-school participants dreamed of superpowers such as becoming invisible, being able to transport themselves from one place to another, or being able to read minds.

As we note again and again, these imaginings of a potential future had no concrete blueprints for action. For us, this underscored the distinctive feature of dreams.

Many of our participants (15%) dreamed of making a difference in the world through philanthropic activities. They wished to give back to their community or the world at large. Often, these philanthropic initiatives grew from personal trials. For example, Idina was a new immigrant to the United States preparing for citizenship. She was also a cancer survivor. She dreamed of establishing support groups for cancer patients:

> I had this dream for a long time. But it became more important three years ago when I got cancer and I noticed the importance of helping or supporting people with this kind of disease—especially children. I don't know exactly how I can make this happen, but it would be a wonderful thing.

Javier, a middle-aged man rendered homeless by Hurricane Maria, dreamed of helping other homeless people:

> I would start a homeless shelter at the YMCA. It's about, well, not only because those people are less fortunate, they just need more shit. There are people that build and have family and, at one time or another, something went wrong

and they didn't have the help. I want to offer some kind of help.

Animals often played a central role in many philanthropic dream stories. Shirley, in middle age and recovering from cancer, told us,

> I know what my dream is. I see a farm. I'm in California near Big Sur. I see a specific type of boxer dog. My farm is filled with them—rescued boxers. I think I will be rescuing horses too. I see certain kinds of horses that need help.

Sometimes, people's philanthropy was attached to career goals. For example, Kevin, a part-time college student, hoped to help people as a life coach:

> I went to a Tony Robbins event and it made me realize I can do anything I set my mind to. I would do so many different things in my life so I could show every person that if you set your mind to something, you can do it. You fail not from a lack of resources but from a lack of resourcefulness.

And Nancy, a graduating high-school senior, hoped to enter the medical field so she could discover a cure for type 1 diabetes:

> Well, I mean, just because, like, I understand the demands of the disease; I can sympathize with other diabetics and [*holds back tears*] being able to kind of, like, take away that pain would bring me incredible joy and also for myself.

A smaller group—about 11% of our study participants—dreamed about improving some aspect of the self. Jenny, an immigrant preparing for citizenship, dreamed of speaking English fluently like a native speaker:

Right now I'm looking for a job and trying to learn how to speak English very well. Maybe after that I could go to college. I'm not going to give up.

Established businessman Patrick dreamed of taking more risks in his life, seeing "playing it safe" as a weakness in his life:

It's a personal development project for me. I'm the oldest in my family and I am hardwired to feel responsible. So it's always been a little hard for me to think about having fun on a consistent basis. I have always dreamed of loosening up and trying new things whenever I want.

And Sarah, a young executive, dreamed of improving herself by simplifying her life in a healthier setting:

We live in a small house. And it's so hot here. We would like to be up north and be able to grow our own food and be more at one with the outdoors. I think we'd be better people for it.

Will these things happen? As we will see, most people believed there was a high likelihood they would. But like our other dream themes, few people were doing anything to move these ideas forward.

Family-oriented dreams, the least widespread dream theme, were expressed by 9% of our participants. Such dreams took different forms: building a family, recovering one, keeping one together. For example, Theresa, a wife and mother in her thirties, told us,

Just wanting to have a baby. It's a scream because when I was younger, I didn't want to have children. And then life kicked in and that biological clock started ticking. Oh my God, I really do want to have kids. But I didn't have a husband. So

I was waiting to meet my partner. Now that I have one child, I really want another. Feelings change.

Belinda, a senior citizen, told us,

My oldest child. I haven't spoke to her in five years. And it hurts, so my outlook and what I want for my family has changed. Family is the most important thing. We can always come back together. Love should always be in a family. As long as I'm alive, there's a chance we'll get back together.

Paul, a midlife man who was currently unemployed, dreamed of a perfect vacation—one that was perfect because it was all about family:

I envision us together, all my family, children, parents, maybe even brothers and sisters vacationing together at the beach. Just reconnected and building family. We're playing games, swimming, we're cooking out. We're singing and telling stories.

Beautiful sentiments, but again, little in the way of planning, thus distinguishing the family-oriented dreams from any sort of aspiration and project.

Feasibility

After listening to our study participants, we classified the feasibility of people's dreams. We found that people's dreams existed on a continuum of sorts. Some people's dreams were quite realistic, even if they had no concrete plans for achieving them. However, generally, these dreams fell far afield from people's current life paths. Still others described dreams that were, theoretically, possible to achieve, but were improbable. Then, there were those whose dreams were simply fantastical in nature. Note that our study participants gave us their own take on whether they had the skills needed to accomplish their dreams; they also assessed the probability of achieving their dreams. We will report that later in the chapter. But here, we wanted to gauge, from sociological work on people's life chances, the feasibility of the dreams people shared with us.[11]

About 45% of the dreams we heard were realistic; they could be achieved if participants pursued the needed steps or took a detour in their current life paths. Such dreams included becoming doctors, lawyers, professors, actors, artists, starting businesses, traveling, working as animal rescuers, finding a loving mate, or helping the sick or the poor. Of our participants, 25% described dreams that, technically speaking, were possible, yet accomplishing these dreams was highly unlikely. These dreams included traveling to the moon or other planets, finding a cure for cancer or diabetes, learning all of the world's languages, or becoming president of the United States. Finally, 30% of our participants presented dreams that we considered fantastical. In our estimation, these dreams had no chance of coming true. These imaginings include levitating one's self, being able to fly, time traveling, owning a pet giraffe, attending a walk-on tryout for the New York Giants and being picked as the new quarterback, reading minds, ending all violence, ending all wars, or eradicating all economic inequality.

The feasibility data showed us two sides to dreaming. On the one hand, many people dreamed within the confines of their current possibilities. However, they did not choose the paths their dreams required. Rather, they tucked away their dreams, thinking about them as a "place" to which it might someday be possible to go. Others took their dreams to another level. There were no holds barred on such imaginings—anything was possible. And while the chances of fulfilling these dreams were slim or nonexistent, people nevertheless imagined these places as potential sites for their futures.

Reach

We asked our participants whether their dreams carried them far into the future or whether they dreamed of things that would be accomplished in the short term. Whether we talked about people's first-, second-, or third-ranked dreams, the majority of dreams—almost two-thirds—reached far into the future.

Consider Reggie, a senior citizen, whose dream cast him as president of the United States. He told us he had held the dream nearly his entire life and, for as long as it took, would continue to pursue it:

> I've had this dream as long as I can remember. Since I was a little kid. I have this memory of being in front of the TV and my mother was crying because Kennedy had been shot. I remember that and I thought, what a great person he was! I thought, I would like to be that person. It may take time, but it's still a dream of mine.

Jenny, a woman in her forties who dreamed of opening a specialty bakery, told us,

> It started when I was with my girlfriend. We baked cookies, so many cookies, from one end of the room to the other. We were in our early twenties; we always would say, we'll do it when we get older.

Carl, a high-school student who dreamed of becoming a well-published poet, saw his dream as a long-term endeavor:

All my life, I wanted to be a poet or a writer. I used to think I could write a poem and just send it somewhere and get published. But after looking into things, I realize I need a literary agent or something. It will probably take a long time. So for me, this is a dream that's way out in the future.

Perhaps Beth, a woman in midlife, captured the tendency for long-term reach the best: "A dream is a goal without a deadline."

These answers and others like them tell us that when it comes to reach, most dreams typically stretched far into the future. The dreams represent a place people journey toward, fueled, in part, by past or present experience. But because the core of these dreams reside in the distant future, with no observability but in the mind's eye of the dreamer, it can be constructed and reconstructed according to one's needs and desires, with no sustained concern for potential concrete obstacles.

Clarity

How clearly did our participants "see" their dreams? Were their dreams pictured in great detail, or were they vague and abstract? Among our study respondents, people were twice as likely to describe detailed dreams as opposed to vague or abstract stories. For these people, the "place" where dreams reside was visited frequently, allowing people to "furnish" it with many specifics and particulars. For example, Abraham, a college senior, dreamed of being a rock star. He told us that each time he thought of the dream over the years, it became more and more detailed:

I'm coming off the stage after an awesome concert. It's an outdoor stadium. Lots of people are storming me, especially women, voluptuous, gorgeous women, and they want my autograph. [*Others in the group laugh, one saying, Only your autograph?*] It's loud, really loud. People are grabbing me. My friends and family are there with me. They think it's cool. I think it's crazy mad and I love it, but I feel like I need some privacy too. I'm strained sometimes. I can feel that. Exhilaration and fatigue all at once, right in the pit of my stomach.

Alexa, a young adult in her twenties, describes her adventure of living abroad with great detail:

I see myself living in Berlin. I've seen pictures of it. I'm in a building on the corner, in the top-floor apartment; it's a six-story building with a slate roof. Real pretty. I've painted the wall a bright lemon yellow and the apartment has lots of light. I have a chair by the window where I can read or people watch. The apartment is nicely furnished so I can welcome friends. It's open but with lots of character. There's a bakery nearby, and when I sit at the window in the morning, I can smell the goodies. Oh, I love it.

Laura, a senior citizen, dreamed of brokering peace in the Middle East. She described the negotiations:

I can picture the players, the world leaders that would have to be there. I see them seated in a conference room. It's a huge table and it's a fancy room. Lots of rich wood. So smooth. Everyone has water, and pads, pencils. Everyone has aids sitting nearby. They're all whispering or passing notes and documents. We're wearing earphones in our ears for translations. I know what I would propose. I could give you my agenda right now! The only thing I can't envision is the responses.

For some participants, just under a third of our dreamers, dreams were so clear that they could actually be physically felt.

It was as if the dreams were, in the words of social theorists like Pierre Bourdieu, or later, Loic Wacquant, "inscribed" in their bodies.[12] Maria, a senior citizen who wants to motorcycle across the country, shares her physical reactions:

> I'm going with my granddaughter—she's game. We have matching leather jackets, it's going to have "We're on Harleys"—mine is huge, black, and very shiny; hers is red. I can almost run my hand down them now and feel how smooth they are. [*She runs her hands up and down her arms.*] Ooohh. When we're riding, I feel the wind in my hair. I can feel it right now. I'm going fast with nothing but road and pretty country around me. I can smell the fresh air and the grass and the flowers. Like heaven.

Keith, a man in his twenties, dreamed of winning an Olympic medal in skiing. He felt the details of his dream:

> I'm looking at the mountain we're going to ski on. I can see snow whipping around. I can feel it on my face. It stings a bit. I feel kinda cold as I describe it. I see the trophy that's up for grabs, and I feel myself in the gate waiting for the gun—tense like—wanting to fly. Everybody is smiling and clapping. I see my teammates, know we have been practicing all the time. My stomach is a little queasy, but I'm also tingling with excitement. Geez, I actually feel that now!

And Cooper, a man in midlife, describes the feel of being a member of the New York Giants:

> I'm coming out of the tunnel and running out onto the field. I'm in the uniform . . . THE uniform. I'm so, so proud. It's early fall, so it's still hot. I smell the grass and I feel the sweat coming down my back. I see me running down the field in a

Giants uniform. I am hitting someone so hard. Oh, I felt that one. The guy's down. I'm jumping up and down for tackling him. Everyone is screaming. I can hear it. It's so loud. [*He cups his hands over his ears.*] The crowd is roaring right through my body.

These answers and others like them suggest that the places our dreams take us can often be elaborate and comprehensive. The rarity of vagueness underscores the importance of these imaginings—their palpability as we embellish and bring color to these spaces each time we visit them. We can hold tightly to these dreams and continually enhance them with parts of our most core self. Even if there is no concrete path to our dreams, people can still see and feel the details as if they may someday live them. Indeed, details might actually enable a virtual experience of one's dreams, bringing people that much closer to a feeling of lived experience.

Social Scope

Who or what is included in people's dreams? We know something about the "what" by reviewing the themes of participants' dreams: new careers, having adventures, acquiring fame, wealth, and power, being philanthropic, improving one's self, or building, mending, or helping family. But who was with our dreamers on their journeys? For whom were they dreaming, and what props or objects seemed important to their stories?

When we examined the "cast" included in our participants' dreams, we find that, overall, people's dreams most often presented a solo performance. That is, when envisioning a dream and telling its story, people most often saw themselves living it and enjoying its fruits as a solo actor. Indeed, our participants were roughly four times more likely to see themselves dominating the dream. To be sure, people saw others (such as family, friends, sometimes, strangers, even animals) in their dreams, but they were in the background or, as one participant described it, just "extras."

We wondered, Would the theme of one's dream change that focus? Would dreams about family or philanthropy, for example, be more likely to involve other people? The answer was no. No matter what type of dream participants described, they were more likely to envision the dream as a solo endeavor. So while participants may have been dreaming of something that would be done for others, or something inspired by others, they, as doers, were the central focus of the dream. As Chaz, a man in his twenties, explains it,

> My dream is to ski . . . ski jump on the Rockies or the Alps. I started skiing at thirty on a dare. So I guess someone else is partially responsible for my dream. But getting it, no, I am alone.

Similarly, Dora, a woman in midlife, dreamed of living in Tuscany for a year.

> RESEARCHER: Can you tell me about the dream?
> DORA: I see myself in a cottage or a villa in Tuscany. I'm reading, bicycling into town for bread, going to museums, and taking Italian lessons, the whole nine yards.
> RESEARCHER: Is anyone with you in the dream?
> DORA: Occasionally, I see visitors and relatives, maybe my husband. But mostly, in my visions of it, I'm alone. This is *my* time, know what I mean?

These findings suggest that others may occasionally play a role in dreams, but overwhelmingly, dreamers cast the story with themselves as the sole starring character. It may be that these solo "scripts" allow people to more effortlessly change and alter their dreams, making them easier to manage as desires and wants evolve. Solo dreams might also reflect core cultural values focusing on individuality, independence, and autonomy.

Flexibility

Recall that we asked participants to identify their top-three dreams. Were participants' list of dreams fixed and singular in focus, or were they varied and assorted? When we posed questions on this issue, we found that our participants seemed to follow two dreaming "styles." About half of our participants could be characterized as *concentrated* dreamers. These people reported dreams confined to a single category—that is, the three dreams they shared with us were about the same theme, be it career, family, and so on. Mike, a man in midlife, explained the tight focus of his dreams:

> Once we had children, things became real clear. It's all about family, everything I think about. So when I dream, it's about the safety and security of my family. You know, working hard to get my kids through school, and mostly, getting them real nice things I probably could never afford. I want to see them land jobs they will always like, start their own families. Maybe that's impossible. But it's about my wife and me being able to feel good about our family, feel like we did our job, you know?

Jill, a high-school senior, talked about her concentrated attention to career:

> I'm at a point where career comes first. I have to get on track. Once I do that, I feel like I'll have time to think about other

things, other dreams and desires. But until then, I have to set my sights on achieving my dream job and all that comes with a great position like a big corner office or an assigned parking space. That's where my thoughts go.

Jill forwards the idea of freedom born of achievement: only after she gets on track can she expand her dreaming horizons. We found similar sentiments among other concentrated dreamers. By talking with participants about the way they ranked their dreams, we saw that concentrated dreamers thought sequentially—a style that conforms to Tavory and Eliasoph's concept of temporal landscapes. There was a definite progression for concentrated dreamers. Many told us that only after "arriving" at their primary dream themes would they be likely to move on to a new set of dream themes. Alan, a senior citizen, explained the progression this way:

> When I was younger, *all* of my dreams were about career. I thought once I succeeded in my career, I would be free to consider other ideas. Over time, that's what happened. *All* of my dreams moved from career to family. As you get older, you find that family, in the long run, is all that matters.

Andy, in midlife, noted a shift over time as well:

> As a kid, you want to be daring and maybe do something that people tell you—hey, you just can't do that because maybe you'd get hurt or sidetracked. As I got older, I gave up on adventure and started dreaming about advancing my career. That is my adventure now.

Thus, concentrated dreamers were disciplined and narrow in focus. Their approach was to take on one theme at a time and build a sequence of dream themes over the course of a lifetime.

The remaining half of participants were *diverse* dreamers. These people spread their dreams across various categories. Still, in examining the data, we found that the dream "sets" of the diverse group were not randomly organized. Rather, we found patterns here. For example, people who prioritized career dreams or self-improvement dreams tended to "balance" their offerings by describing adventure dreams as their second or third choice. In this way, these participants combined a serious focus with one oriented toward action and fun. Similarly, people who prioritized dreams about family often balanced that selection with more self-serving dreams of fame, wealth, and power; they distributed their dreams between self and others. Mike, a high-school senior, explained, "I tried to think about what I would want to do in all the parts of my life. I want to be serious in my achievements, but I want to have fun as well." Kerry, a woman in midlife, reported diverse dreaming as well, saying, "I'm kinda all over the place because I am dreaming about things I wanted to do, but didn't. That's covering a lot of ground. It's showing all the parts of me"

These comments suggest real differences between concentrated and diverse dreamers. The former saw their field of dreams as a narrow space with limited albeit exciting outcomes. The latter—diverse dreamers—used dreams to paint a more balanced future, a field of dreams that was broad and reflective of multidimensional selves.

Longevity

We wanted to learn whether people would ever give up on their dreams or whether they anticipated holding on to them for the long haul. It turns out that, for most respondents, dreaming is a lifelong endeavor, and many hold on to specific dreams for a very long time. About two-thirds of our participants told us that when it came to their top-ranked dream, they would never give up on it. About 55% of our participants felt the same about their second- and third-ranked dreams. They would keep striving for their dreams even if they did not accomplish them.

How did people explain this long-term commitment? Most reached for a central lesson of American culture: the popular adage that "one should never give up." Dehlia, an immigrant in her thirties, tapped the adage in describing her dream of getting a high-school degree:

> I am going to start soon and I'm not going to give up. Never. Always I look. Once I was watching TV and there was a ninety-year-old man who didn't want to die until he got his high-school degree. That's very encouraging and I always look for that kind of people, never giving up. I don't give up. I would like it to happen in five years, but if it takes longer, and it probably will, I will do it. One day it will happen.

Ivana, in midlife and recovering from cancer, dreamed of starting her own business—one that involved motivating and educating people about cancer. Despite her illness and an uncertain future, she too used the "never give up" mantra to fuel her dream:

> I was always taught that you don't give up your dreams. They may not always come to fruition, but dreams lead us places. Not necessarily a concrete place. But you have to hold on to it and see where it takes you. Never give up. That's it.

Mary, in midlife, dreamed of winning a national Scrabble competition. As she shared her dream, she told us,

> I've always felt that if you want to do something you have to try and go after it. That's why successful people are where they are. I'd rather take my chances than give up my dreams.

And Caleb, a college man who dreamed of starting his own business, saw the possibilities for delay, but nothing more:

> If I get someone pregnant, I may have to delay my dream. But overall, I don't think it will inhibit my goals and visions, but it would take more time to achieve.

For these participants, commitment to the dream was central to accomplishing it. Without commitment, nothing was possible.

Of course, some participants did envision giving up their dreams. But interestingly, dreams were sidelined only when an undeniable obstacle entered the picture. For example, some of the participants who dreamed of becoming star athletes or dancers told us that their dreams were likely impossible, citing prior injuries as obstacles: "I busted my knee," or "I have a bad back now," and so on. They still dreamed of such accomplishments, but in a more fantastical, or perhaps, an escapist way. Others talked about giving up a dream because of the risk presented by a potential future injury. For example, Robin, in midlife, always dreamed of being a professional figure skater. She told us, however, that she really didn't think this was realistic anymore:

> I've always been afraid of getting hurt, and that has never changed. It's gotten worse in fact. Oh yes. I haven't done it by now and it's the injuries. I know there are people who do it. I know a ninety-year-old who does it, but I know I won't. The ramifications are too great. The dream had a shelf life.

Changing obligations tempered dreaming for some. For example, Joe, in midlife, wanted to create a company that invested in other smaller businesses, but, he remarked,

If my wife lost her job, then we would lose the flexibility. Right now, she's working so we can take some risk. But if she lost her job, I would have to stop. At that point, I would have to deal with the here and now.

And for some, the unexpected made it impossible to continue dreaming. Brittany, in midlife, said her dream was to finish high school, but her dream was displaced by Hurricane Maria:

I guess maybe I should have given up the dream a long time ago. I have too many kids now. Since I dropped out, I went back once, but it wasn't good enough. For me, I know it's never going to happen because I lost everything.

It appeared to take a major force or obstacle for people to abandon their dreams. The overwhelming number of people who spoke of clinging to their dreams shows the power of culture in our imaginings of the future—something we will discuss at length in the next chapter. The value of stick-to-itiveness in the American story provides a potent message: dreamers simply do not relinquish their dreams until forced to by a concrete event. We are taught that dreams are so fundamental and so critical to our core that we must hold fast to them.

Transportability

What if you can't achieve your dreams? As it turns out, most participants want their dreams to live on—with or without them. Our participants were nearly twice as likely to say they would pass on their dreams to others as opposed to letting their dreams fade. This was especially true with regard to the dreams people identified as most important to them. The tendency to pursue one's dreams, even if it means relying on someone else to carry the dream forward, exemplifies, as did dream longevity, the tenacious nature of what it means to dream.

To whom would people pass their dreams and why? As one might guess, most participants—60%—wished to pass their dreams to children, grandchildren, or even siblings, forming a genetic bridge between themselves and the future. Tracy, a senior citizen, told us she is already passing on her dream of coaching women to success:

> I have three daughters that are incredibly different. Each one of them is an incredibly strong, motivated woman. I preached to them in the car ever since they were small girls. They were captive audiences. Now I have granddaughters, I use email or FaceTime with them. They are very young, but I want them to drink the Kool-Aid—you can do this, there's a bright future for you. Don't feel limited.

Shane, in midlife, said of his dream to be an inventor,

> I would pass it on to my offspring because people emulate, so to aspire to be an inventor and know you made something pretty great, that's something I want my kids to feel, to say they did something that mattered.

Addie, a college student interested in a singing career, told us,

> If I'm not able to live up to my singing dream, I would help my brother become a huge actor. I sing, he acts. That way, one of us might become rich and famous and live one another's dreams.

Family members are not the only people selected to carry on a dream. Almost a fifth of our respondents wanted to pass their dream to a nonrelative—someone they could consciously mentor, forming a pedagogical bridge between their dream and the future. For example, Chris, a man in midlife, dreamed of biking across the country. He thought he might pass the dream to someone he could coach:

> If I were in a position, I mean with resources and time, I think it would be fun to coach someone who would want to do this and see my dream through them. It's a plan B. But if I can't get this done, it's still exciting to see your dream through someone else's eyes.

Halle, a woman in her twenties, felt the same about her dreams of acting:

> If I don't make it on the stage, I could direct at a community theater and pass on what I learned. If I were to have kids, I would want to let my kids do what they want to do. But I would introduce them to the importance of art.

Still others, about a fourth of respondents, saw themselves passing their dream to a broader social group as a way of effecting social change. These participants were building a communal bridge between their dreams and the future. Ileana, a woman in midlife, dreamed of improving the foster care system and possibly opening several homes for foster children.

> If my idea works, I could try to get others to follow my lead. I would like to encourage the people in charge of the foster care system to fix what's broken and try to make it better. I would be the seed of a broader movement.

Chris, in midlife, dreamed of world traveling. Would he pass this dream on?

> Yes, absolutely. Think of all you learn by traveling! We have the responsibility, as humans, to make things better for the

people who come after us. We learn lessons so we can pass them on to people, to other generations.

Still, not everyone wanted to pass on their dreams. Some saw their dreams as highly personal, and therefore, felt their dreams would be of little or no interest to anyone else. Others felt that passing on a dream was too controlling. As Dave, a senior citizen, told us, "I don't want to force a business or anything else on my kids that they don't want." Most striking were those who felt that passing on a dream was akin to failure. Consider Evelyn, a woman in midlife, who dreamed of starting health centers for postcancer women:

> Passing it on is like giving it up, and that is not an option for me. In Japan, we aren't into support groups yet, so I would like to start that for women who need help.

The preponderance of those who sought to pass along their dreams suggests, like our findings on longevity, the tenacious nature of dreaming. Once you have developed a dream, you are reluctant to relinquish it.

Grounding

We heard many dreams during the months we spent in the field. Yet we wondered, How realistic were these dreams? Did our participants feel their dreams were grounded in reality? And did they see them as realistically achievable? Earlier, we presented *our* estimation of the feasibility of our participants' dreams. Now, we hear our respondents' views on the matter.

To explore this issue, we presented our participants with two queries. First, we asked participants to estimate for us the probability of achieving their dreams: "On a scale from 0 to 100, where o means 'I'll never achieve this dream' and 100 means 'I will definitely achieve this dream,' how likely is it that you will achieve your dream?"

Over two-thirds of our respondents gave a probability of 50% or higher, meaning they saw at least a fifty-fifty chance of achieving their dreams. Further, more than half of our respondents—55%—felt that the chances that their dreams would come true was 70% or higher![13] Thus, the large majority of our participants assumed that their dreams, no matter what they were, really could come true.

We tapped the realism of dreams in a second way. We asked people directly, "How realistic is this dream? Is it grounded in reality? Do you have the skills and talents to achieve it?" As unrealistic as some dreams seemed to us—learning to speak every known language, becoming president of the United States, levitating one's body, becoming a star shortstop for the Yankees, traveling to Mars—our participants were twice as likely to assess their dreams as realistic and achievable versus simply a "pipe dream." Thus, our study participants were much less likely than we were to view their dreams as improbable or fantastic.

How did people explain these assessments? Many used a longstanding cultural lesson as proof they would prevail: if you work hard and do your best, you will achieve your goals. Alecia, a high-school student whose dream was to learn all the languages of the world, cited hard work as the key to achieving her dream:

My dad always tells me if you have passion for something and you work hard, you can do it. And I have the passion. You can take that unrealistic dream and make it realistic. If I think about my dream, I get really passionate. I feel like this is awesome and I am so happy I found something I really like. So when I get stressed or upset, I just, like, start looking at vocabulary words or watch a movie in another language. I like the sound of it and I try to remember this is what I truly want in life.

Jackie, a man in his twenties, dreamed of becoming the mayor of a large urban city. He too saw lessons about hard work as the ticket to accomplishment:

I know I can become a mayor because of what I'm doing now and how far I came. Currently, I'm the vice president of Hall Council [a post in his apartment building]. That is honestly the first board that I've sat on. Just being on it for just this little amount of time has changed me dramatically cause I'm the kind of person who don't check emails and like I've never done it and I've missed opportunities because I don't check emails. But now, I check my email almost every hour. I'm more focused and I work hard. I'm more involved and I just pay attention to a lot of things, and it, like, changed my views on society.

Alecia may have to study hard and Jackie may have to become more organized, but realistically we know that much more would be required to succeed in achieving these dreams. Neither were actively planning for these outcomes, but that did not stop them from believing that their dreams would come true.

Even when people's dreams seemed fantastical, hard work was offered as a means of achievement. Robbie, a man in his twenties, dreamed of starting his own railroad. We asked him about the realistic potential of accomplishing this task:

RESEARCHER: That's a big, big task, a very challenging one. Railroad lines seem to be disappearing rather than growing.

ROBBIE: My dream is soooo based in reality. I am going to work so hard. It is so going to happen! Once you set a goal, you make it happen. I'm just going to go for it!

Artie, a man in his early thirties, had a similarly expansive dream—to redesign the U.S. economy and distribute wealth in a more equitable manner. Did he think he could do it?

I would need to expand my knowledge on politics and economics. Those subjects are so expansive, you need to learn how society works, how each social class works as well. When you think about it, like usually the people that handle this type of situation are economists and that's years of extensive study that they did. It's something that I could do, I would just need more knowledge.

Maria, a woman in her forties, had a big dream as well—but one that was much more personal. She lost her home in Hurricane Maria, and she dreamed of returning to Puerto Rico and buying another house:

It's more puttin' your mind to it and working to get it. That's what I say. I've done it. That's it. But I'm older now, I don't have the money. I'm on a fixed income. But if I work it out, there's a fifty-fifty chance I could do it again. Gotta stand up and work hard. Even though I can't work. I'm handicapped now. I had an accident, a couple of years ago. But you never know. . . . God is good.

And Reggie, a senior citizen who dreamed of becoming president, told us,

It could come true, but I equally have to dig deep and go all out. Major key things would have to fall into place. But look—Trump became President. Things can happen when you work hard!

Over and over again, we heard the notion that if one works hard, one will prevail. The type of dream was irrelevant. Rather, personal effort, no matter the potential obstacles, proved to be the primary "fuel" of future imaginings.

While hard work was, by far, most often cited as the means for achieving one's dreams, some invoked the fates, luck, or even God (remember Maria—God is good!) as the necessary ingredient for success. John, a man in midlife whose dream was to open his own restaurant at the beach, told us, "A couple of lucky breaks and some momentum and it becomes a reality." David, a man in his late thirties, dreamed of playing for the New York Giants. He echoed that "luck of the draw" approach, saying "circumstances might just break my way. If there's a lock out, I would do a walk on and get drafted." As for God, Rolanda, a senior citizen who wanted to grow old with her husband and share their life story with their grandchildren, saw God as pivotal to her success:

> I keep praying to the Lord that he will let it happen. I try to keep myself healthy. But as far as living, it's up to the Lord. I pray that it will happen. I do everything I can on my part.

Control

The overwhelming belief in hard work as a facilitator of dreams makes it clear that most of our respondents felt they were in control of their dreams and their futures. This sentiment came up repeatedly in focus groups and interviews. Jonathan, a college student, told us,

I can do anything. If you don't know that, it's like saying you can't do anything. You lack control. But you have control. That gives you depth. So have ambition!

Mary, a senior citizen who was struggling financially, still wanted to start her own clothing line. She told us,

I'm in control of this. I worked in the fashion industry for twenty-seven years before I went to government. I know I have the skills, more than anything, I have connections. I just need location. I'm on my way to North Carolina, and I'm going down there to help my daughter for a couple of weeks. I think we could probably figure this out. I know it.

And Kevin, a man in his twenties who dreamed of being a life coach, saw himself in complete control:

I believe in *The Secret*. You know, the book. If you see it, you can get it. I want the money to show people that you can start from nothing and get everything you want. If you actually ask for anything you want in life, you will get it. If you have the talent and the skills, it will happen. You're in control, so just seize it.

Even those who referenced the fates or God saw some role for themselves in the mix. They felt they had the ability to pray for what they wanted or to seize opportunity when the fates presented it. As Patricia, a senior citizen, told us,

I do, every day, read in a book called *Jesus Calling*, and I'm assured to trust in God and Jesus that things are going to work out all right for me.

For most of our respondents, nothing was really out of their hands.

Importance

We ended every focus group and interview with two final questions: "Do you think it is important to dream? Is it a positive thing?" An overwhelming proportion of our respondents gave us a resounding yes. Eighty-six percent of study participants thought people *must* have dreams. Participant after participant drove this point home. "If you don't have dreams," said Tina, a woman in late midlife, "you may as well be dead." Dominique, a college student, saw dreaming as a lifeline. "Dreaming makes one hopeful in a negative world." Keith, a man in early midlife, said, "Dreams are extremely important. A no-fail dream lets you strive to get to points." Sarah, a woman in early midlife, told us, "Anything that can get me to dream is good because it takes you in the direction of who you are and want to be." And Abe, a man in late midlife, felt dreaming was an obligation—part of a lesson for his family: "It's important that my son see that I'm continuing to dream. The legacy aspect."

Despite the fact that the dreams expressed might never come true, people saw the very act of dreaming as a vital, positive practice. Dreaming ignited passion, revealed one's core, and brought direction to one's life.

What People Didn't Say

It seems useful to focus for a moment on answers we rarely heard. To be honest, we were expecting a sizable group of people to dream of things like winning the lottery or becoming billionaires—dreams that represented quick ways to a life of luxury. Only three of our respondents mentioned the lottery, and only two discussed becoming billionaires. We also thought we would hear dreams about possessions—owning a mansion, a yacht, an island, or perhaps dreams about acquiring some sort of fantastical power—becoming invisible, being able to fly, or to time travel. Only two of our adult participants and five of our third and fourth graders mentioned such things. More often than not, we found that, even among the youngest participants, wealth or power was something to be earned—the product of commitment and dedication. While these respondents may not have had a plan for getting what they wanted, they believed work would be called for. For example, Angie, a third grader, told us she wanted to become a doctor so she could make enough money to run for president. Lani, a fourth grader, voiced an interesting path to wealth:

> First, I wanna be a famous softball player. I'm good at it and then be a great artist. Once I make a lot of money doing those things, I can get an elevator in my house and heated floors in my kitchen.

Zek, a fourth grader, also connected wealth to directed efforts:

> ZEK: If I become a millionaire . . .
> RESEARCHER: How would that happen?
> ZEK: I'm not sure. But then I'd work really, really hard to double it to be a billionaire. Then, I would make a list of everything I want to buy.
> RESEARCHER: What's on the list?
> ZEK: The Eiffel Tower.

What explains the lack of "overnight millionaire" sort of stories? Given how rare these sorts of answers were, we often asked people specifically if they had thought of these "big money" dreams. Manny, a man in his twenties, told us, "Money comes and goes. I dream of things that will last and move me somewhere." Alice, a woman in early middle age, said,

Dreams are about things you can be, not things just given to you. You do it, something fantastic, you arrive and feel proud of yourself. It's not just having something handed to you.

Even Enrique, a grammar-school student, told us, "Being a millionaire would be nice, but it's superficial; it's not a long-lasting thing."

The things about which people failed to dream tell us something important. There are limits to what is considered appropriate for dreaming. And appropriateness appears to be tied to the cultural lessons people learn about what and how to dream. Dreaming limits are another way in which dreams are socially and culturally patterned.

So What Does This All Mean?

Like us, our study participants saw dreams as visions of things that have not yet happened, that may never happen, and that reside not in concrete reality but in the life of the mind. Under such circumstances, what characterizes the dreams we build? Building on the work of cultural sociologists, we were able to explore several factors that inform our understanding of future imaginings: dream themes, feasibility, reach, clarity, social scope, flexibility, longevity, transportability, grounding, and control. We learned of the overwhelming belief that dreaming is an important activity. And by exploring the things that were rarely if ever mentioned, we learned that there are limits to what people see as acceptable dreaming.

The dream patterns we found can be clearly stated. First, the breadth of our participants' dream themes was rather narrow. Recall we found six major categories in which nearly all dreams could be classified. To be sure, there were variations within each of those categories, but the types of dreams people shared with us were fairly limited. Thus, people's dreams, while not always feasible, are not unbounded. Rather, there appears to be an acceptable range of things appropriate to dreaming. We also found that most people engaged in long-term dreaming; the stories they shared with us typically reached far into the future, suggesting that dreaming represents a journey to a new circumstance and a new space. Our work showed that while people's dreams had not yet happened, they were clear in the mind of participants—most people's dreams were filled with detail. In fact, some dreams were so realistic that participants reported actually feeling them whenever they thought or spoke of them. Next, we explored the social scope of participants' dreams to see who or what they included, and we found that, for most people, dreams were individualistic. Friends or family were sometimes involved, but only in a tangential way—as one person put it, they were cast as "extras," with dreams more heavily revolving around a solo performer. Our participants were equally divided on issues of flexibility. About half of the people we spoke to dreamed about a single, concentrated theme, while the other half were much more diverse in their dreaming, focusing on a combination of themes. We also discovered that dreams have "legs." Most of our participants said they would never give up on their dreams—even those that seemed fantastical. That led us to transportability. Dreams often transcended a person's lifetime. Most of our respondents said they would like to pass their dreams on to a family member, a mentee, or a relevant community. Transporting a dream to other actors became a bridge to achievement. Also important, we found that most participants saw their dreams as firmly grounded in reality. From this perspective, any dream was achievable. But unlike "cousins" of dreams such as aspirations or projects, our participants were not actively planning ways to achieve their dreams. Rather, dreams were imagined scenarios that people jumped into and inhabited. Overwhelmingly, our study participants felt in control of their dreams. No matter how fantastical they may have been, most people believed they had the power to achieve their dreams. When we consider the full array of findings, it should come as no surprise that 86% of our participants saw dreaming as a positive, highly important, even a mandated practice that ultimately benefited individuals. This is a sentiment that we will hear spoken and elaborated over and over in the chapters to follow.

As we review our findings, we begin to answer one of the main questions driving this study: are dreams highly personal and unique, or are they socially and culturally patterned? This chapter suggests an order or pattern across the dreams people share with us. As interesting as that finding may be, it invites other questions. Where do these patterns come from? And are these patterned parameters the same for people in different social locations? The chapters that follow examine these very issues.

Chapter 3

Cultural Lessons as Guidelines
for Dreaming

In the last chapter, we discussed the types of dreams that people shared with us in focus groups and interviews. Some clear patterns emerged in the dreams expressed by our study participants. Broadly speaking, the breadth of our participants' dreams was rather limited, suggesting some unspoken rules regarding the acceptable range of things appropriate to dreaming. We also found that, in the majority of cases, people's dreams were more fantastical than feasible, were long-term, highly detailed, and individualistic in nature. And no matter how fantastical the dream, most participants saw their dreams as grounded in reality and under their control. Dreaming was, according to 86% of participants, a positive, even a mandated practice that ultimately benefited individuals. Most told us one should never give up on dreams because dreaming keeps one striving. And if people could not personally accomplish their dream, many felt it should be passed on to someone who could. Dreaming, it seems, is a mission.[1]

These patterns suggest that people hold something akin to cultural guidelines for dreaming: what one can dream about, the parameters of those dreams, even, to some extent, how to dream. How can we explain these strong patterns when we are talking about something as seemingly personal as dreams? Work in cultural sociology helps us answer the question.

The Role of Culture in Dreaming

When individuals try to make sense of the world around them, when they attempt to plan or interpret their actions, they use culture. Cultural sociologists argue that there are two kinds of culture: "public culture" and "personal culture." Each form of culture impacts dreaming in different ways.

At one level, we are influenced by "public culture"—a group's values and beliefs; the concepts, scripts, story frames, and narratives by which those values and beliefs are expressed and given meaning; and finally, the customs, practices, and rules that guide behaviors and organize the social contexts in which we interact. As sociologist Ann Swidler describes it, public culture is "publicly available systems of meanings that define what it is possible to say,"[2] and, we would add, that provide lessons on what it is possible to do or imagine. Thus, public culture helps define an appropriate gift for one's best friend versus one's employer, the arguments that underpin your political allegiances, or how you understand love within a marriage. The components of public culture can be institutionalized via a set of behavioral and relational patterns such as those that exist in the institutions of family, religion, government, and so on. To be sure, public culture can change from context to context and from group to group. But at any given time, public culture structures the meanings that people encounter in their social environments, making those meanings coherent and organizing them as a blueprint for action.[3]

Culture can also influence us at another level. Personal culture becomes ingrained in body and mind. One element of personal culture consists of what sociologist Anthony Giddens called "practical consciousness"[4]—that is, the skills and "know how" we acquire from our repeated experiences. The knowledge that comprises practical consciousness is at the ready to help us automatically react to environmental prompts. It does not involve conscious awareness, and once acquired, it cannot necessarily be explained by those who apply it. Rather, practical consciousness operates reflexively when people perceive a signal from other actors or a cue from their environment that requires a response. Think of how, once knowing the procedures involved in riding a bike, your body comes to know exactly what to do. Once on the bike, the "feeling" of it takes over and you just simply ride. And even after years of nonriding, one can get on a bike and successfully ride again. Now, think about racial stereotypes. When we encounter people who are different from us, we often automatically conjure up ideas about what they are like and what their intentions might be; we may even automatically feel those ideas, experiencing fear, loathing, distrust, and the like.[5]

"Discursive consciousness" represents a second element of personal culture—the things that people verbally express about facts, events, and other aspects of the social world.[6] Discursive consciousness derives from explicit, symbolically mediated information (such as language) acquired through limited exposures. People use it in a slow, deliberate, and reflective manner. It comes into play when people carefully and consciously classify people, places, objects, or events, when they reason through problems and potential solutions, when they build justifications or rationalizations for their opinions or actions, or when they tap established rules to evaluate information, actions, or possibilities.[7] Thus, when someone asks you how to ride a bike, you revert to discursive consciousness and try to explain how you learned to ride or explicitly teach others your skill. Similarly, when someone asks you why you are tense or afraid when encountering someone different from yourself, you quite deliberately reach for narratives and justification that legitimate your reactions.[8]

We take the time to explain the various types of culture because each of these cultural forms plays a specific role in what and how people dream. Moreover, these types of culture are linked. Thus, when people use culture to make sense and meaning, they do not simply use each element of culture in isolation. Rather, they experience the relationship that connects public and personal culture. In the sections that follow, we elaborate on these points and illustrate culture in action.

The Public Culture of Dreaming

Let's take a look at what American public culture has to say about dreaming. What symbols, scripts, and narratives give us lessons on dreaming? What customs and rules govern the act of dreaming? To examine these issues, we did numerous web searches to review the extensive storehouse of cultural lessons on dreaming. We used key words such as "dreams," "dreaming," "future imaginings," "fantasies," "wishes," and "desires," and we linked these with words and phrases such as "public symbols," "heroes," "books," "films," "television," "songs," "poetry," and "quotations." These searches provided us with hundreds of examples, allowing us to analyze the contents of the messages their creators conveyed about dreaming. Specifically, we read and viewed the words and images contained in these lessons on dreaming and coded those messages as positive or negative. We also looked for thematic categories that distinguished the various lessons we found.[9] In so doing, we discovered several longstanding and widely shared lessons on dreaming.

Four Positive Lessons

Public culture presents us with four dominant and quite positive lessons regarding both the appropriate fodder for dreams and the appropriate ways to dream.

Positive Lesson 1—Opportunity Is Boundless: If you live in the United States, you are familiar with the "American Dream." You may view it as alive or dead, as real or mythical, but you cannot escape its place in public culture. The central tenet of the American Dream is that America is a land of opportunity. You can achieve anything if you work hard and put your mind to it. America is where dreams come true. That lesson is a powerful part of American public culture, and it is spread through iconic symbols, historical narratives, books, songs, pictures, and films.

Some of our most famous national icons support lessons of boundless opportunity. The Statue of Liberty embodies the message—especially for immigrants. To pass Lady Liberty's threshold is to be welcomed to a land of opportunity. As Lady Liberty's inscription proclaims,

> Give me your tired, your poor,
> Your huddled masses, yearning to breathe free,
> The wretched refuse of your teeming shore,
> Send these, the homeless, tempest-tost to me,
> I lift my lamp beside the golden door.
> —*Emma Lazarus*

Similarly, the iconic Gateway Arch in St. Louis, Missouri, commemorates the westward expansion of the United States and symbolizes the boundless opportunities the West offered American pioneers.

Historical chronicles of American business icons convey the same message: Andrew Carnegie, John D. Rockefeller, Henry Ford, Thomas Edison, and, later, Ray Crock, Steve Jobs, Bill Gates, and Mark Zuckerberg. So too do the stories of political and social figures who triumphed over difficult circumstances— Frederick Douglass, Abraham Lincoln, Harriett Tubman, Susan B. Anthony, Bill Clinton, Shirley Chisholm, or Michelle Obama, to name just a few. Popular celebrities' "rags to riches" stories are part of boundless opportunity lessons: Elvis Presley, B. B. King, Dolly Parton, Jay Z, Lil' Kim, and Oprah Winfrey represent just some of those in this large category.

In fiction, fairy tales read by so many American children— *Cinderella*, *Aladdin*, and *The Little Engine That Could*—teach lessons of boundless opportunity. Classic rags-to-riches stories like *Jane Eyre*, *Great Expectations*, and *Oliver Twist* place the lesson on elementary- and high-school reading lists. The Horatio Alger Myth, first presented in Alger's 1868 book *Ragged Dick*, centralized a rags-to-riches script that became common to future American novelists. On Broadway, we followed the rise of Peggy Sawyer (*42nd Street*), Eliza Doolittle (*My Fair Lady*), Little Orphan Annie (*Annie*), and Frankie Vali (*Jersey Boys*). Hollywood heroes like Rocky Balboa (*Rocky*), Katherine Johnson (*Hidden Figures*), Christopher Gardner (*The Pursuit of Happyness*), and Jamal Malik (*Slumdog Millionaire*) show us how to go from nothing to something. Television game shows from *Queen for a Day* to *Who Wants to Be a Millionaire* and competition shows like *American Idol* and *America's Got Talent* are fed by the boundless opportunity script.

These examples represent the tip of the iceberg regarding cultural lessons that celebrate the notion of endless possibilities. If you set your sights, the lesson teaches, nothing is impossible.

Positive Lesson 2—Dream Big: Lessons in public culture teach us not simply to dream, but to dream big. As Jiminy Cricket instructed Pinocchio, "If your heart is in your dream, no request is too extreme."[10] Of course, the dream-big lesson extends beyond cartoon characters. We tell those with new ideas or wishes to "go big or go home." In schools and universities, we inspire students and future workers with accomplishments like the Pilgrims' establishment of the Plymouth Colony, the Lewis and Clark expedition, and later, the moon landing, the launching of the Mars rovers, or the Human Genome Project. We focus students on the successful completion of game-changing structures such as the Brooklyn Bridge, the Transcontinental Railroad, the Hoover Dam, the Suez Canal, or the Freedom Tower. We remind people of the big dreams behind inventions such as the cotton gin, the telephone, the automobile, penicillin, personal computers, or the Internet. And we beckon people to dream as big as those who developed self-driving cars, space rockets, intelligent robots, or medical innovations such as the Gamma Knife or CRISPR.

Of course, dreaming big is a central mantra of self-help books, with online booksellers touting thousands of titles on the subject—especially in books designed for children. Perhaps the late minister and motivational speaker Robert Schuller best summarized the dream-big adage: "you can often measure a person by the size of his dream."[11] The lesson is so pervasive that we cast popular cultural characters who fail to dream big—television characters like Jerry, George, Elaine, and Kramer

FIG. 3.1. The Freedom Tower—A "Dream Big"
Structure (Copyright Karen A. Cerulo)

(*Seinfeld*), Phoebe Buffay (*Friends*), and Haley Dunphy (*Modern Family*)—as failures and jokes.

Positive Lesson 3—Never Give Up on Your Dreams: American public culture teaches us that opportunity must be accompanied by determination and tenacity. To underscore the lesson, sites like Twitter's "Motivational Quotes" (over 900,000 followers), Instagram's "positivemindsetdaily" (over 500,000 followers), and literally hundreds of others offer daily reminders to persist in dreaming. Some "never give up" lessons come from national icons. "You're never defeated until you surrender," said Albert Einstein. Thomas Edison echoed the sentiment: "Our greatest weakness lies in giving up. The most certain way to succeed is always to try just one more time." Abolitionist and writer Harriet Beecher Stowe agreed: "Never give up, for that is just the place and time that the tide will turn." But the lesson is taught by successful people in all walks of life. Business mogul Conrad Hilton warned, "Successful men and women keep moving. They make mistakes, but they don't quit." "Winners never quit and quitters never win," proclaimed noted football coach Vince Lombardi. Author Maya Angelou advised, "There is no failure as long as you learn from your experience, continue to work and continue to press on for success." Activist Jesse Jackson offered similar counsel: "If you fall behind, run faster. Never give up, never surrender, and rise up against the odds." And famed rapper Nicki Manaj offers the same "truth": "Your victory is right around the corner. Never give up."[12]

The never-give-up lesson floods self-help books: Jim Collins's *Good to Great*, Randall Lane's *You Only Have to Be Right Once*, Manny Khoshbin's *Driven*, Joyce Mayer's *Never Give Up*; even Donald Trump promotes the lesson, naming his 2008 bestseller *Never Give Up: How I Turned My Biggest Challenges into Success*. The mantra spans the generations. Nearly every film made by director Frank Capra—e.g., *Mr. Smith Goes to Washington*, *It's a Wonderful Life*—touts this lesson, which is repeated through the years in films such as *Fame*, *Flashdance*, *The Shawshank Redemption*, *Precious*, *Castaway*, *Life of Pi*, and *Unbroken*, to name just a few. And in music, from Van Heusen and Cahn's "High Hopes" to KRS-One's "Never Give Up," lessons promoting stick-to-itiveness are critical to achieving dreams.

Positive Lesson 4—Optimism Makes Anything Possible: Several year ago, author Karen A. Cerulo[13] wrote about cultural lessons promoting blind optimism, a sentiment central to American public culture (and many other cultures worldwide). In *Never*

Saw It Coming, she found that, overwhelmingly, people are much better at imagining best-case scenarios than worst-case scenarios. This is especially true for dreaming about the future. Cerulo based her conclusions on a wide variety of data, including interviews, surveys, artistic and fictional accounts, media reports, historical data, and official records that addressed key elements of social life—for example, intimate family relationships, key transitions in our lives, the places we work and play, and the boardrooms of organizations and bureaucracies. Her research showed that most groups and communities adopt elaborate cultural practices that fortify and concretize the central position of excellence in culture. We banish, seclude, or shun the worst—prisoners, the sick, the mentally ill. We cloud the worst in vagueness or shadow it in a barrage of best-case images. (Ever notice how best of this-or-that lists outnumber worst lists more than twenty to one?) We recast and redefine the worst so that it seems better than it is. (Make lemons out of lemonade, right?) Cerulo argues that public culture encourages the storage of sunny-side images in individual memory. This makes best-case scenarios easiest to access when faced with social events—including disasters and traumas. Moreover, as these practices become institutionalized, they establish blind optimism as a group or community's modus operandi.[14]

Barbara Ehrenreich elaborates on this theme in her book *Bright-Sided*. Ehrenreich contends that blind optimism is so central to public culture and so ingrained in many people's minds that "people can be counted on to impose it on themselves." She continues,

Leading proponents of positive thinking are entrepreneurs in their own right, marketing their speeches, books and DVDs to anyone willing to buy them. Large companies make their employees listen to the speeches and may advise them to read the books; they may fire people who persist in a "negative attitude."[15]

Cerulo and Ehrenreich are not alone in their contentions. Social and cognitive psychologists have shown repeatedly that people have an "optimistic bias" when it comes to envisioning their futures.[16]

In American public culture, the history of blind optimism is a long one. It motivated the early settlers to push westward in the search for gold and oil. It set the stage for the building of the transcontinental railroad and the search for the Northwest Passage. But in recent decades, lessons of blind optimism have been fueled by iconic motivators like Norman Vincent Peale and Robert Schuller and kept alive by contemporary figures such as Tony Robbins, Oprah Winfrey, and Joel Osteen. Research findings from positive psychologist Martin Seligman, the academic guru of a positive thinking research agenda, have also made their way into the broader culture. Politicians play a role here too. The sunny optimism of presidents such as FDR ("The only thing we have to fear is fear itself"), Ronald Reagan ("It's morning in America"), and Barack Obama ("The audacity of hope"; "Relentless optimism") helped build their iconic status.

Are There Lessons to the Contrary?

To be sure, American public culture relays other lessons on dreaming as well—lessons that are decidedly more negative. Two, in particular, surface repeatedly.

Negative Lesson 1—The Higher They Rise, the Harder They Fall: This cultural lesson teaches that the relentless pursuit of dreams, particularly those involving fame, wealth, or power, may ultimately backfire on the dreamer. High risers, it is thought, likely engage in shortcuts, careless mistakes, or exploitation that leads to their demise. There is a "correct" way to achieve dreams, and those who ignore the rules will pay dearly.

The warnings to high risers begin in the moral lessons of religion. Countless scriptural passages caution against those who focus on a climb to wealth. The book of Proverbs tells us, "Those eager to get rich will be punished" (28:20–22) for "he who trusts in his riches will fall" (11:28). The evangelist Luke, quoting Jesus, warns, "Take care, and be on your guard against all covetousness, for one's life does not consist in the abundance of his possessions" (12:15). The book of Timothy continues the script: "Those who want to become rich bring temptation to themselves and are caught in a trap" (6:8–12). The Quran also warns against dreams of fast or ill-gotten wealth: "And those who hoard gold and silver and spend it not in the way of Allah— give them tidings of a painful punishment" (9:34).

High risers fall hard: the lesson pervades much of the literature so central to American education. *Macbeth* teaches that dreams involving a singular pursuit of power ultimately end in misery. In *The Great Gatsby*, dreams of material wealth and obsessive love prove the recipe for Gatsby's ultimate downfall. *The Sun Also Rises* uses the exploits of Jake Barnes and Lady Brett Ashley to warn of the moral and spiritual bankruptcy that awaits high risers. In films and theater too, we regularly witness the destruction that visits those who pursue dreams of wealth and power at all cost: Charles Foster Kane (*Citizen Kane*), The Wicked Witch of the West (*The Wizard of Oz*), Sara, Harry, Tyrone, and Marion (*Requiem for a Dream*), Michael Corleone (*The Godfather*), Tony Montane (*Scarface*), Darth Vader (*Star Wars*), Bud Fox (*Wallstreet*), and Jordan Belford (*The Wolf of*

Wall Street). Even television characters obsessed with a rise to the top never experience happy endings: consider Walter White (*Breaking Bad*), Daenerys Targaryen (*Game of Thrones*), and Tony and Carmela Soprano (*The Sopranos*). And if film, theater, or television don't convey the message, news stories about financial scoundrels can get the job done—think of Bernie Madoff, Michael Milken, Martin Siegel, Ivan Boesky, Charles Keating, and Ken Lay, just to name a few.

Negative Lesson 2—The Deck Is Stacked; the System Is Rigged: Many of the lessons found in public culture warn that dreaming is pointless because "the deck is stacked and the system is rigged." Opportunity is not available to all, making dreaming a futile proposition. When the deck is stacked, dreaming may actually prove harmful, for it fills one's head with impracticalities and impossibilities.

There is, of course, a factual basis to the stacked-deck lesson. In *Nickel and Dimed*, Barbara Ehrenreich[17] stepped away from her journalist's desk and began working a number of unskilled jobs including being a maid, a waitress, and a nursing home aide. She showed us that no amount of hard work could lift these people from a life teetering on poverty, making things like decent living conditions, home ownership, adequate health care, childcare, or any form of a financial cushion or emergency fund simply out of reach. Ehrenreich's study is not simply anecdotal. Mathew Desmond's[18] work on U.S. evictions leads to similar conclusions. Evicting those who can't make their rent only ensures that they will *never* make their rent, that they will never be lifted from poverty. Many other social science studies illustrate the massive and growing inequality that invades the U.S. economic system and reinforces a "rigged" social structure.[19] As economist Joseph Stiglitz summarizes the condition,

When poor-boy-makes-good anecdotes get passed around in the media, that is precisely because such stories are so rare.... America has long outdone others in its level of inequality, but in the past 40 years it has reached new heights. Whereas the income share of the top 0.1 percent has more than quadrupled and that of the top 1 percent has almost doubled, that of the bottom 90 percent has declined. Wages at the bottom, adjusted for inflation, are about the same as they were some 60 years ago![20]

Most recently, we have seen the deck stacked against the poor and those of color when it comes to contracting COVID-19, having access to vaccines that fight the disease, and COVID-19-related unemployment. Meanwhile, financial "benefits" of COVID-19 have been enjoyed by those in the wealthiest class.

To be sure, lessons describing stacked decks and rigged systems permeate American public culture. Historical images and descriptions of the 1932 Bonus March, growing urban ghettos, the plight of migrant farmworkers, homelessness, and movements like Occupy Wall Street keep the lessons front and center. In literature, stacked decks and rigged systems are a common theme. During the Great Depression, John Steinbeck (in *Of Mice and Men* and *The Grapes of Wrath*) described the stacked deck experienced by the poor. After World War II, Arthur Miller's Willie Loman brought the lesson to the foreground (*Death of a Salesman*). In the mid-twentieth century, Ralph Ellison's *Invisible Man* underscored how people of color are excluded from the opportunities of which dreams are made. The theme was repeated by many authors, including Lorraine Hansberry (*A Raisin in the Sun*) and Toni Morrison (*Song of Solomon*). More recently, a number of award-winning films, such as *Roma, Moonlight, When They See Us,* and *American Son,* remind us how a stacked deck can kill the dreams of the poor and those of color.

The cautionary lessons contained in narratives guided by the "deck is stacked" and the "system is rigged" themes, like those contained in "the higher they rise, the harder they fall" narratives, counter the positive lessons on dreaming. But do they overpower them?

Choosing Lessons from Public Culture

We can see that the public culture on dreaming offers us conflicting lessons—some lessons praise and promote dreaming, while others demean and discourage it. For cultural sociologists, such contradictions are not surprising. Ann Swidler contends that public culture is not a unified system. Rather, culture is diverse, providing a "tool kit" filled with varied information. People select from the toolkit as needed to inform or legitimate their thinking and actions. This means that people "know how to do different kinds of things in different circumstances" and that people "know more culture than they use" at any given time.[21]

As we review the cultural tools related to dreams, we must ask, Are people familiar with the public culture of dreaming— both its positive and negative lessons? To answer that question, we must revisit our groups' discussions and interviews. What did our participants verbally express with regard to public culture's lessons on dreaming? Which of the many lessons did they use to make their case?

In speaking with our study participants and reviewing their written answers, we found, across our sample, that people were familiar with both the positive and negative cultural lessons on dreaming. However, our participants ultimately embraced only

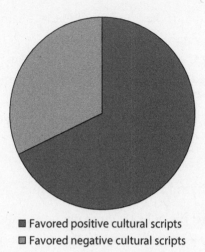

■ Favored positive cultural scripts
☐ Favored negative cultural scripts

FIG. 3.2. Proportion of Study Participants
Favoring Public Culture's Positive versus
Negative Lessons on Dreaming

one of those categories in building their dreams. There was no middle ground. Figure 3.2 shows that just over two-thirds of our study participants favored public culture's positive lessons on dreaming.

What was particularly striking about people's positive takes on dreaming was the automatic way in which these lessons were voiced. Such answers reflected the practical consciousness we mentioned earlier in the chapter. In other words, the statements were "matter of fact," offered almost as "settled law," with little deliberation or circumspection. For example, platitudes about "boundless opportunity" were sprinkled throughout participants' comments. Jack, a businessman in midlife, told us, "I believe in the reality of opportunity." Kevin, a college student, stated, "If you live in America, you have won the lottery. There's so much opportunity, you can achieve anything." And some like Kiko, a recent immigrant, said, "You know this country. America *is* opportunity." Hard work was often an aspect of boundless opportunity. Terry, a high-school senior, told us, "You have to get real and work for what you want." Della, long retired, noted, "You have the ability to make anything possible. Just keep at it." Ruth, unemployed, echoed that sentiment, saying, "Technology has made it possible to learn anything, so get going. A lot of what is possible keeps growing." And Jose, a homeless man, said of his dream, "Work hard enough. It will happen." Study participants repeated these statements over and over, as if they represented "natural" or "everybody knows" aspects of dreaming.

Our participants were also very much aware of public culture's "dream big" directive, and they often referenced it with little or no extended reflection. Diedre, a nurse in midlife, told us, "You have to dream big. Life will temper down your dreams if they're too big, but you certainly have to start big." Al, an accountant in midlife, maintained, "You have to have ability, but also the confidence to reach for something; it should be something big. Dream with no barriers." Liz and Nick, two high-school students, were on the same page:

LIZ: You have to start by thinking about something without any limits attached; you aren't thinking like there's no way I could ever do that so you let your mind go places you might not otherwise.

NICK: Right: Have really big dreams, to be like the hero, to do something on a larger scale; less tied to specifics of the moment.

Here, too, one can see the matter-of-fact nature of people's belief in this aspect of dreaming. These platitudes seem to jump from people's lips with no reflection or extensive deliberation.

When it came to the "never give up" lesson, we heard the same singular thought over and over throughout the study.

Ernie, a college student, said, "Be dream driven and have success in your mind and know if you fail you will keep trying." Tallia, in midlife, declared the same: "Till I'm down underground, I'm still going to keep trying." And Rydell, a man in his thirties, said, "Failure teaches you to work hard and get up. Your dreams don't fail. You can, though. You have to keep chasing the dream." Max, a man in his twenties, placed the "never give up" lesson in historical perspective:

> Inventors keep failing and learn from the mistakes. They say, let me fix this thing and try again and they keep going and that's how society is nowadays. People learn from their mistakes and keep going. That's why history is important.

In group after group and interview after interview, the "never give up on your dreams" lesson was frequently repeated like a mantra, like a strict, internalized rule of successful dreaming.

So many of our subjects also immediately gave voice to the blind optimism that makes one feel anything is possible. This idea was confidently voiced with little debate or careful examination. In many cases, the answers seemed automatic, almost robotic. Jonathan, a college student, told us,

> At some level, you gotta be blindly optimistic. I can do anything. If you don't know that, it's like saying you can't do anything. You lack control. Optimism gives you depth. Have ambition!

Hannah, a woman in her twenties, expressed similar sentiments. "Dreaming is about optimism. I'm a very optimistic person and put 100% in something, and if it doesn't work, you can put 100% into plan B. But you have to keep positive." For our participants, blind optimism was a tool of survival. In Dana's words (a man in midlife), "Thinking of possibilities is important. It makes you hopeful in a negative world." Yolanda, a senior citizen, echoed the sentiment:

> Once you leave this earth, what are they gonna remember you for? Is it gonna be positive, negative, or just, you know, you just kinda like gone with the wind, going through the motions? I never wanna be complacent where I'm stuck in no growth. So it's all about legacy, growth, and optimism.

Despite these many positive takes on dreaming, we also heard some of public culture's more negative lessons on the subject. For just over 30% of our study participants, these negative themes dominated their answers. We were struck by the fact that those voicing negative sentiments on dreaming seemed more deliberative in expressing their thoughts. It was as if these people were quite aware that they were "breaking the tide." Such answers reflect the discursive consciousness we mentioned earlier in the chapter. In other words, people reasoned through their answers, creating detailed legitimations of their dreams—legitimations frequently tied to their personal experiences.

Consider the "higher they rise, the harder they fall" theme. People applied this lesson to make a careful argument. It went something like this: many Americans expect something for nothing; such a thing is not feasible; but even if one is able to rise without effort, such rewards will likely quickly evaporate. Richard, a man in midlife, told us,

> You may rise high, but eventually, you're gonna fall. [*pause*] I see this all the time with the kids I coach in little league. Everyone wants a trophy and when they just get it, everyone thinks they've hit the big leagues. They feel like they're riding high. They get cocky. Then, when they lose a game, they

crash. [*pause*] Frankly, as I think about it, I think it's good when you lose because if you dream of being the best, it's got to be a long-term, consistent effort. Just look at some of these phenoms on major-league teams. When they get swept up in one good season, in the next year, they often drop to the bottom of the barrel.

In a similar vein, recall the participants mentioned in chapter 2 who dismissed the idea of dreaming about the lottery, arguing that lottery winnings would be the result of mere luck and lacked the foundation of purpose. Anita, a nurse in midlife, said,

That's why so many lottery winners lose all the money! I've seen this on the news. They win big and think they'll be on top forever. Then they fall hard. [*pause*] I don't think you can just assume you'll always be on top. Success or riches don't just fall in your lap and stay there. [*pause*] I wonder how many lottery winners stop and make a plan. Maybe that's why they tumble down the ladder of success. You can't just leap to the top of the pile and expect to stay there.

Some participants felt that high-rising dreamers were selfish, perhaps dishonest, and would eventually fail. Elio, a driver for UPS, reflected,

I think about this a lot. I deliver lots of packages to some of the big shots in New York. Some of those people, like the stock traders, shot up like a bolt of lightning. But some of this stuff is so shady. We learned that in the last recession, right? [*pause*] People did things that made them quick money and got them high status. But it didn't last for many of them. [*pause*] I see people come and go from those doorman buildings. I wonder sometimes how it happens to people who should know what they're doing.

Claire, a high-school student, had a similar take:

> I saw *The Great Gatsby* and it was so elegant and rich and I decided I want to be rich. Then I read Thoreau and it really changed my mind. [*pause*] When people just grab for the money, they're gonna ultimately fail. We see that so often. [*pause*] I don't want to just grab for the money. Anyway, Gatsby was sort of a thief, right? And really unhappy too.

These respondents felt one cannot magically catapult to career heights, fame, or any other dream without a cost. And in articulating that negative lesson, they were quite deliberate in making their case.

When it came to negative cultural lessons on dreaming, most striking were participants who voiced the idea that "the deck is stacked" and "the system is rigged." These people deliberated on personal experience, using it to explain and legitimate their ideas. Laura, a senior citizen, told us,

> I have the skills to broker peace in the Middle East, but I just don't have the opportunity. [*pause*] You need to have influence to accomplish a dream like that. I'm not that educated and I don't really know important people. [*pause*] I'm not sure how I would get into the right social circle of people to help me. I think about it, but I don't see a break for me. I'm not in the right, um, place—socially speaking.

Augusto, a man in his twenties, elaborated on this point:

> The way that society and economics is made up right now, like politically, you have so many rich people who have control of the country. Usually those big companies with rich people, they pretty much control everything that happens. [*pause*] I think about it, and I think if you want wealth equality

in the world, it's first managing those people who have a large say in how things work. This has been an ongoing thing. I just feel fixing it is unrealistic. Greed takes up a lot of the country. It's hard to know how to break that pattern.

Jesse, a homeless man in midlife, expressed similar concerns:

I see a lot of hurt in this world. I see people that are willing and don't have, well, I mean, doors close on them. It's hard for them. [*pause*] Nowadays a person alone can't make it. It's very hard. That's another thing—you have to fight. OK, but when you start fighting and the doors close, it brings you right back down. [*pause*] Look at the pay work is giving people. What kind of opportunity you got? [*pause*] Having a chance is not giving someone enough barely to eat, barely to live. You know? That's livin' as a slave. That's the way I look at it.

Quotes illustrating the use of positive versus negative lessons on dreaming are indicative of a broader pattern in our study. Indeed, these findings tell us something important about the relationship between public culture and the two forms of private culture. Recall that in the book's introduction, we posed the following questions: Are people's dreams something about which they consciously deliberate and can easily articulate? Or are they somewhat unconscious, seemingly automatic responses that people make without being able to fully explain where the dreams come from or what they truly mean? These questions emerge from a broader debate among cultural sociologists. Do we form attitudes, ideas, opinions, reactions, and behaviors automatically and unconsciously (i.e., is practical consciousness involved), or are there conscious deliberations behind our attitudes, ideas, opinions, reactions, and behaviors (i.e., is discursive consciousness involved)? The differences we saw among those embracing positive versus negative cultural lessons on dreaming suggest an interesting answer.

American culture and many cultures worldwide are plagued by a commitment to blind optimism. People learn cultural lessons that edify optimism and background worst cases from sight. Indeed, for most people, worst-case scenarios exist only in the recesses of their minds. This has implications for dreaming. Positive cultural lessons dominate the public culture on dreaming. Cultural lessons directing us to emphasize the positive prioritize the storage of sunny-side images in individual and collective memory. That means that best-case scenarios will be most prominent and easiest to access when faced with notions of the future. Knowing this, it is not surprising that those who build their dreams upon positive cultural lessons do not think twice about the oozing optimism of their dreams. Such thoughts come to them automatically. The positive nature of their dreams "feels" right and seems obvious in a bright and buoyant world.

Those who build their dreams on negative cultural lessons are challenging dominant cultural messages. Thus, they must become more deliberate in explaining or justifying their position. Among those who invoked negative cultural lessons on dreaming, we heard more reflective, expansive discussion, more reasoned explanations, and fewer platitudes; these respondents were much more contemplative. In essence, these participants dug deeper to challenge the status quo of blind optimism and to understand and articulate their pessimism and doubt. Thus, weaving negative lessons into one's thinking on dreaming—what dreams should be about and how easily they can be accomplished—requires greater work and a conscious "thinking through" as people battle the overpowering presence of positivity.

Who Uses What Culture
Lessons . . . and When?

Why do different dream lessons—positive versus negative—resonate with different people? There are several possible explanations.

We must always acknowledge that our study participants' propensity for positive cultural lessons on dreaming may be tied to our methods of measurement. One might worry that we "primed" people to think positively by the very question we asked: *If you knew you could not fail, what would you do . . . or where might you go . . . or what might you want to have . . . or what might you be?* In essence, our question took failure off the table. While we recognize this possibility, two things speak against it. As we mentioned earlier, in pretests of our interviews, we asked the question we ultimately used in this study along with several other questions about dreaming. We did not notice a decrease in the use of positive messages no matter what question we posed to pretest participants. Optimism and positive cultural lessons ruled the day no matter how we approached discussion of future imaginings. Second, the use of positive public culture was not universal. We did find variation. That suggests our final choice of question left ample room for answers linked to both positive and negative cultural lessons.

If not measurement, what else might explain the cultural lessons people invoked in building their dreams? Cultural sociologist Ann Swidler suggests that people use culture differently at different social moments. She is particularly interested in comparing how culture works in settled versus unsettled times. Settled times refer to stable, orderly periods within a group, community, or society at large, while unsettled times refer to periods of turbulence and social transformation. Swidler suggests that in settled times people "profess ideals they will not follow (e.g. Do onto others as you would have them do onto you) and utter platitudes without examining their validity (e.g. A rising tide lifts all boats)."[22] In other words, people are most likely to automatically express cultural ideas that represent the dominant traditions of the period. Using Swidler's reasoning, settled times should find people favoring positive cultural lessons in building their dreams, as these are the dominant lessons of the period. In unsettled times, Swidler expects to see a different approach. When people face a lack of stability, they will likely be more conscious and deliberative in using culture. Indeed, they may use culture that challenges the dominant lessons of the day, devising new strategies of action designed to transform society. In the case of dreams, Swidler's work leaves room for the use of negative cultural lessons on what and how people dream, for in unsettled times, one can challenge the dominant cultural lessons.

Was the period in which we collected our data settled or unsettled? It is difficult to say. From a political point of view, the time was quite unsettled. Americans were living in a highly partisan world. Donald Trump's election exacerbated a "them versus us" way of seeing the country. Zachary Neal shows that the U.S. Congress had never been more polarized, with working relations between members of the two parties either absent or negative. Among the broader population, studies by cultural sociologists Arlie Hochschild or Robert Wuthnow are just two of the scholars who described a growing political divide, with Democrats and Republicans, progressives and conservatives living in bubbles that excluded those with different views or different backgrounds.[23] These differences were visible on the public stage during our data collection period. Large-scale protests on contentious issues were exemplified by the Women's

March and the March for Science. The same was true for the
Charlottesville rally that pitted White supremacists against
proponents of racial justice. Contention marked nationwide
protests organized by Black Lives Matter—especially with
reference to police shootings. The same can be said of demon-
strations against the establishment of sanctuary cities and challenges to the rights of refugees and immigrants. One could not
use any form of media without encountering the great political
divide. Cable news outlets, political Internet sites, and social
media posts all underscored the partisan nature of the political
arena. National polling data tells the same story.[24]

Our data collection period represented an unsettled period
regarding the impact of climate change as well. Extreme weather
events, floods, hurricanes, excessive heat waves, droughts, and
wildfires have increased significantly over the last few decades,
but especially over the last five years. In 2017 alone, we saw three
major hurricanes; the year was also on record for the most rapid
intensification of hurricanes.[25] During this same period, 2017–
2018, we saw the highest numbers of wildfires in recent history:
129,582.[26] These disasters were in the forefront of the public
mind. Polling done on people's visons for the future showed
that two-thirds of respondents saw climate change as a very serious or somewhat serious threat to global safety.[27]

In contrast, most characterized the United States as enjoying
an economically settled period at the time we collected our
data. Unemployment dropped to the lowest rate since 1968, and
the Dow Jones average set 70 record point highs.[28] Real median
incomes for American households (i.e., income adjusted for
inflation) rose 2.51%, a continuation of an ongoing trend; the
nation saw increases of 8.49% in real median incomes during
the three-year period from 2015 to 2017.[29] The GDP growth rate
was 2.48% for our data collection period—the healthiest

number since 2014. Existing home sales and housing prices continued to show slow but steady increases. The number of first-time home buyers began to grow, rebounding from the lean years of the Great Recession, with first-time buyers showing greater diversity than current homeowners by age, race, and marital status. When collecting our data, the United States was in the midst of a steady rise in new residential construction. Since the height of the Great Recession, foreclosure filings and rates have been trending down, hitting a thirteen-year low in 2018—shortly after we ended data collection. The consumer confidence index also rose, moving from 111.6 to 123.1 during our data collection period. To be sure, it was not a perfect economy. Income inequality and, for some, stagnating wages, were still major problems.[30] But overall, the economy presented a strong, positive picture. And we might note that both Democrats and Republican were embracing the good economic news, though they disagreed about which party deserved the credit for the positive numbers.[31]

There is evidence to suggest that a growing economy spells stability to people, and, for our purposes, can make them more likely to feel optimistic about dreaming. In a strong economy, people tend to buy more, travel more, enjoy more leisure activities, and take more risks—all things upon which dreams are built. For example, vacation spending topped $100 billion for the first time in 2017. Similarly, business start-ups, always a risky endeavor, were trending upward. Total capital expenditures across all U.S. businesses were on an upward trend.[32] In multiple polls taken as we were in the field, four times as many Americans showed optimism about the country's future versus pessimism, while 82% of Americans said their American Dream has already been achieved or was in reach. Sixty-seven percent of those responding to national polls said they were optimistic about their personal futures, especially their lives within their local communities. Even among minority groups, who are most likely to face structural disadvantages as they work toward achieving their dreams, optimism ran high—sometimes higher than it did among Whites.[33]

What we have here is a mixed bag at the macro level. As we collected our data, politics, group relations, and climate were quite unsettled, while the economy appeared more settled for most. With such inconsistencies, the relationship between broad social moments, settled and unsettled times, and what and how people dream is difficult to determine. Swidler may indeed be correct in her hypothesis, but the events that characterized our data collection period make it impossible to confirm her ideas with any confidence.

One last school of thought may best help us understand who chooses positive versus negative cultural lessons on dreaming. Recall that cultural sociologist Pierre Bourdieu argued that a person's experiences, and the culture involved in those experiences, depends on the social spaces in which people think and interact. As people's contexts and experiences differ, so too do the cultural lessons that they acquire, store, reproduce, access, and apply. Thus one's personal experience vis-à-vis the broader society is important to understanding what and how people dream. This means that more than large-scale conditions, the culture ingrained in people—the lessons they come to declare—may be guided by where things such as one's social class, race, gender, stage of life, and social circumstance "locate" people. Social location gives people a certain perspective on the world that may prove important to their future imaginings. Thus in the chapters to follow, we turn our attentions to unpacking the relationship between various aspects of people's social location and what and how they dream.

Chapter 4

Where You Stand and
How You Dream

We have talked quite a bit about people's social location, suggesting that it can alter the way someone remembers the past, views the present, and, most importantly for our study, dreams of the future. As we noted earlier, most people understand that class, race, gender, as well as age or life narrative disruptions can create inequities in life's opportunities. But we are told that in dreaming, anything is possible. Can social location really invade our private imaginings of the future?

The motivation for this question is rooted, in part, in the work of French phenomenologist Maurice Merleau-Ponty. Phenomenologists study the development of human consciousness and self-awareness—our view of the world as experienced from the "first-person" point of view.[1] Merleau-Ponty used the term "point-horizon"[2] to refer to a body's location in space. The horizon refers to what a person can see, or more importantly, what the person perceives from that location. As one moves through space, one's perspective changes. The location of the "point" always results in a different view of the horizon—indeed in a different horizon. Drawing on this idea,

Merleau-Ponty theorized body, mind, and the social environment in which they are situated as a unified entity that contributes to our perception of the world.

Sociologist Pierre Bourdieu took this idea to new places.[3] Bourdieu spoke specifically about *social* space rather than physical space per se. He believed that one's social class, most powerfully signified for him by one's income and education, gave a person access to different types of "cultural capital." Cultural capital includes the possession of different material things, different educational degrees and occupational ranks, and different skills, tastes, and mannerisms. For Bourdieu, the rich versus the poor, professionals versus laborers, the well-educated versus those with little education possess different types of cultural capital, which in turn shapes their view of the world and how it works.[4]

Bourdieu did not neglect the role of the body in his work. He used the term "habitus" to describe the physical embodiment of cultural capital. He argued that the cultural capital made available in one's social class location becomes deeply ingrained in our bodies and minds such that we come to have an automatic "feel" for the social situations we regularly experience, where we belong within those interactions, and how we should navigate through social space given the cultural objects and practices we possess. We experience cultural capital whenever we talk about feeling in or out of place, in or out of our element.

Since Bourdieu's original writings, many of those influenced by him argue that it is insufficient to think of social class as the sole factor impacting one's cultural capital. Now, many suggest that one's race, gender, age, or other life events are as important as social class when it comes to the cultural capital that becomes an integral part of our thoughts and actions.[5] By exploring the dreams of people in different social locations—locations that go beyond class—we are adopting that approach in our analysis.

We can think of everyday examples that bring abstract concepts like cultural capital, habitus, and their links to social location down to earth. Imagine someone wants to buy a shore home. That person's social class will greatly influence whether such a purchase is affordable at all! If she or he can afford to buy, social class will influence what and where the individual can buy, how the surrounding social and cultural environment will be experienced, and where she or he will envision fitting in. Someone with few resources and limited cultural capital will likely be unable to afford this purchase or only able to purchase something small, possibly in need of work, blocks off the oceanfront, perhaps on a busy street in a small, somewhat neglected town. But for that person, the purchase may be enough. According to Bourdieu, the habitus will, in a way that may feel unconscious, determine the individual's satisfaction with the purchase and the impression of what it "feels" like or what it means to live at the shore. For someone with limited cultural capital, the shore home may simply represent something different, an escape from the day to day. The buyer may be willing to endure lesser comforts for the opportunity to "get away." In contrast, those with the means to live in more expensive neighborhoods will buy where they feel more comfortable vis-à-vis their lifestyles. Someone with wealth and the type of cultural capital that accompanies it will likely be able to afford a large oceanfront property that affords peace, quiet, and a spectacular ocean view. Indeed, such a person will accept no less! For the economically privileged, living at the shore means extravagance, leisure, access, and exclusivity—characteristics that demonstrate one's stature. The habitus of such people ensures that they "know" exactly where they belong, what they expect from others with whom they interact, and how to behave in a privileged setting. In this example, where individuals (and their houses) stand in social space will influence their view of the physical environment as well as the social and cultural relationships and practices within that environment.

Now consider another example. If individuals are part of a privileged race (e.g., a White person in the United States and many other countries), opportunities may seem boundless. The cultural capital ingrained in those from a privileged race means that they likely experience the social environment as colorblind and fair.[6] But if people are members of a nonprivileged race, their experience with bias and discrimination may lead them to view the environment as hostile and unwelcoming, with limited opportunities. The notion of color-blindness may feel foreign to such individuals, with fairness perceived as a false concept. Thus, when racially privileged people see a police officer, they may feel the officer is approachable and concerned with their safety, whereas members of a nonracially privileged group may see the officer and feel that they are under suspicion and in danger of abuse.[7] Similarly, if a racially privileged person seeks to buy a new car, the salesperson may assume she or he has ample resources, aggressively pursue the sale, and give such a person a very enticing price. In contrast, a customer from a nonprivileged racial background may wait longer for service, have her or his credit checked before even taking a test drive, and be charged more than the racially privileged customer.[8]

One can envision how other elements—gender, age, or certain life events and the cultural capital associated with them—might also influence one's vision, one's feel of the past, present, and future. Building on Bourdieu, we argue that where one stands in social space—rich or poor, highly educated or not, White or a person of color, male or female, young or old—influences the cultural lessons to which we are exposed and the cultural capital deposited in us. We suggest that these things may, in turn, very well shape one's ability to envision the future and one's ideas of striving and possibility. Social location and the habitus within may powerfully impact the substance of one's dreams, how someone engages in the very practice of dreaming, and whether or not one sees dreaming as a good investment of one's time and emotion, as something that will "pay off." In this chapter, we explore that possibility, looking specifically at the social class, race, and gender of our respondents and the relationship of those characteristics to dreaming.

Social Class and Dreaming

When sociologists speak of social class, they refer to an individual or group's position in a society's hierarchy. Where does one rank (socially speaking) in comparison to others? Class definitions are generally based on one's wealth, power, prestige, or levels of education.

Why should class make a difference in how people envision the future and what and how people dream? It is because class matters greatly when it comes to life outcomes, including mortality, physical and mental health, susceptibility to risk, disaster, criminal victimization, and other negative life events, and access to quality education. Social class can result in a habitus that centralizes either hope or despair, optimism or pessimism, possibilities or roadblocks in one's vision of the future.

A Brief Review of Social Class Realities

Sociologists have repeatedly demonstrated that people in different social classes can have varying experiences regarding mortality and health. Among Americans, the gap in longevity between those who rank in the top 5% versus the bottom 5% of household earnings is quite striking, with the former averaging a lifespan of 89.4 years and the latter averaging 79.7 years of life. At the other end of the life spectrum, rates of infant mortality are nearly four times higher among the economically disadvantaged than they are among the privileged.

The link between poverty and mortality stems, in part, from issues of health care. People at the bottom of the U.S. economic hierarchy face the greatest risk of contracting illness. Moreover, they are more likely than the economically privileged to die from their ailments—including cancer, heart attacks, and strokes, as well as influenza, stomach ulcers, and syphilis. These economically based health patterns hold true even for diseases nearly eradicated by modern medicine (e.g., tuberculosis). Moreover, those in the lower social classes are least likely to be inoculated for preventable diseases such as measles, mumps, and rubella. These class-based patterns become painfully obvious when examining COVID-19 pandemic rates. Those of the lower social class are more likely to contract and die from COVID-19 than those in the middle or upper ranks of the class hierarchy; those in the lower class are also less likely to be vaccinated against this virus.[9] Poor delivery systems and a lack of informational resources sometimes made the poor (and people of color) unable or reticent to be vaccinated.[10]

Social class can also negatively influence mental and emotional health. Thus, lower-class individuals are more likely than those in middle and upper classes to report worrying all or most of the time that their household incomes will be insufficient to meet their basic family expenses. Similarly, those in the lower class are less likely than their wealthier counterparts to report feelings of happiness, hope, or satisfaction. As a result, lower-class individuals are more likely to greet the day with trepidation, despair, and depression than with enthusiasm, drive, and stamina. In addition, lower-class individuals are less able to cope effectively with life's struggles; their support networks are largely limited to family members, while such networks for the more privileged consist of friends, neighbors, colleagues, and Internet-based groups. The restricted outlets of the lower class are not without cost. Research indicates that these individuals experience less security in social exchanges with nonfamily members and greater distrust and fear of the "outside world" than those in higher class locations.

Regardless of health, mere membership in a society's lower class increases the risk of premature death. The sinking of the *Titanic* in 1912 offers a stark illustration of this phenomenon. Among passengers on that ill-fated ship, social class was a major factor in survival or death: approximately 40% of first-class passengers, 58% of second-class passengers, and 76% of third-class passengers perished in this disaster. What explains the discrepancy? Historians tell us that first-class passengers were better positioned on the ship for ready access to life boats. Third-class passengers were more remotely located and found it more difficult to make their way to the top deck.

Of course, we do not have to travel back to 1912 to see the lessons learned from the *Titanic*. Research on natural disasters in the United States from 1920 to 2010 shows that disasters reinforce economic inequality. Consider, for instance, that Hurricane Katrina was particularly devastating to low-income and Black residents. Evacuation plans depended on having some means of transportation out of New Orleans, leaving lower-class individuals at a tremendous disadvantage. Those left in the city to face the brunt of Katrina were overwhelmingly poor and Black. In the postevacuation period, those with low resources were more likely to endure forced relocation, and, for those who remained, the lack of essential services in poor New

Orleans neighborhoods lasted for years after the storm. The COVID-19 pandemic provides one additional example linking social class and disaster outcomes. The virus victimized the lower class so brutally because the homeless could not self-isolate, and those in low-income jobs such as nurse's aides, grocery-store clerks, product-delivery people, and the like could not work remotely or self-isolate without losing life-sustaining income.[11]

The link between poverty and mortality haunts every corner of American life. In the United States, lower-class membership doubles one's chances of being murdered or raped and quadruples one's chances of being assaulted. Members of the lower class are more likely than others to die as a result of occupational hazards such as black lung, machinery injuries, and the like, and are most likely to experience divorce, job loss, and unemployment. Among children, those of the lower class are more likely to drown, die in fires, be murdered, or be killed in auto accidents than their more affluent counterparts. And during wars, the sons of the poor are most likely to serve in the military and therefore most likely to be casualties.

Finally, in a nation that has long held education as a great equalizer, social class location tells otherwise. Approximately one-quarter of U.S. students attend high-poverty schools—a designation defined by the percent of students entitled to free or reduced-price meals and by limited resources, including student homelessness and a lack of Internet access and "in-area" faculty. These learning conditions impact many outcomes of educational achievement, including standardized math and reading scores as well as graduation rates. While high-school graduation rates are at all-time highs, the rates for low-income students are below national averages. Moreover, students from low-income high schools are less likely to transition immediately to college. Graduates of low-income high schools have the lowest six-year college completion rates—25% versus 50% for those in high-income high schools.[12]

In the face of disease, depression, unrest, or danger, it becomes hard for those in the lower class to summon the motivation or enact the strategies necessary for upward mobility. And when we consider the different class experiences relative to the overall quality of life, we must explore how the realities of social class could affect one's dreams for the future. It is quite reasonable to expect that the things one feels comfortable imagining, how and when people feel able to dream, if they feel compelled to dream or feel dreaming will pay off in the end, can be dramatically affected by one's expectations for a healthy, peaceful, and long life.

Measuring Our Study Participants' Social Class

Sociologists measure class in a variety of ways. One might create a self-reported measure, offering study participants some class designations—lower, working, middle, upper—and asking individuals to locate themselves in one of these categories. One might also consider a person's occupation along with well-established prestige ratings associated with that occupation.[13] Sometimes, sociologists consider people's income or level of education as proxies for class.

We used several of these measures in our work, though not without running into some difficulties. We found that many respondents were reluctant to share their income, a problem that often occurs in research—particularly when one is involved in one-on-one interviews or small focus groups. Thus, the amount of missing data in our income measure made it an unreliable variable for this analysis, and we ultimately dropped

it from our analysis. However, the idea of income was not totally absent from our research. We built a self-reported social
class measure by asking our respondents to identify their social
class as lower, working, middle, or upper class relative to their
annual income, their assets, and their educational experience.

We also collected the occupational prestige scores and re-
corded years of education for each study respondent. As it
turned out, our self-reported class measure was very highly cor-
related with the occupational prestige and level of education
measures. Thus, for the sake of clarity and succinctness in reporting our findings, we restrict our discussion to the self-
reported social class variable.

How many of our respondents fit into each social class category? Nine percent of our sample identified as lower class, 21%
identified as working class, 60% of participants identified as
middle class, and 10% as upper class.[14]

Connections between Social Class and Dreaming:
What We Discovered

To determine the impact of social class on dreaming, we considered all the dimensions of dreaming described in earlier
chapters and explored the associations between these factors
and people's social class location.

We begin by exploring the relationship between one's self-
reported class and the theme of one's dreams (see Figure 4.1).

We were struck by the fact that career and self-improvement
were the two most popular answers both for those who self-
identified as lower class *and* those who self-identified as upper
class. Among the former group, a third of the dreams were
about career and a third about self-improvement. Among the

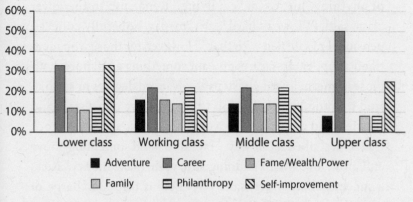

FIG. 4.1. Dream Themes by Social Class

latter group, half identified career dreams and a fourth reported self-improvement dreams. For both groups, the remaining respondents were evenly sprinkled across the other dream themes—except for two notable exceptions. Upper-class respondents *never* dreamed of fame, wealth, and power. Many upper-class respondents told us they had already achieved these things. Lower-class respondents *never* dreamed of adventure. Many of these respondents told us that adventure was too frivolous a dream when struggling to make ends meet.

Resemblances between the upper and lower class may, at first, seem to contradict Bourdieu's thinking on social class and habitus. But once we dug deeper into the meanings people of different social classes brought to concepts such as career and self-improvement, our findings became clearer. For those who self-identified as lower class, career meant getting a job and making gradual advancements within a limited tract—no matter what the job. As Nelson, a lower-class respondent, told us, "Once I get my foot in the door, I'll work hard and move up the ladder bit by bit. I'm not looking to take over the company or anything. Just to make a living." Rena, also in the lower class, said, "I'll work hard, earn my pay, hopefully collect a pension. I'm satisfied with that." However, for those who identified as upper class, career meant something a bit more grandiose. It meant a series of steps—advanced degrees or specialized training, improving job titles, growing office sizes and salaries, and a love for the work. Meredith, a wealthy stock trader, described it this way: "I want to build something, move and grow, love what I'm doing and, yeah, make money." Rick, a successful architect, said, "My goal is to be in charge of something I built." Different interpretations were also prevalent in reviewing answers from those who dreamed about self-improvement. Lower-class respondents talked about making *themselves* better, whereas upper-class respondents spoke about improving *their position and work/home environments.* Thus, on the surface, the social classes at opposite ends of the scale may seem more similar than different. But a closer look at respondents' answers suggests different perspectives at work in each group. As argued by Bourdieu, the habitus ingrained in people from opposite sides of the class spectrum is quite different. Those differences had a discernible impact on people's dreams.

When it came to the dream themes, those who identified as working class and middle class, while very similar to one another, differed from their upper- and lower-class counterparts. Career was still among the most popular answer for members of these two classes. But only about one-fifth of these respondents chose the career theme—a number far lower than those in the lower and upper classes. Philanthropy emerged as the second most popular dream theme for those in the working and middle classes, with about one-fifth of each class group falling into each category, nearly double the percent of lower- and upper-class respondents reporting philanthropic dreams. Among the remaining working- and middle-class study participants, respondents were about evenly split between the remaining dream themes: adventure; fame, wealth, and power; family; and self-improvement. The distribution of answers given by those in the working and middle class suggests that these individuals dream a bit more expansively as compared to their lower- and upper-class counterparts; all six dream themes are more evenly dispersed in these groups' answers.

Working- and middle-class respondents identified career in ways similar to the upper class, focusing on steadily improving their positions. However, in contrast to upper-class participants, building empires was rarely mentioned. In terms of philanthropy, people in the working and middle classes mentioned several paths to philanthropy, including starting service-oriented businesses, jobs that involved caring for others, or joining organizations devoted to philanthropy. No one saw themselves as having sufficient funds to start a foundation or make a sizable contribution to an existing charity, something that many of those in the upper class mentioned as possibilities. When we take these patterns into account, the approach to dream themes taken by members of the working and middle classes suggests that the habitus associated with these classes involves a different perception of future possibilities than those associated with the other social classes.[15]

We also explored the links between social class location and the lessons about dreaming that one draws from public culture.[16] Recall that in chapter 3 we described both the positive and negative lessons on dreaming to which people are exposed. On the positive side, there are lessons such as "opportunity is boundless," "dream big," "never give up," and "optimism makes anything possible." On the negative side, there are lessons such as "the higher they rise, the harder they fall," or "the deck is stacked and the system is rigged." Bourdieu argued that these lessons are part of the cultural capital ingrained in our bodies and minds, and that the lessons most prominent in mind and body will vary by social class.

We found notable differences between the lessons on dreaming adopted by those in the lower class compared to all other classes. Eighty-five percent of lower-class respondents expressed negative cultural lessons on dreaming. Quan, for example, a new immigrant to the country, referenced the "higher they rise, the harder they fall" lesson:

> Sometimes I scared because to be a famous people these days, you have to be around people who don't share your values. [*pause*] You have to be ready to be around people in secret societies and stuff like that. Successful people don't share my faith and ideas. They want everything in a hurry. I'm a Christian and I want to stay a good Christian. I don't want to compromise my faith. I want to achieve my dreams the right way. [*pause*] I don't want to hurt nobody to get famous. I think that comes back at you. You fall fast.

Anthony, a young, lower-class male, was similarly negative as he lamented a deck stacked against accomplishing his dream of changing the economic structure:

> This is something that needs to be fixed immediately. But in my personal opinion, it will never happen. [*pause*] The way that things work, like politically, you have so many rich people and they control everything, just everything. [*pause*] So the regular person doesn't have a chance. The deck is stacked against us. The wealthy run the world.

Regina, a lower-class senior citizen, echoed this sentiment:

It's nice to think about getting big dreams. But it's not realistic. The deck is stacked against people like me. We can try, but we're going to be disappointed. Just look around. Who do you know that went from rags to riches?

The dreams of our lower-class study participants stood in stark contrast to those in the remaining social classes. Sixty percent of working-class respondents and roughly two-thirds of those in the middle and upper classes favored positive lessons on dreaming. Jennifer, a middle-class college student, spoke of boundless opportunity. "There is no telling how far you can go [*pause*] no limits if you believe. Opportunities are all around us." Michael, a middle-aged man from the working class, talked of never giving up. "I don't know if I will get my dream, but I know I will never give up. Your dream is possible as long as you don't give up on it." And Jill, a young adult from the upper class, told us, "Optimism is the key. You have to think positive always. Do that, and you'll get what you want."

These answers indicate a broader pattern in our data. When it comes to social class, where one stands in social space impacts the type of cultural lesson—positive or negative—ingrained in people's minds and bodies. Our lower-class respondents were more often guided by negative lessons on dreaming. But even a small boost up the class ladder was associated with a greater tendency to embrace positive lessons. This suggests that the culture of positivity we discussed in earlier chapters seems to trump any diminished cultural capital held by those in the working or middle classes. Only lower-class members exhibit a view of the world that centralizes negative lessons on what, how, or even if to dream.

We examined several other aspects of dreaming. Often, we found important class differences. For example, did people's dreams reach far into the future, or were they more immediate? Roughly two-thirds of those in the lower class identified their dreams as long-term visions, with many telling us it would "take time" or would "require patience" before they could achieve their dreams. Those in the working and middle class also favored long-term dreaming, though by a smaller margin—55%. The reverse was true for upper-class respondents; only 45% saw their dreams as long-term imaginings. Many of those in the upper classes told us their resources could potentially speed their progress toward achieving their dreams or create conditions that allowed them to focus solely on their dreams. These numbers suggest that as class levels increase, the lessons on dreaming ingrained in minds and bodies display differences as well. While achieving a dream presents a long, hard road for those in the lower class, the dreams of those in the upper class take on a greater sense of possibility; they appear more doable in the short term.

We looked at the flexibility of people's dreams. Were people's dreams concentrated on one theme, or did they encompass a diversity of themes? Class mattered here as well. As we moved up the class ladder, dream flexibility broadened. The starkest contrast rested in comparing lower- and upper-class participants. Roughly two-thirds of those in the lower class favored concentrated dreaming—that is, their dreams fell into a single theme. In contrast, two-thirds of those in the upper class were diverse dreamers, with their dreams spanning two or more themes. Lower-class respondents described concentrated dreaming as "correct" or "the right way to do it," while those who identified as upper class expressed the "freedom" and "ability" to dream in a diverse way. Those in the working and middle classes were evenly split between both styles of dreaming.

How long did our respondents feel they would stay committed to their dreams? Here, too, social class had an impact. While those in the lower class identified their dreams as reaching far into the future, those in this group were least likely to express a long-term commitment to their dreams, with only half of the group saying they would never give up on their dreams. As Robert, a survivor of Hurricane Maria, told us, "How can you say? You never know what will happen." Jessica, recently unemployed, expressed a similar sentiment. "Life can throw you curves. You can't necessarily plan long term." For these respondents, the road to accomplishing a dream could appear unpredictable and potentially treacherous. Such uncertainty influenced the commitment to the dreams of many of our lower-class respondents. This attitude stood in contrast to the rest of our respondents. Two-thirds or more of those in the working, middle, and upper classes said they would never give up on their dreams. They expressed a determination—even in the face of potential obstacles. As Martin, a businessman, told us, "When bad things happen, you have to get up, keep your eye on the ball, and keep going." Similarly, Grace, a minister, said, "If you give up on your dreams, you give up on the future." In contrast to our lower-class participants, many of our working-, middle-, and upper-class respondents felt they had something "in reserve" and embraced the mantra of "if at first you don't succeed, try, try again."

Recall that we asked people if they thought their dreams were grounded in reality. Only 40% of our lower-class respondents felt their dreams were realistic or under their control. Moreover, only 15% of lower-class respondents felt they had a 70% chance or greater of achieving their dreams. In contrast, 80% or more of the respondents in the remaining social classes identified their dreams as realistic and under their control; two-thirds of these participants also felt they had a 70% chance or higher of achieving their dreams. Once again, we see that the cultural capital embedded in lower-class members discourages the belief that dreams can come true. But a small step up the class ladder finds a very different perception of the world, one in which dreams can, and likely will, come true. The culture of positivity seems to overpower the reality of all but those in the lower class.

There were some areas in which social class bore no impact on dreaming. Roughly two-thirds of all respondents reported highly detailed versus vague dreams. Two-thirds or more of every class group described their dreams as individualistic or narrow in scope—our respondents were the "stars" of their dreams, with others simply functioning as props or supporting characters. When it came to passing on dreams, about two-thirds of all groups said they would like to pass on their dreams to someone else. Finally, across all social classes, 80% or more said dreaming was of vital importance. Thus some aspects of dreaming—the necessary detail, the individualized scope, the ability to pass on dreams, and most strikingly, the importance of dreaming—are so firmly ingrained in all people, indeed in culture at large, that class location cannot overcome their impact.

Takeaways from Our Social Class Analysis: Earlier, we wrote about the social realities of living in various social class locations. Study after study remind us of the concrete disadvantages that lower positions in the class hierarchy present. How far do the effects of social class position go? Do social class positions and the cultural capital that accompanies them ingrain in people different visions of the future, different possibilities and opportunities? We found clear class patterns regarding what, how, and even if people felt free to dream. Class, for example, is associated with different dream themes, themes that differ both in type and meaning among the lower class, versus the working and middle classes, versus the upper class. Class is also associated with the lessons one absorbs from the public culture on dreaming. Negative lessons are most often ingrained in those of the lower class, while positive lessons are more often ingrained in those of the working, middle, and upper classes. As we compared the responses from members of various classes, we found that the higher one's social class, the more diversely one dreams, the more likely one is to engage in short-term dreaming, the more reluctant one is to give up on a dream, and the more likely one is to see a dream as realistic and doable. Of course, there were some aspects of dreaming that showed no differences by class. Yet, overall, our findings suggest that the habitus associated with certain class locations differs substantially, providing not only the appropriate substance of one's dreams, but some suggestion as to how the practice of dreaming should ensue. Thus here, in the world of the mind where dreams live, social class shapes the still unlived future one imagines.

Will race, like social class, have a distinct impact on what and how people dream? We turn our attention to this question next.

Race and Dreaming

The differential treatment of Asians, Blacks, Latinxs, and Whites is an indisputable part of American history.[17] And just like economic inequality, racial inequality has profound impacts on lives. The array of inequities that characterize race in the United States are relevant to the everyday aspects of living—health, criminal victimization, housing, educational opportunity, and wealth. Racial inequality also has a powerful impact on one's overall life chances. Here, we argue that these inequalities could also be integral to the ways in which people imagine the future. Where one is located in the racial landscape may indeed influence what and how one dreams, or if one dreams at all.

FIG. 4.2. Barack Obama, the Inspiration for Many Participants' Presidential Dreams (Copyright Karen A. Cerulo)

A Brief History of Race Realities

One of the classic dreams of young children (indeed of many adults in our study) is to one day become president of the United States. Surely this dream was reinforced for people of color with the election of Barack Obama in 2008, and many thought the event might temper the history of racism in the United States. Indeed, shortly following that momentous occasion, only 13% of all Americans said they worried "a great deal" about race relations. But by 2016, that number had jumped to 35%. In 2020, the perception of race relations proved especially stark when comparing Blacks and Whites. As Newport tells us,

> White and black Americans perceive the world through separate lenses, with blacks describing a much more challenging set of experiences than what whites perceive. . . . 67% of whites versus 30% of blacks perceive that blacks have as good a chance as whites to get any kind of job for which they are qualified. . . . Whites and blacks differ as well on views of blacks being treated less fairly at work, while shopping, at bars and restaurants, in getting healthcare, and in dealing with police. A little more than half of whites are satisfied with the way blacks are treated in society, but only 18% of blacks agree. Fifty-four percent of whites say that relations between whites and blacks are good, compared with 40% of blacks.[18]

The social protests of June 2020, motivated by the murder of George Floyd, provide additional evidence for the belief that injustice is a hallmark of race relations in the United States.[19]

Are the different perceptions held by people of different races an accurate reflection of reality? Scores of studies show how racial location can impact one's life, including one's health and mortality, one's risk of violent crime victimization, and being arrested for committing such a crime; racial location can influence one's housing opportunities, access to quality education, or overall wealth. Thus, like social class, race can result in a habitus that presents a vastly different view of the past, present, and, most important for our study, a vastly different view of future potentials and possibilities.

Consider racial disparities in health and mortality. These differences begin in early life. In the United States, the infant mortality rate per 1,000 live births is higher for Blacks than for any other racial group: 10.97 for Blacks versus 3.63 for Asians, 4.86 for Latinxs, and 4.63 for Whites. At the other end of the spectrum, life expectancy is lowest for Blacks (74.9 years) and highest for Asians (87.3 years), with Latinxs (81.8 years) and Whites (78.7 years) falling in between these two groups.[20] Health outcomes vary greatly across racial groups as well. While the incidence of diabetes has increased in all age, sex, racial, and ethnic groups, steeper increases have occurred among Asians, Blacks, and Latinxs. As has been true for many years, Blacks and Latinxs have the highest asthma rates, deaths, and hospitalizations in the United States, and Blacks are more likely than those of any other racial group to die from all forms of cancer.[21]

In the face of global or national health disasters, certain racial groups stand at a great disadvantage. For example, in 2021, the Centers for Disease Control and Prevention (CDC) showed that Asians were equal to Whites in deaths from COVID-19. However, Blacks were 1.9 times more likely and Latinxs 2.3 times more likely than Asians and Whites to succumb to the disease. The disparities in hospitalization are even more dramatic, with Blacks and Latinxs roughly three times more likely than Asians and Whites to be hospitalized due to COVID-19. Overall, COVID-19 has cost years of potential life loss for Blacks and Latinxs that are estimated to be 2–3 times larger than for Asians and Whites.[22]

Racial disparities are also evident in criminal victimization and arrest. The percentage of violent victimizations reported to police (including murders, rapes, and assaults) was lower for White victims (37%) than for Black (49%) or Latinx victims (49%). In a related point, Blacks, Latinxs, and Asians (those that are part of the Non-Pacific Islander group) are overrepresented in arrests for violent crimes.[23]

Beyond issues of health, mortality, and crime, race impacts housing and living arrangements and, by extension, social interactions. This is important because what one sees in the day-to-day environment can have profound implications for dreaming and imagining future possibilities. For example, take a look around your home block or neighborhood. Chances are you will see people who resemble you. Today the average White person lives in a neighborhood that is 80% White, while 50% of Blacks and 40% of Latinxs live in neighborhoods without a White presence. These discrepancies are due to a long-standing systematic racial bias in U.S. residential patterns, one linked to zoning policies of the 1920s. The policies effectively kept Black and, later, Latinx families out of middle-class neighborhoods. Some localities such as Los Angeles had zoning laws aimed at segregating the Chinese as early as 1908. Over time, jurisdictions across the nation began to adopt "zoning" regulations that ensured segregated neighborhoods for decades to come.[24]

Not surprisingly, the impact of residential segregation seeps into the educational sphere. Unless parents can afford otherwise, their children attend local schools, thus reinforcing the segregation patterns of neighborhoods. While our nation's courts once championed school desegregation efforts, the tides have turned. Since the 1990s, courts have declared many school districts as "unitary," thus releasing them from previously mandated desegregation plans. In June 2007, the Supreme Court delivered a blow to school diversity when it ruled against the use of race-based admission policies in public schools pursuing voluntary integration strategies. Today, many school districts look exactly as they did before the monumental 1954 *Brown v. Board of Education* decision.

While some expected that the rise in charter schools might yield progress on the diversity front, this has not been the case.

Thirty-five percent of public charter schools are high-poverty schools versus only 24% of traditional public schools. The racial composition of high-poverty schools is particularly telling: 45% of both Black and Latinx public students attend a high-poverty school, compared to only 8% of White public students. Recent efforts like the Equity Lab (a group working to disrupt racial and ethnic inequity within organizations) are directed at students in high-poverty schools. Such initiatives demonstrate that if given the opportunity many of these students can excel. But absent those opportunities, such students never realize a high-quality education. As one Equity Lab participant from Gallup, New Mexico, put it, "Harvard isn't part of the conversation—you don't even hear that word in Gallup."[25]

Educational outcomes also vary by race. While improving in recent years, in 2018, high-school completion rates were higher for Asian (92%) and White students (89%) than for Black (79%) and Latinx students (81%). As educational levels increase, so too do racial disparities. College enrollment rates in the same year were higher for Asian (59.9%) and White high-school graduates (42%) than for Black (37%) and Latinx (36%) high-school graduates. Six-year college graduation rates are higher for Asian (74%) and White students (64%) than for Latinx (54%) or Black students (40%). Given educational conditions, it is not surprising that the economic payoff of higher education varies by race as well. In 2019, the median annual earnings for those 25–34 with a bachelor's degree were $59,910 for Asians and $59,600 for Whites as compared to $44,300 for Blacks and $45,160 for Latinx.[26] In essence, Black and Latinx students are stuck on the lower rungs of the income ladder—something that could greatly affect what and how one dreams.

Where there is housing and educational disparity, one will also find occupational disparity. We see this in the idea of "spatial mismatch"—a gap between where jobs are located and where people live. This gap, spurred on by urban sprawl, hurts both the poor and racial minorities by lowering weekly median earnings of full-time workers.[27] Such wage differences create racial disparities in overall wealth.[28] While median wealth has risen for all groups between 2016 and 2019, the gap between Whites and other racial groups is substantial. White families enjoy the highest median family wealth at $188,200. Black and Latinx families have considerably less wealth than White families, with Black families at $24,100 and Latinx families at $36,100. Asians are part of a diverse group including those identifying as Asian, American Indian, Alaska Native, Native Hawaiian, and Pacific Islanders. This group, as a whole, displays lower wealth than White families but higher wealth than Black and Latinx families.[29]

It is clear that race, as an element of social location, presents different future horizons and carries different cultural capital. How do these differences impact people's dreams?

Measuring Our Study Participants' Race

Social scientists identify race as socially constructed rather than biologically based. Thus, we asked our study participants to self-identify their race. We provided our respondents with seven categories: Asian, Black, Latinx, Mutiracial, Native American, White, and Other. Respondents indicated the choice that best described them, and we used those answers to make racial comparisons. The racial composition of our sample was as follows: 7% identified as Asian, 15% as Black, 13% as Latinx, 8% as

Multiracial, and 57% as White. None of our study participants identified as Native American or Other.

Connections between Race and Dreaming: What We Discovered

To explore the impact of race on dreaming, we analyzed the association between various racial groups and all of the dimensions of dreaming that we have discussed throughout the study. We begin by exploring the relationship between one's self-identified race and the theme of one's dreams (see Figure 4.3). Race had a noticeable impact here. Asian respondents expressed very limited dream themes. Eighty-four percent of this group were equally divided between career and self-improvement dreams. The remaining Asian respondents (16%) described philanthropic dreams. None of the remaining dream themes were mentioned by Asian respondents, making their range of dream themes the narrowest of all racial groups. Interestingly, the same two themes—career and self-improvement— were the most frequently mentioned dream themes among Latinx respondents. About a third described self-improvement dreams, and somewhat fewer (22%) described career dreams. However, unlike Asian respondents, the Latinx group entertained other themes as well. This group was equally likely to mention dreams of fame, wealth, and power; family; and philanthropy—about 14% in each category. A small minority (4%) reported adventure dreams.

We think it is important to visit the seeming similarities in the dream themes of Asians and Latinxs. In recounting the realities of race, Asians often appear as equally or more privileged than Whites, while Blacks and Latinxs are comparatively less

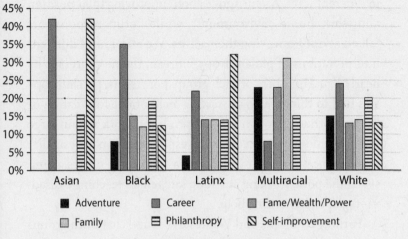

FIG. 4.3. Dream Themes by Race

privileged than Asians and Whites. Thus, similarities between Asians and Latinxs surprised us. But when we dug deeper into the dreams voiced by members of these two groups, differences proved more prominent than similarities. Recall that in our social class analysis, we found that career and self-improvement meant something different for people in the upper and lower classes. That same distinction characterized the answers of Asian versus Latinx respondents. Asians expressed grandiose meanings of career, such as building million-dollar businesses and working in highly professional settings—for example, law offices, medical practices, and corporate management. Latinx respondents, in contrast, reported less lofty dreams. They longed to start a business like a small restaurant, a flower shop, or a beauty salon. They hoped to get college degrees so they could get a good job—though with no specific field in mind. Some spoke of military careers or careers in law enforcement. Asians and Latinx respondents also defined self-improvement in different ways. Asians spoke about improving their position and work/home environments, while Latinx respondents talked about improving themselves. We also found different interpretations of philanthropy, a dream theme expressed by nearly equal numbers of each group. For Asians, philanthropy was tied to things such as starting a charitable foundation or helping others through limited pro bono work within large medical or legal practices. Latinx respondents spoke of smaller one-on-one efforts that would give a quick lift to others: counseling the poor, working at a soup kitchen, or teaching a disadvantaged child needing help.

Turning to Blacks and Whites, we found that both groups most often spoke of career dreams (35% and 24% respectively), and both groups described philanthropic dreams as their second most popular theme (19% and 20% respectively). Among the remaining Black respondents, 8% described adventure dreams, while the rest were equally distributed across the themes of fame, wealth, and power; family; and self-improvement. The remaining White respondents were equally distributed across the four remaining categories. Thus, these two racial groups, contrary to our expectations, looked quite similar in their answers. Despite the dramatic differences of the Black and White experience in the United States, the themes our respondents deemed appropriate for their dreams appeared quite similar. Members of these groups both defined dream themes in similar ways and were most concentrated on similar themes.

Multiracial respondents painted a rather unique picture in comparison to the themes expressed by those of other races. A full third of this group chose family as their most popular dream theme, a proportion much higher than any other group. Some Multiracial respondents explained that they were focused on the hard work needed to achieve a unified family across racial groups—something they saw as critical to a happy future. Multiracial respondents were equally split among adventure and fame, wealth, and power dreams (23% for each theme). Fifteen percent described philanthropic dreams, and only 8% spoke of career-themed dreams—the lowest we have seen in the study. No one in the Multiracial group spoke of self-improvement dreams—again, a first in the study. Thus the growing acknowledgment of Multiracials as a significant social group and the growing social attention to the unique experience of Multiracial people in the United States manifests in a different cultural experience and a different view of the future than those in the other racial groups we analyzed.[30]

We went on to explore the lessons on dreaming that different racial groups drew from the public culture. Latinx respondents were particularly notable here. Sixty percent of this group referenced negative cultural lessons—the only racial group to prioritize the negative. Ivana, who dreamed of being a psychotherapist, adopted a "deck is stacked" outlook:

> It's impossible. Never in my life. Not here at least. I could never be a psychotherapist here because I need to speak fluently, much, much, much good English. I don't have this. Second, I need to reach out to a university to get a diploma and get certification here. That's impossible here. Not for me, not here. No chance here for someone like me.

Jorge voiced the same outlook, saying, "You'll want to keep going. But if your chances are slim, if you know you'll fail, what's the point? Opportunity ain't equal in this country."

Only 40% of Latinx respondents referenced positive lessons on dreaming. This stood in contrast to other racial groups, all of whom favored positive lessons. That includes 60% of Black respondents, about two-thirds of Multiracial respondents, and roughly 80% of Asian and White respondents. For example, Yolanda, a Black college student, touted the importance of optimism: "dreaming creates hope to get up every day; it creates happiness that you can pass on." Ruth, a White, middle-aged writer, talked of boundless opportunity: "Once you commit to something, once you can express your dream, it's like your whole universe moves. Dreaming can bring clarity."

Historical circumstances may have played a role in racial differences in participants' responses. Some Latinx respondents were Hurricane Maria victims; others were new immigrants to the country, facing the onslaught of anti-immigration sentiment emanating from the Trump administration. And while Black respondents were overall more likely to embrace positive versus negative lessons, the intense issues raised by both the Black Lives Matter movement and police shootings of Black victims may have made these respondents less positive than Asian and White respondents.[31] But taken as a group, the power of positive cultural lessons on dreaming appears to have eclipsed, at least to some degree, the negative realities faced day to day by our Black respondents.

Race also impacted several other aspects of what and how we dream. For example, the reach of dreams for respondents of color versus White respondents was somewhat different. Just under 60% of all Asians, Blacks, Latinxs, and Multiracial respondents wanted to realize their dreams in the short term. Indeed, there was often an urgency to their dreams. As Igor, a Black man in early midlife, told us, "There's no time like the present. Why not now?" Among Whites, that pattern was reversed, with just under 60% of Whites willing to wait longer to achieve their dreams. Our White respondents shared with us life experiences that showed, with patience, dreams will eventually come true.

As Rosa, a White woman in late middle age, noted, "Persistence is the key. With dreams, you just have to keep at it."

The findings on the short- versus the long-term reach of dreams surprised us at first. But as we continued analyzing the data, we found that the reach of people's dreams seemed related to longevity—the length of time people held on to their dreams. Two-thirds or more of Asians, Blacks, Latinxs, and Multiracial respondents said they had held their dreams for the long term—many for a lifetime. This was especially true for Asians; 83% of the group voiced this response. Thus, these respondents were anxious for their dreams to finally come true. While they were not willing to give up on their dreams, many respondents told us that they felt they had waited long enough. White respondents, in contrast, were about evenly split in describing their dreams as recent versus long-term imaginings. This group was also evenly split on giving up their dreams and moving on to something new. As we spoke to the White respondents, we found that many of them felt they had the flexibility to change their dreams; many others had already achieved their dreams and were developing new ones. As Lenny, a White man in late midlife, related, "I keep dreaming. Achieve one, move on to the next. You always have to move forward." Gina, a White woman in her twenties, said, "Dreaming is about going—keep expanding your dreams." Contrast this with a comment from Xavier, a Latinx respondent: "It takes a long time to achieve your dream. It's hard . . . very hard. But you have to keep at it, and hope it happens soon." Mandy, one of our Asian respondents, voiced something similar: "When you dream big, you have to understand that it may take a lifetime to achieve what you're after. I have done that. I'm ready to see things happen"

We looked at people's tendency to dream in a concentrated versus a diverse way. Race was important here as well. We found that Asian, Latinx, and Multiracial respondents were more likely to be concentrated dreamers—that is, they identified dreams that fell into a single thematic category. However, in talking with respondents, we discovered different thinking behind these groups' approach. For Asian respondents, concentration was tied to a dream with a sequence of steps, each of which led to a bigger and grander outcome. In contrast, Latinx and Multiracial respondents viewed concentrated dreaming as walking a long road to one dream's fruition—a slow path to a single outcome. Thus the Asian respondent might see a sequence starting with a high-paying job, followed by a move to management, followed by corporate ownership. In contrast, the Latinx and Multiracial respondent might dream of becoming a small business owner without specifying steps to achieving that dream. When it came to flexibility, Black and White respondents differed from the other races we studied. They were more likely to be diverse dreamers, meaning the three dreams they discussed with us spanned an array of thematic categories. But again, diversity had a somewhat different meaning for members of each racial group. For Black respondents, diversity meant "covering several bases" (e.g., career, adventure, family) in order to ensure that at least one dream would come true. For Whites, diversity meant clearing hurdles—prioritizing their dreams, one by one, but ultimately accomplishing a variety of different things. Thus, taken together, the findings on focused dreaming suggest a somewhat different view for those standing in different racial locations.

Almost all of the racial groups we studied felt their dreams were realistic and that they had control over achieving them. When we asked, "Is your dream grounded in reality?" 100% of Asian respondents and 80% of Black respondents answered "yes," with Multiracial and White respondents falling in between these two groups. When it came to control, over two-thirds of Asian, Black, Multiracial, and White respondents thought they had a 70% chance or better of accomplishing their dreams. Latinx respondents were less positive on both of these issues. Just over half of Latinx respondents saw their dreams as realistic, and only 41% felt there was a 70% chance or higher that their dreams would come true. These differences seemed clearly connected to the cultural lessons most prominent in the minds of the various racial groups. Latinx respondents were more likely than any other group to voice negative cultural lessons on dreaming. Thus, attaining their visions of the future seemed less probable for Latinx respondents than for those in other racial groups.

One may reasonably wonder if the intersections of social class and race explains some of the findings reported here. The answer is both no and yes. For example, when we examine class and racial groups that appear most distinctive in their approach to dreaming, both lower-class and Latinx respondents stand out. Yet our Latinx respondents were equally distributed among the lower and middle class. Thus the intersection of lower-class membership and Latinx self-identification does not explain the distinctive views of members in these groups. Similarly, while the largest percentage of Asian and Black study participants (58% versus 50% respectively) identified as middle class, the perspective on dreaming offered by both of these groups most often differed. However, among Whites, class does appear to have an interaction effect with regard to dreaming. Seventy-seven percent of Whites identified as middle class, and an additional 9% identified as upper class. Not surprisingly, then, Whites consistently displayed dream patterns associated with class and racial privilege.

In certain areas, race had no detectable impact on the what and how of dreaming, a finding that held true for social class as well.

More than 60% of respondents across all races said they dreamed in great detail. Seventy percent or higher identified their dreams as individualistic and limited in scope, and 60% or more of each racial group said they would pass on their dreams. Finally, over 85% of all groups said that dreaming is extremely important. Thus, despite the different circumstances of people from different races, the culture of dreaming and the lessons it teaches can, in some instances, overcome real-world experiences.

Takeaways from Our Analysis on Race: What can we take away from the findings addressing the relationship between race and dreaming? Like social class, race often impacts what and how people dream or if people feel dreaming is worth their time. In analyzing different aspects of dreaming, races often differed from one another—differences that became especially clear when we looked beyond broad statistics and dug deeper into the data. For example, Asian and Latinx respondents appeared to express the same dream themes. Yet, we found each group interpreted those themes in very different ways. Similarly, Asian, Latinx, and Multiracial respondents appeared to be concentrated dreamers, while Black and White respondents preferred diverse dreaming. However, again, we found important differences in the ways each of these groups defined concentration versus diversity. Asian, Black, Latinx, and Multiracial respondents were similar in that they held on to their dreams for longer than White respondents, but expressed impatience about having to wait to achieve them. Finally, Latinx respondents differed from all other racial groups in two important ways. First, Latinx respondents were more likely than any other group to embrace public culture's negative lessons on dreaming. Second, in terms of realism, control, and probability, our Latinx respondents were least confident about achieving their dreams.

These differences are important. The findings on race show that the habitus associated with different racial locations can often lead to variable visions of future potentials and possibilities. In addition, racial location often ingrains different ideas about how dreaming should unfold. To be sure, there are some aspects of dreaming that appear unaffected by racial location. But the majority of dreaming dimensions examined in this study show that racial location can greatly influence one's imagined future, placing both roadmaps and roadblocks in people's minds, even before the journey has begun.

Gender and Dreaming

Like social class and race, gender locates people in different social spaces—spaces that are often separate and unequal. Boys and girls are socialized in different ways—ways that encourage contrasting behaviors and impact educational opportunities, occupational achievement, long-term wealth, and health. Thus, where one is located in the gender landscape results in different experiences and perceptions. How will such differences influence what and how one dreams? We examine that question here.

A Brief History of Gender Realities

The impact of gender location begins with "gender socialization"—the explicit and implicit lessons by which people learn how to be masculine, feminine, or something more fluid. An enormous number of studies illustrate the different lessons that surround raising boys and girls—lessons that can start at a child's conception. Researcher Kara Smith found that prenatal talk by mothers to children in utero varies by the gender of the baby. Parents, in anticipating the birth of a baby, sharpen their gendered expectations of what it will mean to have a son or a daughter and strengthen the foundation for traditional gender "typing." These different approaches to socializing children continue in infancy. Some studies show that mothers unconsciously reward and reinforce passivity and dependency in girls while rewarding action and independence in boys. Further, when asked to describe their newborn infants, parents favored traditional gender stereotypes. These differences are important, because research on the neural development of infants suggests that infant brains are so malleable that even the smallest differences can become amplified over time as parents (and others) reinforce gender stereotypes, produce a self-fulfilling prophecy, and impact both the nature of and the receptivity to dreaming. Moreover, various studies show that gender stereotypes become entrenched by early adolescence and become stronger with age. Consequently, the window of opportunity for changing gender stereotypes occurs very early—miss it and the consequences can be detrimental and long-lasting. Knowing this, it is easy to see how differences in gender socialization produce different ideas regarding future possibilities for boys and girls and what, how, and even whether they see fit to dream.[32]

Gender stereotypes result in strikingly different educational experiences for boys and girls. Numerous studies document that teachers give more attention, questions, direction, evaluation, and praise to male students. Teachers' response patterns send an implicit message that male efforts are more valuable than female efforts. More importantly, teachers' gender-driven responses also appear to perpetuate stereotypes of learning. Teachers are still delivering and reinforcing gender stereotypes that suggest boys are more skilled at math and science than girls.[33] Some suggest that the decline in girls' math skills and interest during the high-school years occurs because teachers begin tracking boys and girls in drastically different directions. NARST, an international organization dedicated to improving the quality of scientific instruction and learning, has long noted that teacher-student interactions that favor male students are a major obstacle to equity in learning science. These contrasting lessons could point boys and girls to different domains deemed appropriate for dreaming.

The differential treatment of boys and girls extends beyond the classroom. Girls with interests in the sciences, for example, enjoy less support from their friends than do their male counterparts. Parents (and adults in general) endorse gender stereotypes about math and science as does participation in extracurricular activities. Boys are steered to computers, robotics, and math or science clubs, while girls are steered toward reading and dance, music or art classes. Given these dynamics, it should not surprise us to learn that students are still expressing career interests that fall along traditional gender paths. Teaching, nursing, psychology, English, and the foreign languages are still female-intensive disciplines. Science, technology, engineering, and math (STEM fields) are still male-intensive disciplines.[34]

Perhaps the most telling lesson regarding the relationship between gender and education is this: schooling leads to greater financial benefits for males than it does for females. For every level of educational attainment, the average earnings for women are lower than those for men. In 2018, the median weekly earnings for female full-time workers aged sixteen and older were only 81% of their male counterparts. These messages regarding one's value can have a serious impact on the way boys and girls, men and women imagine the future.[35]

On first glance, it would seem that women have made great strides in the work world. For instance, in 2018, 52% of management, professional, and related occupations were held by women. But when reviewing the upper echelons of management, one finds that only 27% of CEOs and only 32% of general managers are women. Within technical and "professional" occupations, women make up only 25% of information security analysts, 21% of computer programmers, and 19% of software developers. Only 15.9% of architects and engineers are women. While half of the legal occupation workforce consists of women, they are not equally represented in all subcategories of legal work: only 37% of lawyers and 32% of judges are women, while 86% of paralegals are women.

One factor that impedes women's progress in the work sphere is the old industrial practice of separating work along gender lines. "Sex segregation" is still a common practice in many workplaces and within many occupations. Ninety-six percent of speech pathologists, 98% of preschool and kindergarten teachers, 97% of dental hygienists, 94% of childcare workers, 92% of hairdressers, 89% of teaching assistants, 87% of registered nurses, 90% of maids and housecleaners, and 87.5% of special education teachers are women. In fact, you might be surprised to see how many common occupations are still "nontraditional" for women, meaning women constitute 25% or less of those employed in such occupations: farmers, chiropractors, clergy, computer programmers, drafters, police patrol officers and detectives, and taxi drivers, to name just a few.[36] Furthermore, the motivation to enter nontraditional occupations is missing, since women who enter nontraditional occupations earn less than their male counterparts. Interestingly, the reverse is not true for males who enter traditionally female occupations.

The financial toll of gender segregation in jobs and occupations is quite profound. For example, in 2020, the median weekly earnings for full-time male wage and salary workers averaged $1,082; their female counterparts averaged only $891. In general, women earn 82 cents for every dollar earned by a man. Over the course of a year, a full-time working woman earns $10,194 less than her male counterpart. Over a forty-year work span (assuming a steady wage gap), a woman would earn $407,760 less than a man.[37] The unspoken rules of what one can do in the world of work and how valued one is can have an enormous impact on what and how one dreams.[38]

One cannot consider the full impact of gender disparities without addressing health. Females are more likely than men to develop Alzheimer's disease, chronic fatigue syndrome, fibromyalgia, Lyme disease, multiple sclerosis, or rheumatoid arthritis. In addition, women's rates of cancer, stroke, and heart disease have increased in recent decades. Yet, several studies show that the female experience receives only secondary consideration by medical researchers and clinicians. In the case of heart disease, for example, women are diagnosed later than men, underprescribed for drugs treating angina or blood clots, and less likely to be counseled about key risk factors and lifestyle changes. As a result, women are more likely to die from heart attacks than men. The COVID-19 pandemic offers another perspective on gender location and its impact on health. As compared to men, women faced greater job loss, disrupted health care, and increased family care responsibilities as the country adopted social-distancing policies.[39] Thus, on several levels, being female can often be a detriment to one's health and, perhaps, a detriment to one's view of future potentials and possibilities.

Measuring Our Study Participants' Gender

To explore the impact of gender on what, how, and whether we dream, we asked respondents to identify themselves as female, male, transgendered, or other. Fifty-seven percent of our respondents identified as female and 43% identified as male. Even at a time when gender fluidity is in the forefront of public discussions, respondents all identified themselves according to these two traditional gender categories.

Connections between Gender and Dreaming: What We Discovered

To understand the impact of gender on dreaming, we explored the association between the two gender categories and each of the aspects of dreaming reviewed throughout the study.

We began by analyzing dream themes. We found that the most popular dream themes for women and men were identical. Career was mentioned by roughly one-fourth of each gender group and philanthropy by roughly one-fifth of each gender group (see Figure 4.4). But once we moved beyond the two most popular themes, gender differences became more apparent, with dream themes distributed along traditional gender lines. For example, men were about twice as likely as women to identify adventure as a dream theme (16% vs. 9%) and a bit more likely than women to speak of fame, wealth, and power (15% vs. 11%). Thus, it was men, not women, who wanted to become astronauts, rock stars, hedge fund managers, climb high mountains or white-water raft treacherous rivers. In contrast, women were almost twice as likely as men to identify family as a dream theme—especially as family pertained to motherhood and family unity (18% vs. 10%). Women were also a bit more likely to speak of self-improvement dreams (17% vs. 15%). But a caveat is needed here. Our focus group discussions showed that women and men talked of self-improvement in somewhat different ways. Women defined self-improvement as a personal project, citing physical appearance and personality as important

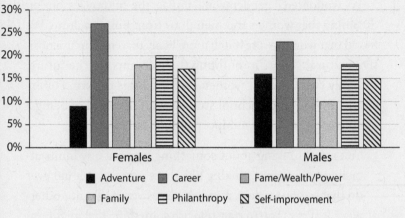

FIG. 4.4. Dream Themes by Gender

areas of concern. As one woman noted, "I want to be my best self—physically and socially." Another woman said, "I dream of being slim and beautiful. Oh, I wish that could happen." (That sentiment was not uncommon among our female respondents.) Men, in contrast, saw adjusting their environments as the path toward self-improvement. One male respondent summed it up this way: "I want to move up and get to a better place."

Figure 4.4 suggests something interesting about gender differences in what we dream. Career continues to dominate the dreams of our respondents, no matter their gender, and philanthropy proves equally important to people of both genders. However, with regard to other dream themes, we see a pattern that mirrors the traditional roles and conditions that we described in our account of gender socialization. Men are more adventuresome and more drawn to fame and power, as gender socialization encourages. In contrast, women are more apt to see themselves as the "keepers of the family," and more heavily focused on appearance in line with gender socialization.

We wondered if gender would impact the cultural lessons on dreaming that women and men draw from public culture. We found that women were much more likely than men to use positive cultural scripts in building their dreams for the future. Roughly two-thirds of women displayed this pattern. For example, Elyse, a high-school student who dreamed of being a famous artist, thought it important to dream big:

> You start thinking about something without any limits attached; you aren't thinking like there's no way I could ever do that so you let your mind go places you might not otherwise. It allows you to start off with something that might not be attainable, but then you can make it more realistic.

Gigi, a senior citizen, spoke of optimism and never giving up: "Dreaming helps you. It helps your state of mind. If you're always thinking, like 'I'll never do that,' it discourages you. You have to keep trying!" Sally, a book editor in midlife, voiced similar sentiments: "I've always felt that if you want to do something you have to try and go after it. That's why successful people are where they are. I'd rather take my chances than give up."

The reverse was true for men. The majority of male respondents (about 59%) quoted negative cultural scripts on dreaming. Zack, a young male, spoke of the high risers fall hard script:

> I dream about becoming a quarterback for the Eagles. I can really picture the details. I see myself moving up the ladder fast—a phenomenon, you know? But in my dream I also see my failure too. I know I'm not fully prepared, I moved too fast. I got hurt in real life and there's no coming back. Maybe I was too aggressive. I think that invades my dreams.

Jonathan, in early midlife, felt the deck was stacked against his sports dreams as well. "When I got my head out of the clouds and lived in the real world, my dream died. I'm not connected. There's no chance for a guy like me." Kevin, a man in late midlife, saw age, time, and responsibility as stacking the deck against his dream to bike cross country:

> I think my dream is wishful thinking. If you prioritize things, it's at the bottom. Maybe I'd do day trips. There's a big difference from biking for consecutive days versus one day. I don't see having the time or the finances to do it. My job and my family make it kinda unrealistic.

There were a number of other areas in which we saw differences in how females and males dream. Like those in the lower social class, women were a bit more likely than men to identify their timeline for achieving dreams as long term (60% vs. 53%), describing the process as an uphill battle. As one woman told us, "It's still a man's world and I know I have to work longer and harder to get my dream." We also found that, like those in the upper social class and like Blacks and Whites, women were more likely than men to be diverse dreamers (53% vs 41%). But unlike upper-class or White study participants, women did not connect diverse dreaming to freedom or "clearing hurdles." They discussed the diversity strategy as a way to "cover all bases"—much the same as Black respondents. One woman mused, "If one dream fails, I can try something different—perhaps something more doable."

While the majority of both groups said they were in control of their dreams and would never give up on them, women were more likely to take this stance (74% vs. 63%). The same was true for the realistic nature of their dreams. Eighty-six percent of women identified their dreams as realistic, versus 74% of men. And women were much more likely to believe there was a high probability of achieving their dreams. About two-thirds of women felt there was a 70% chance or greater that their dreams would come true; only 48% of men felt that way. Finally, both groups believed dreaming was important, but women were much more adamant on this point, with 93% of women advocating dreaming versus 77% of men.

Our findings concerning the public cultural lessons on dreaming associated with women and men, as well as gender differences on the realistic nature of dreams, the commitment to one's dreams, the probability of achieving them, and the importance of dreaming were somewhat surprising. In our class and race groups, privilege was associated with a greater tendency toward these positions. Yet here, females, generally viewed as less privileged than men, were more likely to articulate positive lessons on dreaming, express greater commitment to dreams, greater confidence in achieving them, and place a greater importance of dreaming. To understand these findings, we looked to the interaction of gender, class, and race and the potential impact it might have on these aspects of dreaming.

With regard to class, for example, we found that men outnumbered women in the lower- and working-class categories, while women outnumbered men in the middle-class category. (Women and men were equally distributed in the upper-class category.) Since those in the lower class were most likely to adopt negative dream lessons, an interaction effect may have occurred here. We then turned to the issue of race. Women outnumbered men among Asian and Black participants, while men outnumbered women among Latinx participants. (Women and men were equally distributed in the White racial category.) Since Latinx participants were most likely to adopt negative dream lessons and Asians were highly likely to adopt positive dream lessons, again, an interaction effect may have occurred here as well.

But interaction effects alone do not seem sufficient to explain our findings. With regard to the realistic nature of one's dreams, commitment to them, the probability of achieving them, and their importance, another line of research proved critical—research on "possible selves" and "future imaginings." Several studies show that when asked to envision the future with regard to *specific* topics—e.g., personal finances, economic trends, or job advancement—men are more positive and optimistic than women.[40] However, under more *general* circumstances, the opposite is true. In imagining the future, women pursue greater diversity of both goals and possible selves than men. Women, (like those in nonprivileged classes and races) focus on broad possible outcomes, and are often more vigilant against ideas of failure.[41] These patterns are compatible with the gender distinction our data revealed.

As with class and race, there were areas in which gender had little or no impact on dreaming. About two-thirds of both genders reported highly detailed dreams (66% vs. 65%), and the large majority of women and men described their dreams as individualistic in scope (85% vs. 81%). Women and men were about equally likely to say they had held their dreams for the long term—even for a lifetime (57% vs. 54%), and about two-thirds of each gender group said they would pass on their dreams (63% vs. 66%).

Takeaways on Gender and Dreaming: So what can we take away from the connection between gender and dreaming? The cultural capital and resulting habitus associated with different genders influence many aspects of what and how one dreams. For example, while the two most prominent dream themes were identical for women and men, there were important differences in the other themes about which men and women dreamed.

Women were more likely than men to identify topics associated with traditional womanhood—namely, family and self-improvement—and their ideas about self-improvement (unlike men) had to do with personal improvement rather than improvement of surrounding circumstances. Men, in contrast, were more likely than women to dream of adventure and fame, wealth, and power—themes consistent with traditional images of masculinity. This suggests that while career remains universally impactful for people of all genders, the socialization that ensues in childhood and adolescence—the lessons about what one should strive for and how one should behave—sticks.

We also learned that women are more diverse, more committed, and more optimistic about their dreams than men. The social realities of gender are important here. It may be that women's approach to what and how one dreams is less consistent with the strict lessons of womanhood that emanate from gender socialization and more consistent with the challenging realities that demand women adapt to difficult or discriminatory situations and the need to be solution oriented. Overall, our findings suggest that the parameters of men and women's fields of dreams are drawn early, sustained, and go on to impact their projects and plans.

Conclusion

In this chapter, we witnessed the ways in which one's social class, race, and gender can impact one's cultural capital, shape one's habitus, and influence certain groups' view of future potentials and possibilities. Far from being a private, individualistic phenomenon, our analysis of class, race, and gender shows that what and how one dreams of the future is, in large measure, socioculturally patterned.

Because we did a study that allowed us to talk to respondents at length, our sample is necessarily small. Had we done a large survey study, we could have explored in more detail how social class, race, and gender intersect when it comes to what, how, and if people dream. As it stands, our data allow for only limited analysis on this matter. On the other hand, this study is exploring new terrain. Thus, the kind of detail derived from intensive interviews and focus groups is an important first step in examining a new topic such as the sociocultural dimensions of dreaming.

Even with a small sample, we can draw some important implications. As Bourdieu and others suggest, the culture ingrained in body and mind by virtue of where one stands in social space impacts our memories of the past, our perception of the present, and, in line with our focus, our visions of the future. To be sure, our respondents' answers show that this effect is not universal. Some ways of dreaming, such as their clarity, scope, transportability, and overall importance, were highly similar across all respondents despite their social class, race, or gender. But more often, social location resulted in real differences regarding what, how, and if we dream. The very "personal" nature of dreams that conventional wisdom suggests may not be so personal after all.

If social class, race, and gender impact our dreams, it is highly likely that how members of these groups build their futures and plan their actions perpetuates social differences. Even here, in the life of the mind, opportunity varies in ways that can discourage and depress efforts. Can one's stage of life or the unexpected adversities one may face in life impact dreaming as well? The next chapters help us explore those questions.

Chapter 5

Dreaming through the Times of Our Lives

We were in the parking lot, preparing to enter a senior citizens center. Eight people were waiting for us so we could discuss their dreams for the future. Scheduling dealt us an interesting hand. Our talk with the seniors came right after a visit to a third-grade classroom. We were eager to discover how two groups at opposite ends of the age spectrum would think about dreaming.

Throughout this book, we have been talking about how culture influences what and how people dream. We reviewed the cultural lessons that pertain to dreaming and tried to determine which of these lessons become ingrained in different people. We first examined how broader social conditions and events might impact the ways people use public culture to build their dreams. However, the answers we drew from that analysis were somewhat contradictory and rather limited. Clearly, something more is going on when it comes to explaining dreaming. So we moved on to factors that define people's location in social space, beginning with social class, race, and gender. We found that these factors greatly influence the cultural lessons that become rooted in people; social class, race, and gender are associated with important variations in what and how people dream as well as whether or not they find dreaming worth their time.

In this chapter, we explore another factor that could prove important to shaping people's dreams: age. When it comes to age, we are especially interested in what sociologists call one's location in the "life course." When you think about it, the life course is about sequential spaces—a series of stages and circumstances that people pass through as they move from birth to death: childhood, adolescence, young adulthood, early and late midlife, and old age. Do dreams vary among those in different stages of the life course? And if so, how?

To find out, we talked with people at many different stages of the life course. We started with those who are just beginning the journey—here, third and fourth graders. We then connected with those making the transition to young adulthood—people just about to graduate from either high school or college. We looked next at those who had entered early adulthood—people in their mid to late twenties, most of whom were now a part of the workforce. We moved on to those in early midlife, the majority of whom were married with young children. We next addressed those in late midlife—people established in occupations or careers and many with grown children. We concluded by analyzing senior citizens—those above age sixty-five with different levels of activity and involvement.

The Life Course and Dreaming

Why should one's position in the life course matter with regard to dreaming? Perhaps because research shows us that aging can influence and often change everything in our lives—our beliefs, values, aspirations, and behaviors. The popular tradition of documenting life course milestones via photos, videos, or gatherings offers compelling evidence that we recognize the power of age and its profound impact on our lives.

One's place in the life course also brings expectations with it—expectations integral to how we imagine the future. Children are free to dream about what they see—fantastical dreams of superheroes and princesses or more down-to-earth dreams of firefighters and soccer stars. When we are young, we dream of being older—or at least old enough to drive, get an exciting job, and make our own decisions. When we reach adulthood, many of us continue to yearn for a later stage in life, a time when we imagine enjoying the fruits of our labors. And in those later adult years, when we are working hard and dealing with the trials and tribulations of family and social life, retirement looks like a pretty good deal. In essence, as we move through the life course, our point-horizon changes—each stage of life brings a different view.

The demands and expectations presented to people at each stage of life place them in a different social space. Thus, age is not just about the passage of time or the accumulation of years. Where age locates us in the life course influences the cultural capital we possess. Perhaps considering the normal stages of life development provides the most obvious illustration of this. Newborns and babies lack many skills possessed by older children and adults. Babies must learn how to crawl, walk, and talk and are not expected to perform these behaviors until they are developmentally ready—around eight months for crawling and about eighteen months for walking and talking. If children don't hit these milestones, it is usually a cause for concern in parents. Parents worry that their children will not have the cultural capital possessed by others in their age group. Similarly, we recognize that reasoning and critical thinking skills are development tasks that cannot be logically expected from those who are too young. We typically consider the age of seven as the point where children enter the age of reasoning. We expect to see concrete thinking between the ages of six and twelve and abstract thinking between the ages of twelve and eighteen.[1] Knowing this, we are not surprised to see young children drop their belief in Santa Claus or the Tooth Fairy when they hit the age of seven or eight. Indeed, we view as comical hearing older children or adults who express such beliefs. (Remember the laughter when Buddy, a character in the movie *Elf*, expresses his earnest belief in Santa.) In terms of self-growth and moral development, the connection between aging and things like needs, a sense of belonging, or resolving value crises are part of many developmental theories, including Lawrence Kohlberg's stages of moral development or Abraham Maslow's stages of self-actualization. Thus different locations in the life course—in early development or one's golden years—may result in a habitus that either limits or expands people's dreams and beckons different cultural lessons with which people can paint pictures of the future.

A Brief Review of Life Course Realities

Hundreds of social science studies show how one's position in the life course matters with regard to things such as physical health, mental health, economic security, criminal victimization, social involvement, and risk taking.

Consider the case of the elderly and health. Many negative health issues plague those in the later stages of the life course, including hearing or vision loss, mobility issues, or memory loss. Natural disasters such as hurricanes and heat waves prove more lethal for the elderly versus the young and middle aged.[2] During the COVID-19 pandemic, the elderly faced increased chances of hospitalization and death.[3]

These are gloomy trends, but despite popular notions to the contrary, good health is actually the norm for most older Americans. Indeed, there are some very positive health outcomes of aging. Only 17% of those aged 65 or older suffer from coronary heart disease, and only 7.6% suffer from strokes.[4] Moreover, a growing body of literature shows that emotional control and regulation improve with age. Perhaps reflecting the greater sense of peace with their lives, the suicide rate for those 65 and over is lower than that of any other age group. (Among the young, ages 10–34, suicide is the second leading cause of death.[5]) Many argue that aspects of health and mortality are tied to life satisfaction. Research indicates that life satisfaction bears a u-shaped curvilinear relationship to age. Satisfaction is highest within the younger and older age groups, and lowest within middle age categories.[6] These variations in physical and mental health have the potential to change one's perspective on the world. Such changes may impact one's view of future potentials and possibilities.

Economic security or one's risk of criminal victimization also vary according to one's location in the life course. Compare, for example, the young versus the old. Contrary to popular belief, the elderly are not necessarily the prime victims of poverty. Despite owning this distinction in earlier historical periods, contemporary poverty rates for the elderly hover around 9%; that figure is lower than the 14.4% for those under the age of 18 and lower than the 10.5% national rate.[7] Crime victimization, also stereotypically associated with the old, is actually highest among the young and steadily decreases across the life course.[8] Thus here, too, in both the economic and criminal realms, one's position in the life course presents different risks and different perspectives.

Civic mindedness can change dramatically when one compares those in different life course locations. For example, those

65 and over post the highest rates for voting in political elections. During the COVID-19 pandemic, the prevalence of mitigating behaviors such as mask wearing, hand washing, and social distancing was lowest among the 18–29 age group and highest among the over 60 age group.[9] When it comes to charity, the "silent generation" (those born between 1928 and 1945) proves the most giving—they contribute 25% more often than those from younger generations, and their average annual donation is greater than the average donations from other generations. But when it comes to volunteering, those 35–55 lead the way.[10]

Finally, consider the area of risk-taking. While some research shows risk taking to be more prevalent in youth, other research indicates a u-shaped curvilinear relationship between risk taking and age.[11] (Recall George H. W. Bush's skydiving at his eightieth, eighty-fifth, and ninetieth birthdays.)

Clearly age constitutes a social location that impacts our lives in so many ways. How do age and one's position in the life course influence our dreams?

Measuring Life Course Position

To measure one's position in the life course, we asked our study participants to both provide their age and to self-identify with one of these seven life course positions: childhood, graduating high schoolers, advanced college students, young adults, early midlife adults, late midlife adults, and senior citizens. Table 5.1 shows the breakdown derived from combining our two measures.

We begin this analysis with a picture. Figure 5.1 groups together people at various stages of the life course—third graders and fourth graders, graduating high schoolers, advanced college students, young adults, those in the early stages of midlife, those in late midlife, and finally, senior citizens. This graph serves as

TABLE 5.1: Life Course Category and Age

Life Course Category	Age
Childhood	8–10 years old
Graduating High Schoolers	17–18 years old
Advanced college students	19–21 years old
Young adults	22–29 years old
Early midlife adults	30–45 years old
Late midlife adults	46–64 years old
Senior citizens	65 years or older

a reference point by which we can visually compare the dream themes most important to people in different stages of life. The graph shows an important trend. The dreams of respondents in earlier stages of the life course involved a limited number of themes. In contrast, the dreams of those in the later stages of the life course were more evenly dispersed across the six dream themes. We review these patterns according to our various life course groups.

Children's Dreams: As we planned our study we wondered, At what age should we begin talking to children about dreams? Would a preschooler or a first grader really understand what dreaming was all about? We weren't sure. After consulting with some elementary school teachers, we decided to talk to two third- and two fourth-grade classes—one class of each rank from a public school and the others from a private school. Students in these classes ranged from seven to ten years of age. In hindsight, we feel we made a good choice in our selection of grades because we discovered stark differences between the dreams of these two groups. While the third graders' dreams often seemed a bit fantastical, the fourth graders' dreams were comparably feasible. In comparing the two groups, we felt we

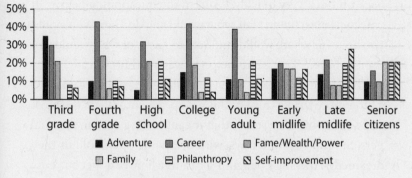

FIG. 5.1. Dream Themes by Life Course Locations

had captured a transitional period among children as they conceive of future possibilities.

It's always a bit nostalgic for adults to walk through the halls of a grammar school. You immediately remember the sound of chalk on a blackboard or squeaky markers on a white board; there is the slamming of locker doors, the sing-songiness of group recitation, the smell of industrial cleaner on the floors. You remember the running, the giggling, the wonder of learning something new, the feeling of carefreeness that the early grades of grammar school so often hold.

We entered the classrooms and crunched ourselves into those tiny desks made for people who are roughly three feet tall. The teachers politely introduced us—always using the prefix "doctor." (This always brought "oohs" and "ahs" from the group.) "Class," said the teacher, "remember I told you we were having visitors today and we're going to talk about your dreams." One little boy raised his hand, saying, "Teacher—I had a really funny dream last night." "No," said the teacher, "not that kind of dream, remember?" (Oddly, we ran into the same problem with our senior citizen groups. A few seniors wanted to talk about their dreams of the prior night. But in each case, we were able to get everyone back on track very quickly.) And so the questioning began. "If you knew you couldn't fail, what would you do . . . or who would you be . . . or where would you want to go . . . or what would you want to have?" Tiny hands began to wave enthusiastically.

Third graders' dreams often straddled fantasy and reality. For a little more than a third of this group, adventure was the most popular theme. For some, that meant having certain unusual pets. Several girls and boys, with eyes wide open, told us they dreamed of owning a penguin, a giraffe, a lion, or a "pet butterfly I could hug." For others, the adventure involved doing something risky. Jeremy stood up with fist raised, saying, "I'd like to ride a bull!" Maria, tightly pinching her nose, told us she dreamed of "being able to hold her breath under water forever." Still others dreamed of impossible adventures like time traveling, flying, being invisible or able to go through walls, being telepathic, and having the power to grant other's wishes. In some cases, the seeds of reality were beginning to bloom. Sarah, a third grader, told us, "I'd like to win a million dollars. I'll live in a mansion, have a pool." But then, she punctuated her dream with something totally unexpected. "And I would own a lot of pickles." It seemed that every dream reported by the group brought enthusiastic oohs, ahs, and looks of wonder.

Of course, not all of the third graders' dreams were fantastical. Some—just under a third—were already on the career track. They wanted to be artists, astronauts, athletes, chefs, doctors, military generals, social workers, teachers, veterinarians, and YouTube stars. About a fifth of the third graders dreamed of "adult" goals revolving around fame, wealth, and power: having a mansion in Hawaii, owning a Lamborghini, an Olympic-size swimming pool, or being the most famous athlete in the world. Slightly less than a tenth of this group were thinking about philanthropy, with most wanting to rescue animals. And a handful, about 5% of third graders, dreamed of self-improvement—but the kind that comes with growing up: getting taller, being able to jump higher, growing a mustache, being free to dye one's hair blue. Family, as a dream theme, did not enter our third graders' discussions.

When we talked with the fourth graders, things got a bit more "down to earth." No one wanted to be invisible, hug a butterfly, or buy lots of pickles. Rather, we began to hear the types of dreams we would later hear from older study respondents. Just less than half of fourth graders dreamed about careers—a much higher number than the third graders. We found several would-be presidents of the United States—among both the boys and the girls (hurray!)—as well as actors, athletes, doctors, graphic artists, lawyers, scientists, teachers, and therapists. Dreams of fame, wealth, and power, the second most popular answer, were offered by just under a quarter of our fourth graders—roughly the same as the third graders. But unlike the third graders who saw these things happening somehow magically, our fourth graders (like our adults) expected to work for their fame, wealth, and power, although they expressed no specific plans for doing so—they had no working goals or projects. Madison donned a very serious face and explained how she hoped to make a breakthrough medical discovery. Carlos and Adam were excited and wide-eyed as they dreamed of joining forces to develop advanced robots and popular "apps." Brittany told us she "wanted to be like the mathematicians in the movie *Hidden Figures*," and many boys and girls mentioned becoming well-known movie stars or prize-winning athletes.

Adventure was far less attractive to fourth graders as compared to their younger counterparts. Only a tenth of the fourth graders dreamed of adventure, and these adventures were much more feasible than those raised by our third graders. No one mentioned flying, time traveling, or owning exotic animals. They mentioned instead living in a foreign country for a year, traveling around the world, or traveling to all fifty states. Indeed, traveling to all fifty states brought lots of thumbs up from the fourth graders. About 10% of students dreamed of philanthropic issues, including things like ending war or running shelters for the homeless or the sick. Meredith stood up and proclaimed that she wanted to help people with disabilities learn to apply makeup and dress in ways that flattered their bodies; she modeled her outfit as an example of the things she could do. Kristen hoped to own a special hospital for injured animals, and Derek dreamed of opening a bakery that would sell only healthy foods.

Self-improvement, a theme for less than a tenth of fourth graders, came in the form of staying in school or working harder. Unlike our third graders, family was on the mind of some fourth graders. A small group, roughly 5% of these children, dreamed of contributing to family operations by learning caretaking skills for younger siblings or learning to cook great dinners for the family. As Jennifer put it, "You know, being like a *Chopped* champion!"

As we compare the dream themes offered by our third and fourth graders, we noted an interesting takeaway. Fourth graders—those students straddling nine to ten years of age— seemed poised at the threshold of "adult" dreaming. This group was the first to express dreams that were more feasible than fantastical, more indicative of who they were or wanted to become. This, we felt, was important. For among those in our sample, it appeared that somewhere around nine to ten years of age, children begin to channel their dreams in ways that fit more common sociocultural patterns. For the fourth-grade respondents, fantastical dreams change from something likely unachievable (like flying or having a pet giraffe) to the still "big" dreams expressed by their older counterparts—becoming president, an astronaut, traveling the world.

Approaching Adulthood: Our high-school and college groups were generally very upbeat, perhaps because, in each case, people were approaching a finish line; they were moving on to college or a job, moving on to graduate schools or a profession. As high schoolers and college students approached graduation, they saw new beginnings and future possibilities. You could almost feel that enthusiasm in the hallways of the high schools we visited as people were practicing for school plays or rehearsing for the band. The gyms and club meeting rooms were busy, and the hallways were full with people talking about what they would do next. The college students were much the same. As two seasoned college professors, we recognized the anticipation and excitement that comes with the spring semester of a graduation year. It is palpable and uplifting.

In comparing the dream themes of our high-school and college respondents, we found many similarities between them. And surprisingly, the two groups—especially the college students—looked quite a bit like their fourth-grade counterparts. (You can see this by reviewing Figure 5.1.) Some of those early cultural lessons on dreaming—the lessons newly seeded in fourth graders' perceptions of the future—were becoming more deeply rooted in the minds of high schoolers and college students.

Career dreams proved most popular for high-school and college students, occupying a third of high schoolers' dreams and just over 40% of college students' dreams. Careers for both groups were similar, including business, law enforcement, medicine, politics, real estate, science, and technology. However, some of our college students were also a bit more grandiose than the high schoolers, also naming things like being the president of a nation, working in a space station, or being highly visible entrepreneurs. Some college students talked about "landing their dream jobs," something we heard much less frequently from the high schoolers.

Fame, wealth, and power was the second most popular dream theme among respondents in these groups: about a fifth of high schoolers' and college students' dream themes fell into this category. Like fourth graders, high-school and college students saw fame, wealth, and power as something they would achieve through some sort of hard work or effort; these things would not materialize magically as they did for third graders. "You have to dream big and work hard," said Justin. "It doesn't just happen." Pete echoed the sentiment. "My dream will come true if I work hard and never give up." Interestingly, however, high schoolers were more likely than their college counterparts to see the potential for failed dreams. They talked about bumps in the road and potential derailments. They entertained negative cultural lessons on dreaming as much as positive ones. As Caren told us, "You know, you have to have a plan B."

High schoolers and college students differed in other ways. High-school students were much less likely than college students to dream of adventure (5% versus 15% respectively). This surprised us a bit, but when we questioned high schoolers, we learned that they felt they still had work to do in order to "position" themselves on a track to success. As Robert put it, "I got lots to do before I can think about extended fun." Becky told us, "High school's over. Now the real stuff begins. You never know how things will turn out." In contrast, our college students felt they had worked hard for their degrees and needed to balance that work with some fun and adventure before settling down. Rocco, just weeks from graduation, said, "I'm just really burned out; I'm ready for some fun." Professors often call it "senioritis." We see a lot of it in our spring semester college classrooms.

High schoolers were much more likely than college students to dream of philanthropic activities (21% versus 12% respectively) and have dreams of self-improvement (11% versus 4% respectively). Dreams of self-improvement for these groups meant solidifying who they were and what they wanted from the future. That could mean excelling at a certain subject, developing a better work ethic, becoming more physically fit, and so on. On the other hand, high-school students were less likely to have dreams about family (0% versus 4% respectively), though neither group was particularly interested in this category.

As we compare the high-school and college groups, we garner another important takeaway. In early life, the dream themes of those at socially defined life transitions—fourth graders on their way to middle school, high schoolers and college students approaching graduation—appear more similar to one another than to those in later stages of the life course. Certain themes, those involving positioning one's self via career or amassing wealth, dominate dreaming, with roughly 60% of dreams falling into these limited categories. The building of skills and resources contribute heavily to who one dreams of becoming and where one dreams of "landing."

Young Adulthood: The next group we tapped were those in young adulthood—people in their mid- to late twenties. We recruited these respondents from a variety of places: church groups, social clubs, recreational teams, workplace settings, and the like. Almost everyone in this group was employed; about a fourth were in graduate or professional school, and a little more than half were newly married. These were people who had taken the first steps in establishing work, and in some cases, family life. And as we discussed their dreams, we noted that they seemed a bit more subdued and reflective than their younger counterparts. At the same time, they were the most connected to the positive cultural lessons on dreaming—boundless opportunity, dreaming big, never giving up, and the power of optimism—more so than any other age group. Angel, fresh out of the military and now working with youth at the YMCA, told us,

> Without dreams, ideas would not happen. That's the way that I see it. Sometimes, you're laying down and you start day-dreaming. I could do this, I could do that, and suddenly an idea pops up and it will happen.

Jessica, studying for a master's degree, echoed the sentiment:

> It's good to be happy, to be optimistic. Everyone has pro-blems. But if you're happy, you know who you are. People say to be happy within yourself, but other people come into your life and other opportunities and help you to be happy. They make anything possible.

In talking with young adults, something struck us. This group was out in the "real world" for the first time, and that seemed connected to the fact that dream themes within this group were more varied than our previous life course groups. To be sure, career dreams were most frequent among young adults (39%), with people mentioning many of the same occupations offered by younger groups. Philanthropy was the second most popular dream theme for young adults; about a fifth fell into this cate-gory. However, young adults' philanthropic dreams were differ-ent from those of the younger groups; they were much more linked to visions of who they would become. Often, their philanthropic dreams came from a personal experience. Jamal, currently a teacher and athletic coach, told us,

> I love helping people to learn. I tutored a lot when I was in college. So I am applying to Teach for America for two years. I want to do that kind of thing—just helping people who need it. Then I want to figure out how to help people for the rest of my life.

Didra was searching for her next step in life, and she found her past shaping her vision of the future:

> I see my own experience with cancer, and so many people were kind to me, helped me and my family, when I was taking chemo especially. I want to help others in some way. That's the future I dream of. If I work hard, I know I can help other people recover and heal.

Eleven percent of young adults dreamed of adventure, but young adults' adventures were less grand in comparison to younger groups. Young adults were not particularly interested in supersonic flight or moonwalks as were some of the younger groups; they were not interested in traveling around the world for a year or two. Rather, their adventures were singular events: to see Paris or Tokyo, to skydive, to bicycle across the country. These narrower adventures came from a pragmatic place. Since most young adults were just recently employed, the idea of an extended adventure did not feel realistic. Moreover, those in this group saw adventure as a sequence of events that would develop as they grew. In describing their dreams, many of these young adults told us that adventure was going to be part of a lifelong lifestyle as opposed to a one-time thing.

Eleven percent of young adults dreamed of self-improvement, focusing most often on learning or becoming more socially attuned or kind. And like younger groups, only 5% of young adults dreamed of family-related themes. In contrast to younger groups, however, young adults were comparatively disinterested in issues like fame, wealth, and power. Only about one in ten young adults dreamed of such issues—nearly half of the numbers exhibited by high schoolers and college students.

For the first time, diverse dreaming was beginning to emerge across the group. The proportion of young adult respondents mentioning each of the dream themes shows less "herding" into two or three categories and much more dispersion across the six themes. We also heard a lot about opportunity, persistence, and optimism from this group—more so than from any other set of respondents. More experience brought more exposure to different cultural lessons, but the positive lessons resonated most with this group, providing an optimistic lens through which to envision the future.

Early Midlife: We next examined the dreams of people in the early phases of midlife. Respondents in this group ranged in age from thirty to forty-five. About three-quarters of this group were married or living with a partner. About a fifth of the group were never married, and the remaining members of the group were divorced. Most of the married couples had at least one child, and about three-fourths of this group were working full-time. (The group included some stay-at-home parents who did not list home work as a job or occupation.) We found these respondents through churches and synagogues, schools, social clubs, and community groups. Respondents in this group were the most difficult to schedule because so many participants needed to arrange childcare or reorient busy family schedules. Interestingly, though, while members of this group told us that other obligations would necessarily limit the time they spent

with us, once they began talking, they always stayed much longer than expected. Next to our senior citizens, respondents in
the early midlife group seemed to have the most to say.

As we listened to the dreams of people in the early midlife
group, we noticed that dispersion in the dream themes mentioned across the group—something we witnessed among young
adults—became even more pronounced. As Figure 5.1 shows,
career dreams were still the most common, but only by a slight
margin. Just about a fifth of this group spoke of career dreams. A
near equal proportion, 17%, fell into each of the following dream
theme categories—adventure; fame, wealth, and power; self-
improvement; and—for the first time in double digits—family.
We heard lots of dreams about family that were simply absent
from our younger groups. Some dreamed of a life that would
allow them to "spend more time with their kids and make lasting
memories." Others dreamed of "owning a family beach house or
vacation home and taking extended family vacations to bond and
build stronger ties." For many in this group, family was a strong,
driving force in who they were or wanted to become—even if it
involved sacrifice. Susan, a minister, told us, "I want to be a really
inspiring lecturer at a divinity school, but now, I have to put that
on hold unless I pick something local. I want to wait until my kids
are out of the house." Manny, an engineer, expressed similar sentiments: "Family is my number-one issue now. Once you have
kids, everything changes. The kids come first."

The dreams we heard about self-improvement dovetailed with
family issues. Phil, a small-business owner, told us, "I want to get
healthier so I can walk my daughter down the aisle someday."
David, studying for his CPA license, said, "I want to become the
kind of parent and husband that my family always feels comfortable coming to with both joys and problems." Our final category,
philanthropy, engaged 12% of our early midlife dreamers. And here

too, philanthropic work often overlapped with family issues. Some spoke of starting charities to help children or single moms. Others wanted to help orphans. Laurie, a stay-at-home mom, told us, "I want to write a book about faith and family, so people can find the kind of help they need to make it through the tough times."

While these respondents were nearly equally dispersed across the six dream themes that emerged from our data, many of these dreams, in one way or another, were really attached to family. Once individuals begin to move ahead in their careers and take on family obligations, dreams of adventure or fame, wealth, and power do not disappear. Yet, they take a back seat to the things that form the foundation of people's local world and moment in time. Perhaps that is why we heard so many cautionary caveats from this group. Dave told us, "Dream—go ahead, but ask people for plans. How will you get there?" Frank, who dreamed of working for the New York Giants, told us,

Let's face it. You really have to know someone to realize a dream like that. That has to be part of it. With a dream like that, at some point, reality has to kick in and you have to realize that something like that isn't going to happen.

And Toni, a teacher, told us,

Big dreams help develop character. It's important to have them. But at some point, you have to get real and work for what you want. Beyond a certain age, it could be harmful to dream . . . too risky to you and your family.

So have a plan—that was Dave's call. Yet, we rarely heard any concrete intentions from this group. As has been true throughout our study, the dreams people shared with us reflected where people hoped to land. Our respondents knew their dreams would require work, but they had not, in any real way, concretized these imaginings as achievement goals or projects.

Late Midlife: Those in the late midlife group ranged in age from forty-six to sixty-five. Seventy percent of this group were married, 27% divorced or separated, and 3% were never married. Here, too, we solicited participants via civic, social, and community groups, churches and synagogues, and the like. Participants in this group were generally active both at work and in extracurricular or volunteer activities. They were also quite reflective in our discussions, and (sometimes) a bit wistful as they thought about life choices they had made along the way.

The late midlife group varied noticeably in comparison to their early midlife counterparts. Here, too, respondents' dreams were dispersed across the six dream themes, but the most popular dream themes shared with us differed from any of the groups we studied thus far. Figure 5.1 shows that, for the first time, career was not the most common dream theme for people at this stage of life; only 22% reported career-related dreams. For many, the "career ship" appeared to have sailed. People told us, "I've achieved my goals," or "I am where I am; it's too late in the game to change." Thus, the career story seemed complete for most.

Self-improvement dreams were most popular among the late midlife group (28%), a first thus far. In dreaming of self-improvement, people suggested things like becoming better spouses or better parents, of improving their outlook on life, becoming healthier, more involved in the community. Most often, these self-improvement dreams involved becoming more resilient or enjoying the satisfaction of a life's work. Greg, a financial advisor, talked about resilience:

My dream is to be impeccably prepared. I guess I just think you have to be prepared to weather the storm. You have to . . . when you go out there, you've got to be prepared that it might not work. You gotta be prepared for everything, even people out there trying to undermine what you're doing. That's just life, so you got to be prepared.

Elle, a writer, dreamed of reaching a sense of self-satisfaction: "I dream of a 'payoff' for all the hard work, like, to finally see all the pieces I've built to become, well, me!"

Twenty percent of the late midlife group dreamed of philanthropy, a number much higher than the early midlife group. Respondents spoke of starting foundations, of supporting groups to which they belonged in ways their current finances did not allow. And, as with other groups, there were dreams of starting animal rescue farms or working with the poor or the sick. Only 14% of the late midlife group dreamed of adventure— a number similar to that offered by the early midlife group. The themes of fame, wealth, and power; and family each occupied only 8% of our late midlife dreamers.

The low numbers on family surprised us a bit. When we probed on the issue of family, respondents told us that they had laid a foundation for their families and now thought the chips would fall as they may. Edgar, an accountant, told us,

You can improve your marriage but your kids are all grown. You're not parenting anymore. It is what it is. You just have to have a good relationship with your kids. I think they look to me for parenting but I don't think I do it. In my mind, the thing is you're sharing, you're almost like done parenting. It's done. You have to know when to give advice and when not to. If they ask, it's easy, but . . .

We took away the following from the late midlife group: dream themes of late midlife respondents were quite diversified; no one theme dominated the group's dreams. Yet, taken together, the dreams of those in this group spoke to arriving at a place of security and self-actualization. Within that framework, however, there was a nagging sense that you could not count on your dreams. Negative sentiments seemed to be in the forefront of so many of the late midlife respondents. As Mark, a construction worker, told us, "My dreams feel more finite now. I have too little time to accomplish them." Cal, a small-business owner, told us, "I have wishes, desires, hopes . . . yeah dreams, but I'm not optimistic about them."

Senior Citizens: We complete the analysis of dream themes by presenting the visions of senior citizens—those over the age of 65. Within this group, 46% were married, 15% divorced, 17% were widowed, and 22% were never married. Only about a fifth of the group were still working full-time. We accessed the seniors via local clubs, senior citizen centers, churches and synagogues, and local community groups. As we did our focus groups and interviews with senior citizens, we found them to be very responsive; they were always on time, sociable, and eager to share. And while many of these respondents suffered physical maladies, they were pleasant, full of energy, and willing to talk about their dreams in great detail.

Seniors' most common dreams involved philanthropy, self-improvement, and family, with over one-fifth of respondents falling into each of these categories. On the philanthropic side, people told us, "Life is more than thinking about yourself; it's reaching out and helping others. We're not here that long." Some dreamed of starting community groups to help the less fortunate in their towns. Others expressed dreams that were a bit more elaborate. Miriam, widowed and retired, shared her dream with us:

> You can get all the people of the world eating and not dying because there are people dying as I speak. Well it would be like curing cancer. It would be such a monumental feat. People would be happy and once they're eating properly, we could get clean water and proper housing. The list would go on and people would live happy.

When it came to self-improvement, people said things like "it's always important to think about making yourself a better person and never be satisfied with the status quo; try to be better, always," or "we have an obligation to learn to be kind." But some dreams were more specific. For Marla, suffering from some disabling illnesses, self-improvement meant regaining her independence:

> I used to live alone. I loved it really. But now my son makes me live with him. Don't get me wrong. He's good to me. But it's not the same. I miss my place, setting my own schedule, eating the way I like. My dream is that I'll get back to living like that. I want my independence. I really, really want that to happen.

For Bobby, self-improvement meant becoming a better husband:

> I just retired and my wife and I are having some trouble getting a rhythm back. I know it's me. I feel a bit out of sync if you know what I mean. But I think about it a lot. How could I be a man she wants to spend time with, do things with? My dream is to be a better partner for her. We could have some really good years ahead.

In the realm of family, many seniors had family fissures that they hoped to heal. They dreamed of reconciling with a child, former spouse, or sibling. Bella, estranged from her daughter for over twelve years, shared her dream with us:

> It's been so long. I don't know what happened to us. I musta done something. But I don't understand what it was. I call her. She doesn't answer. So I start, thinking it's hopeless. But I love my daughter and I have a granddaughter I've never seen. I dream of us all being one happy family. I hope it can happen.

Others dreamed of strengthening already strong ties. As Jake, long retired, told us,

> I have three daughters, and two of them, the oldest and youngest, have called me and asked, "Dad what do you think?" It's amazing cause one of them, the oldest, is quite a powerful business person. That's quite a nice feeling to have her call and ask for advice. I did, as she was going up the ranks, have a lot of conversations with her about what business was like. So having it with the daughters *now* . . . it's family. I really dream about being able to help my daughter's children in the same way. It gives me purpose, relevance, respect. It's the paste of a family.

As we might expect, senior citizens were the least likely of all age groups to engage in career-related dreaming; only 16% of this group reported career dreams. Most felt their career trajectory was set and change was unlikely. Still, a very few individuals dreamed of retooling or starting a new career. As Theresa told us, "I'm not dead yet—there's always time to try something new." In a few cases, seniors spoke of converting a hobby into some sort of a second career, be it playing an instrument, singing, crafting, or the like.

Roughly 10% of seniors dreamed about adventure; the same was true for dreams of fame, wealth, and power. To be sure, those who dreamed such dreams had grand ideas: white-water rafting in the Northwest, motorcycling across country, living on a yacht and sailing across the globe. However, most senior citizens told us the time for adventures had passed, and fame, wealth, and power seemed unimportant to their current lives.

The distribution of seniors' dream themes was among the most varied of our sample. At this age, it seemed as if anything was worth a thought! But like those in other stages of life, people knew what they wanted from the future, yet they had no specific blueprints for achieving it. For these individuals, like all the others with whom we spoke, their dreams were something living in their minds, in an imagined future. While the path to their dreams was unclear, many still hoped—even felt confident—that these things could happen. Yet, they also acknowledged that their dreams might not come true. Our senior citizens were both optimists and realists.

The Life Course and Other
Aspects of Dreaming

In our analysis thus far, we have considered a number of other characteristics that guide people's dreams of the future.[12] What role did life course play here?

In discussing dream themes, we spoke a bit about the cultural lessons on dreaming that people from different age groups drew from public culture. Here, we revisit that issue because the voicing of positive versus negative cultural lessons on dreaming proved the most complex part of our life course analysis. Figure 5.2 shows the patterns.

College students and young adults overwhelmingly embraced positive cultural lessons. Why? In interviews and focus

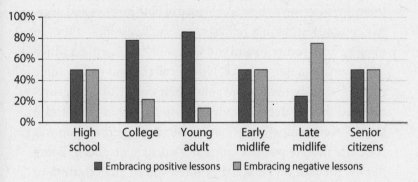

FIG. 5.2. Positive and Negative Cultural Lessons by Stage of the Life Course

groups, we heard the stories of people at the precipice of new life adventures, people who saw the future about to unfold in a very realistic way. Members of these groups seemed heavily focused, indeed attached to the positive lessons that could carry them forward. The story was very different for those in late midlife. These respondents were most likely to voice negative cultural lessons on dreaming. Many members of this group told us that they felt certain things were coming to an end—the chance for career advancement was likely over, retirement was on the horizon, children were leaving home, physical ailments were beginning to set in. Experiencing these "hard knocks" seemed to encourage late midlife respondents to embrace more pessimistic cultural lessons.

High schoolers, those in early midlife, and senior citizens were equally likely to articulate positive and negative cultural lessons on dreaming. The similarities between these groups baffled us a bit. But as we thought through the issue, possible explanations arose. High-school respondents had a long road ahead of them with lots of possibilities. But perhaps, as people with limited life experience, the high schoolers were equally swayed by the positive and negative cultural lessons available to them. In many ways, their acceptance of both positive and negative cultural lessons may represent a default position—they can imagine both scenarios and will withhold judgement on which adages prove more powerful. Now recall that our early midlife respondents seemed to suspend their career or adventure-oriented dreams due to family obligations. Just as their dream themes were tempered by family obligation, perhaps too was their attention to positive cultural lessons on dreaming. Being heavily focused on family, they often voiced an obligation to anticipate both best- and worst-case scenarios for their children and their overall family unit. This would explain the divide on the cultural lessons they expressed. And now to our seniors. Just as a lack of life experience may have encouraged high schoolers to entertain both positive and negative lessons on dreaming, abundant life experience may have made senior citizens feel that good and bad things happen over the course of a lifetime, and both positive and negative cultural lessons must be acknowledged. Our respondents told us as much. After all, it was seniors who embraced positive cultural lessons in dreaming the big dreams of feeding all the hungry, brokering peace in the Middle East, or establishing a national network of homeless shelters. Of course, other seniors were dealing with the impediments of age; circumstance had dampened their enthusiasm. Jason, who wanted to white-water raft the rivers of the Grand Canyon, told us, "It won't happen. I've stepped back to less challenging things. I'll leave it as a dream." Similarly, Iggy, who dreamed of becoming a concert pianist, told us,

Everything is in storage and I'm in an apartment. It would be nearly impossible to get a piano back into my living space. I don't think the apartment people would appreciate it because in the building I live, you can hear everything.

Our seniors, more than any other group, had lived the ups and down of life, something that influenced what they dreamed about.

One's stage of life influences other aspects of dreaming as well. For example, did our respondents' dreams reach far into the future, or were their dreams short-term imaginings? As one might guess, roughly 60% of those in the earliest stages of life—high schoolers, college students, and young adults—saw their dreams as long-term imaginings.[13] Early midlife respondents were evenly split between short-term and long-term dreaming. And roughly 60% of both late midlife and senior citizen respondents viewed their dreams as short-term imaginings. Jean, in her seventies, told us, "If it's gonna happen, it has to happen now. Time ain't standin' still!" Not surprisingly, as we age, our dreams necessarily take on more urgency. Thus, our respondents' stage of life played a role in what they perceived to be the time available to accomplish their dreams.

We found some differences in how flexibly people dreamed across the life course. Our high-school students were the most diverse dreamers, with about two-thirds of the group mentioning different dream themes across their three answers. For them, life was just unfolding, with varied possibilities being presented. This contributed to the diversity of their dreams. As one high schooler told us, "There's so many choices. I don't want to limit myself yet." Our college, young adult, and early midlife respondents were more concentrated dreamers, with just under two-thirds of these groups expressing dreams that corresponded to a single theme. Here, it is worth noting that, among these age groups, "focusing" is an important task. College students must select majors; adults must make career choices. These demands may contribute to more concentrated dreaming. Our late midlife and senior respondents were evenly split between concentration and diversity, perhaps reflecting the different paths people in these groups expressed—life winding down versus beginning new life chapters. So as we examined flexibility among people at different stages of life, there seemed to be a "boomerang" effect. The young dream broadly; those in the middle of the life cycle become more focused, and finally, among the oldest groups, diversity reenters the dreaming picture.

We asked people how long they had entertained their dreams. Were the dreams recently developed, or something they had long considered? High-school and college students were most likely to identify their dreams as recently developed. This was not surprising, as they were in the early stages of dreaming. The remaining groups spoke of their dreams as long-term affairs—imaginings they had held for fifteen to twenty years, or, in the case of midlifers and senior citizens, all their lives.

When we examined all other aspects of dreaming, we found only negligible differences among people at various stages of life. The large majority of each group (60% or higher) saw their dreams in great detail. In this regard, it is interesting to note that about two-thirds of high schoolers and college students told us their dreams were so clear, they could feel them. We found that the majority of all age groups—two-thirds or higher—saw the scope of their dreams as limited and individualistic. People at every stage of life would pass their dreams on to others. About two-thirds of each group responded this way, although high schoolers and young adults felt even more strongly (73% and 80% respectively).

One hundred percent of high schoolers and roughly three-quarters of all remaining groups were sure they would see their dream through to the end. Across all groups, 70% to 90% of respondents saw their dreams as grounded in reality, with high schoolers and senior citizens in highest agreement on that issue. Seventy to eighty percent of each age group felt they had the ability to control the achievement of their dreams because, as previously mentioned, most respondents viewed personal effort as more important to a "dream come true" than luck or fate.

When it came to estimating the probability of achieving one's dreams, all but one of our groups offered high numbers, hovering around 70%. Our senior citizens were different; they thought there was only a 40% chance of achieving their dreams. As one person told us, "If it hasn't happened by now, it probably isn't going to. Yet, I'm still going to try." Even the most positive of wishful imaginings runs into the realities of aging.

Finally, when we asked our respondents if it was important to have dreams, again agreement was overwhelming. Three-quarters or more of all age groups felt dreaming was vital. John, a young adult, explained his answer by saying, "Your dreams don't fail; you can though. You have to chase them, because your dream makes you who you are." Myra, in early midlife, said, "Dreaming is all about self-discovery. Without dreaming, you can't really know who you are." And Patrick, a senior citizen, told us, "You have to say dream big. Who are you? What do you want from life? Dreaming helps you figure it out." No matter the age or stage of life, committing to dreams and seeing dreams through was viewed as a critical task.

These latter findings tell us that some aspects of dreaming remained relatively constant across those at various stages in the life course. In these cases, culture's lessons on dreaming are highly influential, overpowering life course location when it comes to how people's dreams come together.

Takeaways on Life Course and Dreaming: When we think about how dream themes change over the life course, we found several patterns that are important to reiterate. First, in our sample, fourth-graders—those students straddling nine to ten years of age—stood on the threshold of "adult" dreaming. Unlike our third graders, this group expressed dreams that were more feasible than fantastic. For children at nine to ten years of age, those preparing to enter the middle-school years, the broader cultural lessons on dreaming show the first signs of being ingrained in individuals' brains and bodies. Second, the dreams expressed by those at socially defined transitional moments—fourth grade (the move to middle school), high-school graduation, college graduation—appear more similar to one another than they are to those in later stages of development. Certain themes—those about positioning one's self for adulthood or those that paired youth with adventure or fame—dominated dreaming for respondents in these younger groups. Third, people in young adulthood and early midlife began casting their dream nets far afield (although early midlife respondents sometimes linked their dream themes back to family). For these groups, the cultural lessons that guide dreaming appear broader and more dispersed, with people settling in different places rather than herding around limited themes. In later midlife and the senior years, this pattern of diversification became even more pronounced. Thus, as people progress through the life course, they seem willing to consider more expansive possibilities.

Other differences must be noted as well. For example, college students and young adults overwhelmingly embraced positive cultural lessons, while those in late midlife were most likely to voice negative cultural lessons on dreaming. High schoolers, those in early midlife, and senior citizens were equally likely to articulate positive and negative cultural lessons on dreaming. As we moved up the life course ladder, we found that dreams shifted from being long-term imaginings to short-term imaginings. But as we examined flexibility among people at different stages of life, there seemed to be a "boomerang" effect. The young dream broadly; those in the middle of the life cycle become more focused, and finally, among the oldest groups, diversity reenters the dreaming picture. Finally, high-school and college students were most likely to identify their dreams as recently developed. This was not surprising, as they were in the early stages of dreaming. The remaining groups spoke of their dreams as long-term affairs—imaginings they had held for fifteen to twenty years, or, in the case of midlifers and senior citizens, all their lives.

Just as we saw when comparing people of different social classes, races, and genders, one's position in the life course represents a social location. Each location carries varying cultural capital. As such, the habitus that accompanies different stages of life leads to different visions of future possibilities and possible outcomes.

Conclusion

Throughout this book, we have argued that culture is a driving force in people's dreams—both in terms of what, how, and whether they dream. Part of culture's impact rests on the lessons we learn with regard to dreaming. But in large measure, those lessons are tempered by where we are located in social space. In this chapter, we explored how one's stage in the life course might bring about variations in what and how we dream.

We found that where one stands in the life course matters for several aspects of dreaming. One's stage of life impacts the theme of one's dreams as well as whether one chooses positive or negative lessons on dreaming from the cultural lessons available. One's stage of life also impacts the reach of dreams, concentrated or diverse dreaming, how long we entertain our dreams, and the perceived chances of realizing dreams.

Of course, the life course does not evolve so methodically for everyone. As we all know, the progression through childhood, young adulthood, middle age, and senior citizenship can be interrupted by disasters and unexpected obstacles—be they environmental, medical, or economic. So in the next chapter, we focus on such interruptions and how they can affect what, how, and whether we dream.

Chapter 6

Dreaming When Life Is Ruptured

It took us a few extra minutes to get out of the car for this focus group. We knew we were about to interview people displaced from their homes—some by poverty, others by Hurricane Maria. Some had lost family members or pets as well. What would we find? Surely there would be lots of pain and uncertainty in the room. Would it be possible to talk about dreams with people whose hopes had been dashed?

We had similar feelings when we started focus groups or interviews with people facing other kinds of loss—people fighting serious illness (in our case, usually some form of cancer), or those who were unemployed—either recently or for an extended period of time. For these people, life had been interrupted. We wondered how such interruptions would affect people's ability to dream or the kinds of dreams they might have—if any. We wondered, too: what cultural lessons, themes, and images would people use to make sense of their circumstances, and how would people apply those lessons to make sense of their futures? Would people feel that opportunity was boundless, that one should dream big or never give up, that optimism makes anything possible? Or would people feel that climbing the ladder of opportunity only led to an astronomical fall, or that the deck of life had been stacked against them?

Narrative Ruptures

Sociologists have suggested that narratives can be a potent analytic tool, especially when it comes to studying people's personal interactions, plans, or life stories.[1] But narratives do not always unfold in a smooth or continuous fashion. People who write stories, books, or document histories, those who make films or design video games, often use the term "narrative ruptures." Narrative ruptures refer to dissonant events that interrupt or contradict an ongoing story or contrast with one's memory of story events.

If we take a moment to imagine our lives as personal stories, we can also imagine ways in which our stories could be ruptured. You've just been told you are pregnant . . . but later suffer a miscarriage. You've just bought your first house . . . only to be told that you're being laid off from your job. You've lived in a city all your life with no intention of leaving . . . until your property is completely leveled by a hurricane, flood, earthquake, or fire. You and your partner have finally settled into retirement only to learn that your partner is in the early stages of Alzheimer's disease.[2]

In the pages that follow, we explore the dreams of people who faced three different narrative ruptures—those displaced by poverty or a natural disaster, those diagnosed with cancer, and those who had lost their jobs and were now unemployed. When we examined the dreams of these individuals, we found some interesting differences among people in each of these groups, as well as differences between these groups and our sample at large. But before we present those findings, we review some of the realities associated with ruptures to one's life narrative.

A Brief Review of the Realities
of Narrative Ruptures

One of the most serious ruptures to a person's life narrative comes when a natural disaster, an economic catastrophe, the lack of a living wage, or a shortage of affordable housing results in displacement. In the United States, more than a half million people are currently displaced—that is, homeless and living in temporary or transitional housing or sleeping on the streets.

The causes of displacement are noteworthy because they are most often structurally based conditions that require a social rather than a personal solution. So, try as they might, many people simply cannot afford to live outside of flood zones or hurricane-prone areas; individuals alone cannot possibly fight downsizing or resistance to a higher minimum wage, or solve the problem of affordable housing. Thus, those displaced are forced to deal with the well-documented correlates of homelessness: high rates of unemployment, increased health risks, the utilization of emergency health care, shorter life expectancy, high risk of personal harm, high risk of mental-health issues, high risks of depression, anxiety, and self-criticism. While homelessness was trending down in the last decade, the past three years have seen increases in this population. It is expected that the COVID-19 pandemic will result in a major setback in efforts to combat homelessness.[3]

Like displacement, cancer can be a major disruption to one's life narrative. While cancer death rates have seen a 27% decline in recent decades, cancer is still the second leading cause of death in the United States. In 2019, more than half a million

Americans died from cancer. As of January 1, 2019, there were nearly seventeen million cancer survivors. Each year, the risk of males developing cancer in their lifetime is one in two, and the risk for females is one in three.[4]

Consider that cancer is one of the most expensive health conditions to treat. In the last decade, advances in treatment options have meant increasing costs of treatment. Even with health insurance, the out-of-pocket costs of cancer treatments are great. High insurance premiums, copayments, deductibles, coinsurance, and lost wages all contribute to the "financial toxicity" of those undergoing cancer treatment. Furthermore, the out-of-pocket costs of treatment can continue for years after the initial diagnosis. It is estimated that some cancer patients spend 20% of their annual incomes on medical expenses.[5] In order to deal with these expenses, cancer survivors report adjusting their life styles—including things like decreasing amounts spent on leisure activities, food, clothing, or housing. One study has found that cancer survivors are nearly three times more likely than those without a cancer history to file for bankruptcy.[6]

Finally, in a nation that values work and productivity, few things can be more disruptive than the loss of a job. And when that loss is not immediately remedied, its impact can be quite profound. During the recent Great Recession, the unemployment rate hit 10% in 2009, and it did not fall back to the 2007 level of 5% until 2014. From late 2007 to 2009, nearly 8.7 million jobs were lost. Even after economic recovery had started, unemployment rates lagged behind until corporations, businesses, and consumer confidence levels rose. This lag leaves many of the unemployed *hearing* that things are improving, though their personal job situations remain unchanged. Two of the most obvious casualties of unemployment are decreases in consumer spending and loss of wealth and homes. The Great Recession saw the largest decrease in consumer spending since World War II. The average American family lost a third of its net worth during these years.[7] Further, it is estimated that between six and ten million Americans lost their homes as a result of the Great Recession.

Some analysts speculate that many of the Great Recession's aftereffects are still unknown. The delay of "adult life" indicators (having children, buying homes, living on one's own) as well as disrupted career paths may well be among the long-term outcomes of the biggest economic meltdown since the Great Depression.[8] We take the time to review the Great Recession since it provides a critical backdrop and even a life experience for many of our research participants. Though recovery occurred, many Americans had their lives impacted in one way or another in the recession's aftermath. To be unemployed during the time we conducted our study was to be part of a distinct cohort of individuals who were personally experiencing a hardship during a renewed period of job growth.

Each of these life-narrative ruptures have tangible consequences for one's day-to-day living. How might they affect what people dreamed about, how they dreamed, and what they thought about the usefulness of dreaming?

Suddenly, Everything Was Gone

In September of 2017, Hurricane Maria, a deadly category 5 hurricane, ravaged Dominica, the U.S. Virgin Islands, and Puerto Rico. Over 3,059 people were killed by the storm—all but eighty-four of them in Puerto Rico.[9] Many Puerto Ricans affected by the hurricane were relocated to the east coast of the United States. Via relocation organizations and religious support groups, we gained an opportunity to speak with some of the survivors. Some had been in the United States for weeks; others had just arrived. The survivors ranged in age from the midtwenties to sixty-five-plus. These same organizations also put us in contact with people rendered homeless due to economic misfortune. Some had lost their homes during the Great Recession, but most were more recently displaced by a changing economy and shifting labor needs. Like the Hurricane Maria survivors, these respondents had no homes and had limited means of support.

As with all our respondents, we wanted to know the general theme of displaced people's dreams. We found that the dreams expressed by those in this group were concentrated in three main areas. Half of our displaced respondents identified self-improvement as their primary dream theme—the largest proportion we witnessed in the study. But these were not the kinds of self-improvement dreams we were used to hearing. These dreams were built on self-doubt, a sense of deficiency, or, sometimes, guilt.[10] Many of these respondents wanted to improve something about themselves. For example, some of our Hurricane Maria survivors wanted to earn a college or professional degree, thus helping them to learn ways of improving Puerto Rico's resources, fight corruption, or simply have more resources to deal with a future disaster. But the majority of those seeking self-improvement did so because they felt they had, somehow, contributed to their current conditions by not being the best they could be. Edgar, a young adult, told us, "I need to fix all my problems right now. [*pause*] I have a lot of them. And then, maybe, work up to my dream. I'm not prepared yet." Others wanted to become more religious. Bella, in early midlife, told us she wanted to become the "sweetest being in existence," while Riccardo, a man in late midlife, told us, "I have to become

closer to God. I must never allow myself to be parted from him."
For some of these respondents, albeit a small minority, dreams
of self-improvement seemed loosely linked to a negative cultural lesson: what rises, falls. We say this because some of the
displaced respondents had achieved a lifelong dream—home
ownership or working toward a degree—only to see it shattered. They interpreted their shattered dreams as some sort of
punishment. Della, in early midlife, told us, "I just want to go
back and fix all my mistakes . . . change the things I did wrong."

Just over a fourth of our displaced respondents had purely
philanthropic dreams. Despite the devastation of their own experiences, they dreamed of finding a way to help others whose
life stories had been ruptured. Many hoped to someday put in
place some plans or mechanisms to help ensure that such destruction would never happen again—to anyone. Elyse, a
woman in midlife, lost her home. And while she dreamed of
moving back to Puerto Rico and rebuilding her home, she was
just as adamant about helping others to build homes as well.
"Maybe we could build stronger homes that would be strong
against the storm," she said. "We could get some people with
expertise to help us." Similarly, Manny, a young adult, wanted to
return to Puerto Rico to improve health conditions. He told us,

> I want to return to Puerto Rico and help people who have
> cancer. Right now, the medical help is difficult because of no
> power and hospitals destroyed. I want to help fix that. My
> mom had cancer. I know I could help take care of people.
> And systems can be developed to avoid this. I want to help
> others . . . make a difference.

Nearly all of the remaining respondents in the displaced
group expressed career dreams in our discussions. But these
career dreams were strongly linked to philanthropic ends.

Dennis, a man in early midlife, dreamed of being a police officer so he could help others. "I can see myself in that place. I'm going onto a porch and helping someone with a domestic violence call." Ernie, a young adult, dreamed of becoming a computer programmer. "I could fix all my problems with new technologies and then I could help others fix problems—especially with climate change and electrical grid problems." For our displaced respondents, nearly all career dreams were aimed at helping a broader community.

For people who had been displaced, things like fame or adventure were unimportant. For instance, we asked some respondents, "Do you ever dream of winning lots of money? That could fix lots of problems." One person told us, "No. That's unlikely. I have to deal with reality." Another said, "That's about luck. I don't feel so lucky right now." These people were focused on their dream themes and ready to work to achieve them—even though the path from here to there was not clear to them. Remarkably, the large majority of displaced respondents clung to the cultural lesson of "never giving up" and being optimistic as a way of dealing with a ruptured life story.

In some limited ways, our displaced respondents looked like the dreamers in our broader sample. About two-thirds of these individuals had highly detailed dreams—numbers identical to the full sample of respondents. And like our broader sample, about three-quarters of the displaced described dreams that centered on them as individuals and did not include others. They were the stars and the central actors in their dreams.

However, displaced respondents differed from the broader group in important ways. Almost all of these individuals (about 80% versus 69% of the full sample) spoke of the positive cultural lessons on dreaming: "never give up" and "optimism makes anything possible" were mentioned most often. Indeed, they were committed to these ideas. Despite hardship and demise, this group clung fiercely to the ideas of hard work and optimism.

Our displaced respondents were a bit more likely than the sample at large to identify their dreams as long-term imaginings—dreams they held for fifteen or twenty years—perhaps for a lifetime. At the same time, our displaced respondents were more impatient than the people in the sample at large. At this point in their lives, our displaced respondents were nearly twice as likely as those in the broader sample to want their dreams accomplished as soon as possible. What explained this urgency? So many of our respondents were "on route" to their dreams before their lives were ruptured. These individuals now felt pressured to make up for lost time. For example, Elyse, a woman in midlife, recounted,

> My dream did come true. I had my house. But now I lost it. So I got to try and get back up there. I just bought my house four years ago. It's a bad dream right now. When I had it, it was good. I would be with my dad in the same neighborhood. But now, I have to start all over again. Got to start now . . . no time to waste.

Similarly, Ronnie, a man in late midlife, wanted to run for political office:

> I don't have much time left because to win elections, you gotta climb a ladder, network, get funders. Right now, I don't have a lot of rich people in my life. And you just don't suddenly run for president like Trump did. You gotta be rich for that. So if I want to make a difference, I have to get going. Gotta get back on my feet and meet people.

Our displaced respondents also dreamed in a very concentrated way. While our full sample was about evenly split between concentrated versus diverse dreaming, almost three-fourths of this subsample dreamed in a concentrated way, meaning all three of the dreams they discussed with us were on the same theme. For this group, facing environmental destruction or economic hardship seemed to focus them on a narrow solution. They became very single-minded with regard to where their futures lay.

In comparison to our broader sample, our displaced respondents were also a bit more likely to say they would pass their dreams on to someone else and to say they would never give up on their dreams. Betty, who dreamed of getting a college degree, said, "It's never too late, right?" And Jeff, who dreamed of opening a help center for those facing all sorts of disasters, told us,

> My dreams are still the same since I was small. Little by little, I want to get there and make it come true. I'm chipping away at it. It can be discouraging. But I look at dreams that can be accomplished. They need work, but there's always part of it that can be accomplished.

Another important difference between the displaced and the sample at large had to do with whether they saw their dreams grounded in reality and what they identified as their probability of occurrence. In our broader sample, about two-thirds of respondents saw their dreams as grounded in reality, whereas three-fourths of our displaced group felt this way. Based on this first measure, one might be tempted to see the displaced as more convinced of their chances for successfully achieving their dreams. Yet, when it came to gauging the probability of occurrence, just over two-thirds of our full sample saw at least a fifty-fifty chance of achieving their dreams. Among displaced respondents, only about a third felt this way. What explains this difference? We felt the lower probability figures stemmed from the loss of control that comes from living through a natural or economic disaster. Uniformly, our survivors told us that they felt their dreams could not be accomplished via hard work alone. They felt some outside entity or force must intervene. This was quite different from the sample at large. Brittany, who dreamed of going to college and making a better life for her family, sought help from the state or federal government. "The wages here are horrible. They need to address that. You can't always do it on your own." Maria hoped for the help of God:

> I'm older now, I don't have the money. I'm on a fixed income. But if I work it out, there's a fifty-fifty chance I could do it again. Gotta stand up and work hard. Even though I can't work. I'm handicapped now. I had an accident, a couple of years ago. But you never know. . . . God is good. I need God's help.

Joe, a senior citizen who dreamed of becoming strong and healthy again, hoped for the kindness of neighbors and friends:

> I want to be more healthy and not worry too much. My wife died and that destroyed my brain for six months. I slowly, slowly got better. People helped me. Sometimes economic, sometimes I learned by experiences. But you can't do this kind of thing alone. You have to have the help of those around you.

For some, displacement shattered cultural lessons about boundless opportunity born of hard work. The response, however, was not to stop dreaming, but rather to seek a support system to keep those lessons alive and help make one's dreams come true. With some sort of outside help, belief in the culture's positive lessons on dreaming remained alive.

We must note one last important thing about displaced respondents. Despite their trials and tribulations, 100% of these participants said they felt it was important to keep dreaming. Clifford, a man in midlife, said, "Yeah, because it helps me get through. Real isn't very good right now." Patricia, a young adult, told us something similar: "Dreams give me hope." For Clifford, Patricia, and others like them, dreaming is not a frivolous activity. It is a necessity that helps sustain us, defines who we are, and keeps us moving forward. Far from having disaster crush one's wishful imaginings for the future, displacement, no matter how it occurred, only strengthened the importance of maintaining future imaginings in the life of the mind.

As we left our displaced respondents, we saw a group of people who, while challenged in many ways, remained optimistic and willing to try again. The losses generated by events and circumstances did not destroy these respondents' propensity to cling to our culture's positive lessons on dreaming; this suggests that future possibilities and potentials were ingrained in them. Moreover, while needing to rebuild their own lives, they were committed to building other lives as well. This group surely needed a helping hand. But at the same time, they viewed themselves as a helping hand to others.

Will I Make It?

There are many kinds of disasters that can befall people. Displacement is just one possibility. What if you were told that you had a potentially fatal disease? How might that news affect your dreams? Would all your dreams suddenly become more impassioned and animated, more important? Or would you simply feel there was no longer a need to dream? To explore this issue, we talked to people facing health-related ruptures to their life narratives. Most of the respondents in this subsample were dealing with cancer. Some were currently receiving treatment, and others had recently finished treatment. We connected with these people via hospitals or medical programs that ran patient support groups. We received permission from each hospital to solicit volunteers for our study. All our respondents were in the early midlife or late midlife group, and more than three-fourths of the group were women.

We entered each discussion with health-challenged individuals wondering what talk on dreams would elicit from people facing serious, potentially life-threatening circumstances. We wondered what the tone of the groups and interviews would be. In every case, we found that our sessions were upbeat, with people determined to take a positive attitude on their situations. As a result, dreams for the future were vivid for these respondents. The cultural lesson of "never giving up" could not have been stronger. While we understand that a selection bias was most likely at work in these groups (perhaps only the most optimistic patients showed up for a focus group about dreaming), we nonetheless were struck by the participants' overall positivity.

In many ways, the optimism of our health-challenged respondents did not completely surprise us. In earlier work, author Karen A. Cerulo discovered that many health-related professionals encourage their patients to treat medical problems as opportunities rather than obstacles. From migraines to autoimmune diseases, from heart disease to cancers, illness is "an opportunity . . . it's a path, a model, a paradigm, of how you can interact to help yourself and another. By doing so, you evolve to a much higher level of humanity."[11] Among such professionals, optimism is almost akin to a prescription.

Well over a third of the dreams from our health-challenged respondents were philanthropic. What did philanthropy mean to those battling disease? Esti, a woman in early midlife, hoped to start a support group that would help others with cancer.

Wanda, a woman in late midlife, dreamed of establishing a ministry that would have three components: face-to-face service, books, and a radio show:

> You know, I have to start small. So I'll do some face-to-face guidance. I can then see myself writing a book about it all. I've never written a book, but why not try? Then, what I would really love would be to parlay this into a radio talk show. People calling in for help and the people listening getting help too. That could be a big ministry.

After emerging from personal trials, many in the health-challenged group dreamed of comforting others who might be dealing with the trauma of a new diagnosis or the difficulties of treatment. These people were, in many ways, on a mission of service. As Phil, a man just completing treatment, put it, "I made it through the impossible. Now I want to make my second chance count."

Just under a third of health-challenged respondents had family-related dreams. Penny, a woman in late midlife, dreamed of finally getting married:

> I see all the divorces and wonder if I made the right choice not getting married. When I was young, I wanted the fluffy wedding dress and everything. Then I got working, and I just never met the right person. Now, hopefully I'm healthy, and I'd like to rethink it all. I want a second chance at a deep relationship.

Kathy, a woman in early midlife, dreamed of spending more time with her family.

> I have a second chance to spend more time with my family, travel with them, be with them, spend more quality time.

This is always something I wanted to do, but work got in the way. Then you get sick, and well . . . I see us somewhere on a beach, all together, laughing. Having a vacation home at the beach is part of the dream.

These respondents spoke of family as something that had been neglected due to other duties. Their disease reoriented their perspective, with family moving to the center of their future imaginings.

A little less than a fourth of our health-challenged respondents expressed dreams tied to self-improvement. However, unlike the displaced respondents, these people did not see their health issues in any way connected to a personal deficiency. Rather, they felt their treatment could provide them with a second chance at life, allowing them to reboot and dream of things that might make their futures more fulfilling. Michelle, a woman in late midlife, hoped to gain more spiritual enlightenment:

My dream is so vivid. I imagine being in India. I see my teachers from India and Burma. I would go with my teacher to India and learn how to bring peace to people and enlighten myself and others.

Sandra, a woman in late midlife, said she wanted to become a better, more prolific dreamer. "Dreams motivate you to work, and they help you escape bad days. So I want to improve my ability to dream big." And Mark, a self-employed photographer, dreamed of moving beyond portrait work and taking a more creative stance in his future work:

I would rent more expensive space. And take a chance on jobs I want, jobs that are more challenging and interesting, more like being an artist. Things feel so new to me now, and I want to break out and give some new things a try.

Only a small portion of this group (6%) shared career-related dreams, and no one spoke of adventure or fame, wealth, and power. For our health-challenged respondents, dreaming was about using their circumstances—whether a happy ending or continued uncertainty—as a chance to either give back to others or simply be with significant others. There was a gratefulness behind these dreams that placed "connecting" at the center of these respondents' future imaginings.

In some limited ways, our health-challenged respondents looked much like our sample at large. Like the full sample, about two-thirds were able to see their dreams in great detail. Similarly, three-fourths of these respondents described dreams that revolved around the individual rather than a larger group. Finally, about two-thirds of respondents said they would never give up their dreams—a proportion equal to the sample at large.

Overall, however, our health-challenged respondents showed many differences in comparison to the full sample. Taken as a whole, discussions with our health-challenged respondents revealed positive cultural lessons at work—more so than the sample at large. People saw their treatment as an opportunity—a door to a better future; they also echoed the culture of optimism and the importance of stick-to-itiveness. These lessons, in many ways, became strategic tools for repairing the rupture to their life stories.

Health-challenged respondents were much less likely than the sample at large to say their dreams were long held. Less than half of these respondents felt that way, adding more support to the idea that disease offers an opportunity to reboot one's visions of the future. And this group was about twice as likely as the sample at large to feel an urgency to accomplish their dreams.

Recall that the sample at large was split down the middle in terms of concentrated versus diverse dream themes. But about four-fifths of health-challenged respondents were diverse dreamers—that is, they offered us three very different dreams. Here too, the jolt of a poor health diagnosis, coupled with the tendency to reboot, made people rethink their dreams for the future—and to do so in the broadest terms.

Our health-challenged respondents and those in the broader sample were equally likely to see their dreams as grounded in reality. But almost all of the health-challenged group (90%) thought there was at least a 50% probability that their dreams would come true. Similarly, almost all of these individuals felt in control of their futures—perhaps as a result of the optimism that is often so much a part of health treatment and health support groups. We heard talk of using diet, exercise, visualizations, and the like as tools for aiding healing. Some respondents spoke of the importance of tapping one's will to live.[12] Indeed, cultural lessons of optimism were hard at work among these respondents.

Our health-challenged respondents were far less likely than the sample at large to want to pass their dreams on. Disease had people rethinking their lives, making their dreams new and something tied just to them. But like our displaced respondents, 100% of our health-challenged group identified dreaming as an important, even a crucial activity.

Our health-challenged group had faced an event that changed their lives completely. Health issues dramatically changed their point-horizon and altered their cultural capital and the habitus that accompanied it. These changes forced them to rethink and refocus their future imaginings. Amazingly, they came out of these experiences, in general, more optimistic than others in the study. They had a second chance, and the positive cultural lessons on dreaming would now fuel their visions of the future.

What Do I Do with Myself Now?

As we were revising the final draft of this book, the unemployment rate in the United States was roughly 15%—all, of course, due to the COVID-19 pandemic. But when we did our focus groups and interviews and when we analyzed our data, the unemployment rate was headed for a record low. Under those conditions, we wondered: What if you were among the dwindling population who still found themselves without a job? How would it affect your dreams for the future? Would you be willing to dream? Or would you feel your dreams had failed you? To explore this issue, we spoke with a number of people who were unemployed during our research period. We found our unemployed respondents through "job seeker" groups or unemployment support groups. These groups were populated both by people who had recently lost their jobs, or more commonly, by those who had been unemployed for an extended period of time.

As we spoke with our unemployed respondents, we quickly saw that optimism and other positive cultural lessons were not central to their visions of the future. These sessions were the most difficult of our discussions. The rooms were quieter, the respondents sometimes presented as depressed, with many often expressing a lack of focus or purpose. It was understandable. Some were discouraged by all the talk of an improving economy with less unemployment because things weren't improving for them. Some were stunned by a sudden, seemingly unexplained job loss, while others had lost jobs repeatedly and were getting weary of trying.

Not surprisingly, career proved the most common dream theme among our unemployed respondents; about a third fell into this category. Some people reached back to careers that occupied their dreams at earlier times in their lives, wondering if their lives would be different had they followed a different path. Edgar, a man in late midlife, told us,

> You know, over thirty-five years ago, my dad told me I would make a good historian. Instead, I went into law. I regret that. I love history. [*pause*] College classrooms are scary these days, but I could teach history in high school. The give and take of the discussion; telling people how we got to where we are without any spin. You can go back to where this country started. These kids don't have a basic understanding of U.S. history. I could help them.

Others dreamed of starting a business; they were tired of relying on others for their livelihood. Barbara, a woman in early midlife, remarked,

> I've been doing what I do for nine years and I'm tired of going around in a circle doing the same thing. I want my own business. I'm tired of someone telling me to do this or that or that I'm not doing things right. I don't mind taking correction, but the jobs don't pan out. I want to be my own boss. [*pause*] I can see the companies I want to work *with*, but with, not *for*. I want to do it on my own.

Several people dreamed of taking on a job that was completely different from their past jobs and completely different from anything they had thought of before: becoming a professional choirmaster, becoming a sports figure, or being a Tai Chi master. Leslie, a woman in late midlife, said that she wanted to open a gift shop:

> I used to be in real estate, but you don't get to build relationships. People buy a house or don't. People come and go. You

don't establish any ties. If I have a store, I'm there. I create it. I love to shop for merchandise, go to the shows, help people decorate or find gifts. I like being around people and being creative and making money.

And some just wanted to return to the career in which they had been engaged before losing their job—albeit, perhaps, in a more grandiose way. Jesse, a man in early midlife, told us,

I trained consultants. What I'd really like to do is to be a sought-after keynote speaker. It's kind of like what I was doing, but a lot more of it, helping many, many more people. I want to be busy at it. . . . I have topics I want to speak on. Some, I've done before. And I can see the audience and see them rise to their feet as I finish. They light Bic lighters, you know, signaling an encore. We want more, we want more! I'm in auditoriums or corporate learning facilities in New York, Los Angeles, and everywhere in between.

Unlike our displaced respondents and health-challenged respondents, unemployed individuals were a bit more varied in their dream themes. About a fifth of the group dreamed of adventure: biking cross country, living in Europe, or taking up skydiving. The remaining respondents were evenly split among three categories: fame, wealth, and power; family; and philanthropy. Heidi, a young adult, dreamed of living in New York City and becoming a famous actress. Patricia, a woman in early midlife, told us, "I want to meet a partner and fall hopelessly in love and stay with that person for the rest of my life." Jake, a man in late midlife, dreamed of "reconciling with my daughter and getting to know my grandson. You know, to be part of a family." And Carol, a woman in early midlife, wanted to start an animal shelter for homeless animals:

I'm looking at possibilities outside of my former career that would give me more pleasure. Sometimes I think it was a gift I got let go because I wasn't happy. I can't go to school to be a vet. I don't have time or the ability. I'm not educated to be a vet tech or anything, and most of those jobs don't pay a lot. Today, I saw a possibility in a shelter for animals. That appealed to me.

Self-improvement was a somewhat common theme for displaced and health-challenged respondents, but interestingly, no one in the unemployed group expressed self-improvement dreams. We asked our respondents if anyone had thought about things like retooling, getting training, or getting a new degree so they might be in a position to begin again in a new field. That idea did not resonate with unemployed respondents. Some participants told us they had neither the resources nor the energy to do so.[13] But more often, our unemployed respondents were somewhat defiant, telling us that they saw their plight as beyond their control. Thus, changing in any way was not viewed as a recovery strategy.

Our unemployed respondents mirrored our broader sample in only very limited ways. For example, members of this group had a wide variety of dream themes, much like the broader sample. Slightly more than two-thirds of respondents saw their dreams as grounded in reality and said they would never give up on them—numbers similar to the broader sample. But the similarities ended there.

For our unemployed group, hopelessness lurked in the shadows. Unlike the sample at large, the cultural lesson expressed by over half of the unemployed respondents was "the deck is stacked"—an understandable position for people who had been rudderless for prolonged periods of time. For these respondents, the "system" was to blame. Jack, a man in late middle age who has been unemployed for several years, told us, "I did my job well. It was outside forces that led to my job loss—the greed of the recession." Millie, a woman in early middle age just recently unemployed, said, "I don't think I lost my job because of my qualifications. It's just tough times out there. I'm not high enough up the ladder to save myself."

In talking to our unemployed respondents, other differences emerged as well. Our unemployed respondents were a bit more likely than the sample at large to say their dreams had been held for the long term: fifteen to twenty years, or, in some cases, a lifetime. This may have contributed to the quiet sadness of the group. Long-held dreams had not been reached and no longer seemed likely for members of this group. As Larry told us, "I'm just focused on getting a job; my dreams have had to take a back seat." But if their dreams were to be achieved, roughly two-thirds of our unemployed respondents felt this had to happen in the short term—a sentiment similar to our displaced and health-challenged respondents. There was no time left to wait.

For our unemployed group, dreams were also much less likely to be detailed—a first for all the groups and interviews we did. Just under two-thirds reported hazy images of their dreams—something that seemed compatible with dreams lost. For unemployed respondents, disappointment made the future hard to imagine in any detailed way. We also found that *all* of our unemployed respondents saw their dreams as an independent endeavor versus involving others—the highest percentage of any group we spoke to. As Barbara, a woman unemployed for a full year, told us, "At this point, I feel like I have only myself to rely on."

Two-thirds of people in the unemployed groups were diverse dreamers, sharing with us three differently themed dreams as opposed to a collection of consistent dream themes. Respondents told us that they felt the need to "cover all the bases," to imagine happiness in as many places as possible. This uncertainty may explain why only half of the unemployed respondents desired to pass their dream on to another.

Less than half of the unemployed respondents expressed any sense of control over the hand they had been dealt. No wonder, then, that fewer of our unemployed respondents—just over half—as compared to 69% of the full sample thought they had a better than a fifty-fifty chance of achieving their dreams. Matt, unemployed for two years, told us, "You need money. You need math skills. I don't have any of those things. So where am I going?" Ellen, unemployed for just under a year, echoed that thought: "My dream, I think it's just a background thing. I never think about actually accomplishing it. I don't have the time or resources." Kevin, our cross-country biker, said,

> I think my dream is wishful thinking. I mean you're talking to someone who's been out of work for six months, so if you prioritize things, it's at the bottom. Maybe I'd do day trips. There's a big difference from biking for consecutive days versus one day. I don't see having the time or the finances to do it.

And Jesse, a senior citizen unemployed for several years, told us,

> It was always hard to think about making a switch to a dream instead of the thing I was getting paid for. It's become harder now, because I'm unemployed and everything seems impossible now.

Yet, despite that general pessimism, 80% of our unemployed respondents thought it was important to dream—a high percentage, albeit slightly lower than the sample at large and much lower than the displaced and health-challenged respondents.

Members of this group routinely linked dreams to survival. Dean, a young adult, declared, "You *need* dreams and goals; some for the immediate future and some for later." Reenie, a senior citizen, said,

> It's important to look at dreams and say what is it? What's the heartbeat or kernel of it? Because a lot of times we think we're too old or something. A lot of things are possible. Dreams are who we are.

And Jackie, a man in early midlife, gave the strongest statement of a dream's importance: "It's survival and salvation." In this particular way, the cultural lesson that dreams can come true was still ingrained in the members of this group, though not in a sufficiently powerful way to overcome the realities of people's situations.

Comparing the Ruptured Groups

As we close this chapter, we think it is important to underscore some similarities and differences between the three groups of respondents discussed here. Doing so shows us how different types of ruptures to one's life narrative can exact different effects on what, how, and whether people dream. Table 6.1 gives a helpful comparison as we review patterns within the broader sample versus the similarities and differences among the three ruptured groups.

First, we found some interesting similarities between displaced and health-challenged respondents. The dreams discussed by members of these groups emphasized service to others, seeing helpfulness and connectedness as central to their future imaginings. These people, all dealing with life-threatening events that interrupted their life narratives, seemed to reach outside themselves to build and support their dreams. The

TABLE 6.1: Comparing Ruptured Groups with One Another and the Sample at Large

	Full Sample	Displaced	Health Challenged	Unemployed
Most Popular Dream Theme	Career	Self-Improvement	Philanthropy	Career
Positive Cultural Lessons	69% positive	85% positive	80% positive	45% positive
Reach	61% long held 33% do now	67% long held 60% do now	40% long held 63% do now	65% long held 67% do now
Clarity	67% detailed	67% detailed	67% detailed	40% detailed
Scope	78% Narrow	74% Narrow	75% Narrow	100% Narrow
Flexibility	50% diverse 50% concentr.	25% diverse 75% concentr.	80% diverse 20% concentr.	67% diverse 33% concentr.
Longevity	67% never give up	77% never give up	67% never give up	67% never give up
Transportability	67% pass it on	77% pass it on	40% pass it on	53% pass it on
Grounding	67% real	75% real	67% real	67% real
Probability of Occurrence	69% 50/50	33% 50/50	90% 50/50	58% 50/50
Control	69% yes	53% yes	90% yes	45% yes
Importance	86% yes	100% yes	100% yes	80% yes

unemployed respondents, in contrast, were much more internally focused, emphasizing career at the center of their future—either regaining their jobs or successfully trying something new. Perhaps that is why, when it came to the scope of dreams, our unemployed respondents reported the highest proportion of narrow dreams focused on the self.

Displaced and health-challenged respondents displayed other similarities as well. Members of these groups saw their dreams in much greater detail than our unemployed respondents. Indeed, detail eluded a good portion of the unemployed. There was a dampening effect from the persistent challenge of job loss—often long-term job loss—that kept the dreams of the unemployed distant and hazy. Finally, more than any other group, including the sample at large, the displaced and the health challenged felt dreaming was not only a good practice, but a critical one. While the majority of the unemployed group felt that dreaming was a good thing, this sentiment was weaker among the unemployed than it was for any other group of respondents.

We found some similarities between the displaced and the unemployed. Members of these two groups had held their dreams for much longer periods than our health-challenged subjects. And while both of these groups saw their dreams as realistic, displaced respondents and the unemployed estimated a lower probability of their dreams coming true than did the health-challenged respondents. Perhaps this is because the displaced and the unemployed felt less control over their futures, whereas the health challenged believed they had that control.

Finally, we note two similarities between the health-challenged and the unemployed groups. Members of these groups were more diverse dreamers than the displaced. However, the unemployed typically wanted to recreate what they had lost or find ways to avoid such losses in the future. In contrast, health-challenged respondents were looking for new opportunities, for second chances at a new life. We also found that the health challenged and the unemployed were less likely than displaced respondents to express a desire to pass their dreams on to others. For the members of these two groups, dreams seemed a more personal thing.

Conclusion

In the previous chapters, we argued that those of different social classes, races, genders, and those at different stages of the life course occupy different locations in social space. We found that those differences were meaningful when it came to what, how, and even if one dreams. In this chapter, we have learned that ruptures to one's life narrative also alter one's cultural capital; these ruptures often move people in sudden and abrupt ways, changing their social locations and their perspective on the future. Thus, here too, these circumstances influenced dreaming patterns.

These findings show us the power of social location in altering the practice of dreaming. Among those with whom we spoke, dreaming was not unique and simply tied to personal history, nor was it a blind adherence to a broader "American Dream." Rather, dreaming occupied a middle ground. It was systematically influenced by one's position in social space, the cultural capital available in that space, and the habitus that becomes ingrained by virtue of one's social location. Our research on life-narrative ruptures shows that the potentials and possibilities one sees for the future are powerfully embedded in the social point by which one views future horizons.

Chapter 7

The Importance of Studying Dreams

We began this book by asking a series of questions. What does it mean to dream? Does everyone do it no matter what their reality? And what do our dreams look like? Do they unfold in uniquely personal ways, or are they patterned, following some sort of cultural script? We wondered, too: How do people's dreams differ from age to age, from group to group, from context to context? Finally, we asked: Do people ever fail to dream or simply stop dreaming? If so, why?

As we have moved from chapter to chapter, we have tackled each of these questions—looking first at our respondents as a whole, and then exploring certain subgroups of our study participants. In each chapter, we highlighted what we saw as the "takeaways" of our analysis. But here, as we bring our book to a close, we would like to think about some broader conclusions of this study.

Aspirations and Projects . . . or Dreams?

In our introduction, we referenced psychological, social psychological, and economic research on "aspirations" as well as the sociological study of "projects." Moving through the book, we tried to remind our readers how these concepts differed from dreams. Aspirations and projects entail plans or roadmaps for the future; they detail the concrete, often patterned actions people take to achieve their educational, job-related, or familial goals; they involve rational, willful actions and plans made in relation to others and aimed at a specific end.

Among those in our focus groups and interviews, concrete plans were almost always absent—even when dreams involved something such as a career, which typically requires a detailed plan. This is because nearly all of our respondents dreamed of things that were not part of their day-to-day existence. Dreams were things our respondents wished to be true, not things to which they were already en route; their dreams were, for the most part, novel and extraordinary rather than a simple expansion of "business as usual."

Why study dreams, then? Because dreams provide us with a window; they give us a glimpse into a person's essence, their identity and sense of self; they allow us to see what a person truly values. As Thoreau wrote, "Dreams are the touchtone of our character."[1] In dreaming, we can unveil a core of our being that we may not be willing (or able) to otherwise articulate. Certainly, some people will work toward making their dreams come true. But whether or not they do, the very content of their dreams tells us something important about where they see themselves and where they would like to be in the broader social landscape.

Are Dreams, Then, Simply a Personal Thing?

Popular author Rhonda Byrne once wrote, "The life of your dreams, everything you would love to be, do or have, has always been closer to you than you knew, because the power to everything you want is inside you."[2] Her words reflect an image of dreaming that is a part of conventional wisdom. Dreams, it is thought, come from the heart. They are highly personal, future imaginings that are the unique property of every individual.

To some degree, the personal side of dreams has merit. Each person's lived experience plays a role in the final product of her or his imagined future. But if *Dreams of a Lifetime* has taught us anything, it is that people's personal experience is only one element of dream building. Much of what our respondents dreamed was similar—sometimes identical—to the future imaginings found in the hearts and minds of others. This suggests that our dreams are derived from the lessons of public culture and then developed or limited by the social organization that defines the social spaces in which we live. More than a private world that is all our own, our research shows that dreams are as much a sociocultural creation as a personal one.

Our focus groups and interviews powerfully underscored our claim. Over and over, in group after group, interview after interview, we found that people engaged in the same, very limited number of dream themes: adventure; career; fame, wealth, and power; family; philanthropy; and self-improvement. This narrow subject matter resulted in enormous overlap in what conventional wisdom would have us believe are unique imaginings of the future. Our research also showed notable similarities in many of the ways in which people dreamed. In nearly all cases, people's dreams were detailed and clear, individualistic in scope, and something that people hoped to pass on to others should they fail to accomplish their dreams. Especially striking were the repeated claims that dreaming was enormously important, essential, even critical, to a life well lived. Without dreams, most respondents told us, life would be bleak and meaningless.

It did not surprise us to learn that so many people spoke about the importance of dreaming. In the lessons on dreaming one finds in American public culture, positive lessons outnumber the negative and are more appealing to individuals. The power of a culture that promotes positive thinking can be gripping. This positivity translates to specific cultural lessons: opportunity is boundless, dream big, never give up on your dreams, and optimism makes anything possible. Thus, failing to dream would not only be unusual, it would be downright deviant—even stigmatizing.

When we reflected on the similarities in what and how people dreamed, we felt we had to ask, Did we stack the deck? For example, as we mentioned in chapter 3, some might argue that we "primed" people to think positively and fantastically by the very question we asked: *If you knew you could not fail, what would you do . . . or where might you go . . . or what might you want to have . . . or what might you be?* Admittedly, our question took failure off the table. But, as earlier noted, we pretested our research instrument, trying several different questions to capture the act of dreaming. Despite various ways of wording the query we used to initiate a discussion of people's future imaginings, our study participants were consistently more positive than negative in their descriptions of what and how they dreamed. But, keep in mind, our study participants were not always positive, and that leads to a second important point. Positive approaches to dreaming, while dominant, were not universal. We did indeed find variations in what and how our respondents dreamed. Thus we feel confident that the question we chose to trigger discussions of dreaming was not a leading one.

What Were the Variations in Our Study Participants' Dreams?

In addition to providing a glimpse into peoples' essence, identity, or sense of self, our respondents' dreams also told us something about the cultural lessons that saturate the different social locations in which individuals stand. What do people in different social locations value and devalue? What do they strive for? What is an acceptable desire? What can a future look like from different point-horizons? From a sociological perspective, our study showed that the culture within one's social location comes to structure one's very imagination. This is important, and of some concern, because, in essence, culture is building inequalities into the life of peoples' minds even before their plans are made and their actions executed. Thus, one's tangible resources alone do not define future possibilities. The cultural capital that accompanies one's resources creates a habitus that, for some, makes certain dreams and certain future imaginings difficult, even impossible to envision. In this way, culture can either broaden or limit possibilities before action takes place.

You can see this very process at work in our findings. When we concentrated on subsets of our study participants, grouping people by class, race, gender, or stage of life, we found important differences in what and how people dreamed. People from different social classes favored different dream themes, and sometimes interpreted those themes differently. For example, a theme like "career" meant something different to those in the lower versus the upper class. Social class also influenced the lessons our respondents absorbed from the public culture on dreaming. Negative lessons were more likely ingrained in those of the lower class, while positive lessons were more likely ingrained in those of all other classes. We found that the higher one's social class, the more diversely one dreamed, the more likely one was to engage in short-term dreaming, the more reluctant one was to give up on a dream, and the more likely one was to see their dreams as realistic and doable. These patterns confirm what Olympian gold medalist Billy Mills so eloquently stated: economic poverty leads to "the most devastating poverty of all, a poverty of dreams."[3]

When it came to race, we found important differences as well. Asian and Latinx respondents frequently expressed the same dream themes, though each group understood those themes in very different ways. "Self-improvement," for example, meant something different to those in these two groups. We also saw that Asian, Latinx, and Multiracial respondents favored concentrated dreaming, while Black and White respondents preferred diverse dreaming. In addition, Asian, Black, Latinx, and Multiracial respondents were similar in that they held on to their dreams for longer than White respondents, but expressed impatience about having to wait to achieve them. Finally, Latinx respondents differed from all other racial groups in two important ways: they were more likely than any other group to embrace public culture's negative lessons on dreaming and were least confident about achieving their dreams.

Gender differences in dreaming were obvious as well. The two most prominent dream themes were identical for women and men: career followed by philanthropy. Yet beyond that, women were more likely than men to identify topics associated with traditional womanhood—namely, family and self-improvement, the latter usually linked to physical appearance. Men, in contrast, were more likely than women to dream of adventure and fame, wealth, and power—themes consistent with traditional images of manhood. We also learned that women are more diverse, more committed, and more optimistic about their dreams than men.

Our study participants' life course location was also associated with differences in dreaming. Interestingly, those aged nine to ten offered the first examples of dreams that were more feasible than fantastical (though many people's dreams had an element of fantasy). We also found that the dreams expressed by those at socially defined transitional moments—fourth grade (the move to middle school), high-school graduation, college graduation—appeared more similar to one another than to those in later stages of life. And people in young adulthood and early midlife began casting their dream nets far afield, settling in many different places rather than herding around limited themes. In later midlife and the senior years, diversification became even more pronounced; these two groups were more inclined to consider expansive possibilities. Thus age appears to have a liberating effect on dreaming. How about the cultural lessons that guided people's dreams across the life course? College students and young adults overwhelmingly embraced positive cultural lessons on dreaming, those in late midlife tended toward negative cultural lessons, and high schoolers, those in early midlife, and senior citizens were equally likely to articulate both (a complicated finding that we unpacked in chapter 5). We also found that dreams shifted from long-term to short-term imaginings as we moved from the youngest to the oldest groups. Yet, dream flexibility among people at different life stages suggested a "boomerang" effect. The young dreamed broadly; those in the middle of the life cycle became more concentrated; among the oldest groups, diversity reentered the dreaming picture. Finally, we found that high-school and college students were most likely to identify their dreams as recently developed, while the remaining groups spoke of their dreams as long-term affairs.

What about the dreams of those with ruptured life narratives? Displacement, illness, and unemployment had notable impacts on what and how people dreamed. For example, displaced and health-challenged respondents favored self-improvement and philanthropic dreams, while the unemployed focused on dreams about recovered careers. The displaced and health-challenged groups were most likely to tap positive cultural lessons on dreaming, with the former group most likely to say they would never give up on their dreams, and the latter group being the most diverse dreamers and the most confident about achieving their dreams. Unemployment was a major obstacle to dreaming. While the displaced and health challenged could dream with great clarity, unemployed respondents described dreams that were vague at best and fueled by negative cultural lessons. The unemployed also felt least in control of their dreams. And like the displaced, the unemployed were much less certain than the health challenged to believe their dreams would come true.

The associations between different social locations and what and how people dream suggests a new way of considering inequality. Our findings imply that it is not simply concrete opportunities that are limited by one's class, race, gender, life course locations, or by certain ruptures to one's life narrative. The very propensity to dream of things that contradict the stereotypes and expectations attached to a disadvantaged social location can be stifled or squashed by the scripts and beliefs that permeate that disadvantaged space. Such findings broaden the scope of what inequality means. When dreams are blocked by a habitus built from biased assumptions about a person's chances and capabilities, imagining the future can become a painful or futile exercise. Witness that some of our study participants articulated dreams, but, at the same time, viewed them as lost causes. So while most of our respondents believed that dreaming was highly important—even essential—others identified it as a dangerous activity.

To be sure, our analysis is based on a small, purposive sample of study participants. That presents a limitation of the study, making generalizations challenging. But the findings are sufficiently striking as to encourage additional research to determine just when "difference" becomes equated with either advantage or disadvantage, possibility versus impossibility in the life of the mind. In addition, some longitudinal research on dreaming could offer considerable insight into just how malleable our dreams might be over time. Does a habitus developed early in life dominate later future imaginings—for either the good or the bad? Might there be "late bloomers" when it comes to dreaming? Just what is the life course of dreams themselves? We also think it is important to study dreams that fail. What are the consequences of "giving up" on a dream? Do failed dreams undermine the dreaming process as a whole, or is there an adjustment process in which dreams are toned down or modified? And with a nod to Langston Hughes, what happens to a dream deferred?[4] Are such dreams simply abandoned, or is there a more concerted effort to achieve them?

Can Dreaming Be a Bad Thing?

Differences in what, how, and if we dream also suggest a new way of thinking about dreams themselves. True—the future imaginings that reside in the privacy of our minds, far from being personal and unique, are discernable products of sociocultural patterns. But there is something more here. We tend to define dreams as positive things. And for most of our study participants, they were. As we reflect on the dreams people shared with us and all the details that accompanied them, we cannot help but note how enthusiastically attached most people were to their future imaginings. Indeed, we learned from many of our study participants that their dreams were calming, inspirational, motivational, or exciting. Despite some negativity, overall, rich and poor, privileged and nonprivileged races and genders, young to old, those facing serious adversities saw dreaming as important, even vital, to a productive existence. Most felt convinced they would never give up on their dreams. And in most instances, people were convinced that their dreams would come true. That goes for the senior citizen with no political experience who felt he could still become president of the United States, the high-school senior who felt she would get a high-paying job, retire by thirty, and run a nationwide animal rescue farm, or the early midlife man who felt he might still have a chance to become a pro-football quarterback.

Answers like this made us wonder. Could clinging to dreams be a bad thing? Certainly, the culture of optimism entrenched in the United States would offer a resounding no to that question. But we feel compelled to present another possible side to the argument. Can dreaming contribute to blind optimism? As individuals and as a society, we have not been very effective at envisioning worst-case scenarios. We are quite tied to sunny-side images of the future. Consider that despite the statistics to the contrary, people are much more likely to envision a stable, lifelong marriage as opposed to a divorce, to imagine stable employment versus job loss, to anticipate graceful, secure aging versus illness and institutionalization. Despite past experience, local, state, and national governments are dreadfully unprepared for natural disasters, lethal attacks, economic crisis, and pandemics. The handling of Hurricane Katrina, Superstorm Sandy, the 9/11 attacks on the Twin Towers, repeated mass shootings, the Great Recession of 2007–2008, and COVID-19 are just a few recent examples of how blind optimism and the lack of imagination and coordinated preparation sometimes result in negative—even deadly—consequences.

In each of the aforementioned individual challenges and large-scale instances, warning signs were present. But for most people, for most organizations and governments, worst-case scenarios were invisible. Why? As we mentioned earlier in this book, we all learn cultural lessons that promote optimism and background worst cases from sight; indeed, we have developed long-standing cultural practices to accomplish this. These practices have implications. When cultural lessons direct us to emphasize the positive, they prioritize the storage of sunny-side images in individual and collective memory. This makes best-case scenarios easiest to access when faced with social events— including disasters and traumas.[5]

How does that matter when it comes to dreaming? Some of our respondents suggested some possibilities. One man in early midlife said,

> You have to be prepared to weather the storm. You have to be prepared for all of that. [*pause*] When you go out there to pursue your dream, you've got to be prepared that it might not work. You gotta be prepared for everything.

A female young adult told us,

> Dreaming is great. But it has the potential to be harmful. I think fantasizing is OK. If you go beyond fantasizing and you think those are actual goals for yourself, without thinking about the roadblocks you're going to face, you have the potential to do harm there.

And a man in late midlife remarked,

> If you let it distract you from what you need to do day to day, well, living in a fantasy world is not good.

There is wisdom in these comments. They are not the words of "Sad Sacks" or "Debby Downers." Rather, they reflect a certain realism, or at the very least, a dreaming "correction" required by some social situations. Knowing this, we may wish to rethink how we present the role of dreaming in social life. While we applaud the dreamers among us, we urge some caution as well. Balance is key to making dreams productive and beneficial. Really, the prescription is familiar. Continue to dream and hope for the best, but do take the time to plan for the worst.

So What Have We Learned?

Dreams of a Lifetime shows that we live in a land of dreamers. Some dream for enjoyment or escape, some for inspiration and motivation, and some dream because they are, consciously or unconsciously, embracing long-established, dominant cultural lessons. Dreaming starts early, and patterns of dreaming are ingrained at a young age. None of the people we spoke with reported having no dreams at all, and most could not conceive of life without dreams.

But if dreams represent a blind optimism of sorts, should we discourage dreaming? Is that what our book is suggesting? Not really. But we do have some suggestions. First, our dreams demand some reflection. What are we getting from our dreams: escape, thrills, soothing moments, inspiration, motivation? If so, dream on, but understand the dream's purpose. Dreams should not be viewed as a magical tool to success.

Second, if dreams are to be achieved, something more is required. We should not fall prey to beliefs that suggest dreaming will make something so. (Remember the bestselling book *The Secret*, whose author, Rhonda Byrne, contended that thinking about something could make it come to fruition? We respectfully disagree.) We must be fully aware that once formulated, a dream requires transformation. It must become a project. We must plan and make efforts—even when the myths and values surrounding our dreams may convince us otherwise. To achieve your dreams, you must work toward the specific life imagined.

Third, it was clear to us that some study participants never intended to actually pursue their dreams. On the other hand, some respondents did intend to do so. And some were in a better position than others to pursue their dreams. The professional who wanted to start his or her own business was already "on track." Yet, the woman who dreamed of settling the Middle East troubles had no path available to her. The high-school senior who wanted to learn all the languages of the world was already working on mastering several foreign languages. The senior citizen who clung to the dream of becoming president had no traction at all. The thought occurred to us: just as some students need remedial education in order to be better prepared for college work, perhaps we need advisory support for dreamers in disadvantaged social locations. As our data indicate, the dreams of the disadvantaged are different in theme, endurance, perceived probability of achievement, and so on. As a nation that features a culture of positive dreaming, we should attend to helping disadvantaged dreamers accomplish the "steps" required for dream fulfillment. Such guidance might help dreamers become planners or even help disadvantaged dreamers to dream bigger.

Consider, for instance, Dalton Conley's argument: a major consequence of one's social-class position is the presence (or not) of an "envisioning process." Children in advantaged classes are consistently helped to envision positive futures. It happens in the social exchanges that are routine occurrences in their social environments. They meet and learn how to interact with their parents' friends and associates—people who might be judges, physicians, CEOs, and the like. These exchanges help to ready them for dreaming of similar futures. Our point here is simply this: it may not be enough to encourage all to dream big or promote the idea that anything is possible. Based on their social location, some individuals will need more training, an enlarged social network, or an increased awareness of the steps needed to convert a dream into a plan.[6]

Fourth, we hope our readers will take from this book a lesson on the inequality of the dreaming landscape. Our culture encourages all to engage in dreaming. But for many, we block the paths to accomplishing those dreams. When we encourage a child to become a doctor, lawyer, or a business mogul, but restrict the path to achieving such dreams to only those in privileged social classes, races, and genders, we essentially destine people to dream in vain or to abandon their dreams. When we say, "You can be anything you want—even president of the United States," but ignore the way in which politics, money, and power are intertwined, we set the stage for feelings of personal failure and resentment. When we say, "Work hard enough and your dreams of affluence will come true," we deny the fact that hard work may still result in a life of poverty, for hard work alone cannot a privileged life make. (Ask those who work sixty- and seventy-hour weeks at a minimum wage and find themselves too tired or busy to work toward a dream.) Some of our study participants had already learned these painful lessons.

Until opportunities become more equitably distributed, until we level the playing field of potentials and possibilities, we must recognize that, for many, dreams will remain just that— unattainable possibilities and nothing more than wishful thinking. Only when doors are open to all can we recognize the transporting power of dreams. And so we end our book with this wish: We dream of a time when we can confidently say to all the dreamers of the world: dream on for dreams really can come true.

Notes

Chapter 1. If You Knew You Couldn't Fail...

1. Some of the descriptions of concepts, methods, and sampling, as well as a few quotations from study participants, appeared in a previously published article: "Future Imaginings: Public Culture, Personal Culture, Social Location, and the Shaping of Dreams." See Cerulo and Ruane (2021).

2. This literature is truly massive, addressing things such as the role played by families in developing children's aspirations (see, e.g., Archer et al. 2012; Flouri et al. 2015; Huttman 1991; Ion, Lupu, and Nicolae 2020; Rosen and D'Andrade 1959; Turner, Chandler, and Heffer 2009); educational aspirations (see, e.g., Covington 2000; Jang 2020; Khattab 2018; Meece and Agger 2018; Riegle-Crumb, Moore, and Ramos-Wada 2011; Sewall and Shah 1968; Strayhorn 2009; Zipin et al. 2015); career aspirations (see, e.g., Carr and Kefalas 2009; Cassirier and Reskin 2000; Correll 2004; Rainey and Borders 1997; Zhao, Seibert, and Lumpkin 2010); the aspirations of immigrants (see, e.g., Benson and O'Reilly 2016; Crivello 2015; Jung and Zhang 2016; Kim, Mok, and Seidel 2020; Portes, Mcleod, and Parker 1978; Suárez-Orozco and Suárez-Orozco 1995); or those of the poor (see, e.g., Cook et al. 1996; MacLeod 2019; Wilson 2011). Many of these works compare aspirations by gender, income, or race. For good reviews of the aspirations literature, see, e.g., Brunstein and Heckhausen 2018; Eccles and Wigfield 2002; Heath, Rothon, and Kilpi 2008; Hill and Wang 2015; Kao and Thompson 2003; Khattab 2015; Spencer, Logel, and Davies 2016; Winne and Nesbit 2010.

3. For more on projects, see, e.g., Archer 2003, 2007; McAdams 2013; Mische and Pattison 2000; Tavory and Eliasoph 2013.

4. Both Henri Desroche (1979) and Richard Swedberg (2009) thoroughly examine the concept of hope and its importance in the social sciences. In philosophy, Ernst Bloch (1995) offers a comprehensive treatment of hope. For other interesting works in this area, see, e.g., Alacovska 2019; Back 2015; Bishop 2000, 2011; Crapanzano 2003; Estola 2003; Miceli and Castelfranchi 2010.

5. According to Averill, Catlin, and Chon (1990), the probability of attainment distinguishes hope from things such as want and desire. See also Averill and Sundararajan 2005; Miceli and Castelfranchi 2010; Reimann et al. 2014.

6. There is a growing literature that explores the links between hope and health. For some good examples, see, e.g., Benzein and Saveman 1998; Benzein, Norberg, and Saveman 2001; Corn, Feldman, and Wexler 2020; Gengler 2015; Groopman 2005; Herbrand and Dimond 2018; Petersen and Wilkinson 2014; Petersen 2015; Scioli et al. 2016; Snyder, Irving, and Anderson 1991; Taussig, Hoeyer, and Helmreich 2013; Turner 2005; or Turner and Stokes 2006.

7. See Groopman 2005: 26.

8. For more on the culture of optimism, see, e.g., Cerulo 2006, 2020; Ehrenreich 2009. In religion, hope moves beyond optimism and is inextricably linked to goodness. Swedberg (2009) gives an excellent explanation of this.

9. See Beckert 2013: 224. Beckert, of course, is writing about broader economic structures, but his argument about how systems behave is transferrable to work on dreams. Fictional expectations take the form of stories, theories, and discourses (2013: 220). And while they may never materialize, it is clear that these assessments are not out of touch with reality. Fictional expectations must take into account "present empirical information and must appear coherent to create a convincing 'story' of the future development of the phenomena at stake" (2013: 224).

10. Mohr et al.'s (2020) discussion of "aims" is also similar to our conception of dreams.

11. See Samuel 2012: 2.

12. See Cullen 2003: 5.

13. For very readable and well-researched work on the American Dream, see, e.g., Cullen 2003; Jillson 2004; Samuel 2012. See Adams (1931) for the introduction of the term, and Jennifer Hochschild (1995) or Putnam (2016) for problems emerging from the concept.

14. We are indebted to Ann Mische's (2009) essay on projects and possibilities for some of these analytic categories.

15. To some degree, we build on work by Lamont (2000) or Swidler (2001) on the building of attitudes.

16. Good summaries of this work can be found in Cerulo 2018; Cerulo, Leschziner, and Shepherd 2021; Leschziner 2019.

17. Quoted from the Langston Hughes poem, "Dreams." See Rampersad 1994.

Chapter 2. What Do Dreamers Sound Like?

1. We compared the answers given in focus groups versus interviews to ensure that the different methods did not alter people's responses. We found no significant differences.

2. One drawback of self-identified class measures is the common tendency for people to most often self-identify as middle class. Our numbers reflect that tendency. However,

it is worth noting that our sample breakdown is similar to figures derived from nationally representative samples such as those used by the Gallup poll. See Newport 2018.

3. We collected some additional data that, while not central to the analysis, gives our readers additional details on the makeup of our sample. Forty-four percent of our respondents were married or living with a partner, 18% were divorced or separated, and 6% were widowed. The remaining individuals—32%—were never married. Several religions were represented among our participants: 4% were Buddhist, 39% Catholic, 12% Jewish, 7% Muslim, 28% Protestant (including Baptists, Lutherans, Methodists, etc.); 10% of our participants said they had no religious affiliation.

4. See Tavory and Eliasoph (2013) and Mische (2009) for work on future imaginings and the impact of those imaginings on action.

5. See Tavory and Eliasoph 2013: 913.

6. See Tavory and Eliasoph 2013: 916.

7. Here, Tavory and Eliasoph (2013) build on work by sociologist Anthony Giddens (1991), who states that people can imagine multiple futures, but that an overarching order—a temporal landscape at work in one's cultural context—organizes, or possibly, restricts those futures. Mische (2009) takes a similar position.

8. Note that in referencing some of Mische's (2009) factors, we adopted more accessible terminology. We did not use all of her factors (e.g., genre, connectivity, expandability), as they did not seem relevant to our research questions. Finally, we added four factors of our own—elements emanating from our conceptual foundation and our data: feasibility, transportability, grounding, and importance.

9. The remaining 5% of participants expressed dreams involving health, security, and large-scale social change, with less than 2% of respondents in each category.

10. All names are pseudonyms used to protect the identity of our study participants.

11. We had someone unfamiliar with our study objectives recode our classifications of feasibility. Intercoder reliability, the level of agreement between our classifications and those of the outside coder, was 87%.

12. Social scientists refer to these kinds of "feeling" thoughts as embodied cognition. See Cerulo (2019) for a good review of literature on this topic—including works by Bourdieu (1990) and Wacquant (2004, 2015).

13. These data address people's most important dream. But note that the probability predictions for people's second and third dreams were nearly identical.

Chapter 3. Cultural Lessons as Guidelines for Dreaming

1. As mentioned earlier, some portions of this chapter appeared in Cerulo and Ruane 2021.

2. Swidler 2001: 162.

3. Paraphrase of Swidler 2001: 161.

4. See Giddens 1984. For those interested in the history and current state of these ideas, we note that Pierre Bourdieu (1990) used the term "habitus" to represent this element of personal culture; Omar Lizardo (2017) later coined the term "nondeclarative culture."

5. This is illustrated in work on "implicit bias" and race. See, for example, Amodio and Devine 2006; Greenwald and Hamilton Krieger 2006; McConnell and Leibold 2001; Shepherd 2011. Shepherd (2019) gives a good review of this literature.

6. Giddens (1984) coined this phrase as well. Lizardo (2017) refers to this element of personal culture as "declarative culture."

7. For more on types of culture, see, for example, Patterson 2014 and Lizardo 2017.

8. Chaiken and Trope 1999; Evans 1984; Lieberman 2003; Smith and DeCoster 2000; Ullman 2012; these are some of the many cognitive scientists who tell us that the distinctions between types of personal culture have a neurological basis. Practical consciousness is acquired slowly from repeated exposures or recurrent activities; it is located and operates in the amygdala, basal ganglia, and lateral temporal cortex. Discursive consciousness involves limited exposure to symbolically mediated materials; it is located and implemented in the prefrontal cortex, cingulate cortex, and medial-temporal lobe. These neural differences help us understand the automatic versus deliberative aspects involved in using these two types of culture.

9. Ten percent of our content was recoded by someone unfamiliar with our hypotheses. Intercoder reliability was 91%.

10. From the song "When You Wish Upon a Star."

11. Retrieved from Quotes.net: https://www.quotes.net/quote/17378.

12. These quotes were retrieved from brainyquote.com, goalcast.com, goodreads.com, and quoteinvestigator.com.

13. See Cerulo 2006.

14. Cerulo (2020) notes the detrimental role of blind optimism in fighting COVID-19.

15. See Ehrenreich 2009: 203.

16. See, e.g., Gouveia and Clarke 2001; O'Sullivan 2015; Sharot 2011; Weinstein 1980; Weinstein and Klein 1996.

17. See Ehrenreich 2001.

18. See Desmond 2016.

19. See, e.g., Abrams et al. 2019; Amadeo 2021; Chetty et al. 2017; Edin and Kissane 2010; Edin and Shaefer 2015; Ehrenreich 2006; Fontenot, Semega, and Kollar 2018; Heiserman and Simpson 2017; Kim 1998; Kozol 2012; London et al. 2004.

20. See Stiglitz 2018.

21. See Swidler 1986: 277. Cultural sociologist John Levi Martin makes an even more radical claim, writing, "Culture may at sometimes function as a tool kit, but

more generally I suspect it is more like a junkyard, full of sharp bits of rusty metal, in which children happily play. . . . Like items in a junkyard, the vast majority of culture is unused. It is not just unused at any instant, it is unused, period. Most books sit in libraries unread, most vistas go unseen, most of our rituals are forgotten, most of our memories are not shared" (2010: 240).

22. See Swidler 1986: 280.

23. See Hochschild 2018; Neal 2018; Wuthnow 2019. Braunstein 2019; Chua 2019; Inglehart and Norris 2017; Silva 2019; Van Duyn 2018 offer more support of the political divide.

24. See Brenan (2019) or Pew Research Center (2017a) for specifics on these polls.

25. See Leahy (2017) or Levitt and Komminda (2018) for more on this topic.

26. See Insurance Information Institute 2020.

27. See Rzepa and Ray 2020.

28. See Amadeo 2019, 2021.

29. Real median family income and real per capita income rose as well, though at slightly lower rates.

30. See, e.g., Chetty et al. 2017; Fontenot, Semega, and Kollar 2018; Saez and Zucman 2016.

31. See ATTOM Data Solutions 2019; Investing.com 2019; Joint Center for Housing Studies at Harvard University 2019; Statista 2019; U.S. Census Bureau 2021a.

32. See *Lodging* 2019; Reed and Crawford 2014; U.S. Census Bureau 2019, 2021b.

33. For more on these findings, see, e.g., Abrams et al. 2019; Associated Press-NORC Center for Public Affairs Research 2013; Berman 2015; Cannon and Bevan 2019; Graham 2018; Norman 2018; Smith 2017.

Chapter 4. Where You Stand
and How You Dream

1. David Woodruff Smith 2013.

2. See Merleau-Ponty (2013 [1945]).

3. Wacquant (1998) notes the influence of Merleau-Ponty on Bourdieu, and Marcoulatos (2010) speaks of the complimentary nature of these two scholars.

4. For more on Bourdieu's thinking, see Bourdieu 1984, 1986.

5. For a good review of this literature, see Lin 2000; McDonald and Day 2010.

6. Of course, some Whites living in economically depressed environments hold a different view. See, e.g., Hochschild 2018; Kimmel 2017.

7. For some evidence of this, see, e.g., Bennett and Plaut 2017; *Economist* 2019; Edwards 2016; English et al. 2017; Fryer 2019; Kahn et al. 2017.

8. Some interesting studies have been done on racial discrimination in sales. See, e.g., Alkayyali 2019; Ayres 1995; Brewster, Lynn, and Cocroft 2014; Henderson, Hakstian, and Williams 2016; Pittman 2017.

9. By "lower class," we refer to those living at or below the poverty line. In the United States, that is roughly 12% of the population; see Semega et al. 2019.

10. See NurseJournal 2021.

11. For more on the Titanic, see Maltin 2011; Zuckerman 2020. On Katrina, see Garfield 2007; Manove et al. 2019. On COVID-19, see Zanolli 2020.

12. For more on the links between social class, mortality, and life expectancy, see, e.g., Bor, Cohen, and Galea 2017; Chen, Oster, and Williams 2016; Cherry and Heininger 2017; Chetty et al. 2016; Cockerham 2017; Hill and Jorgenson 2018; Venkataramani, O'Brien, and Tsai 2021; or Weinstein et al. 2017. For more on the links between social class and health, see, e.g., Cockerham 2017; Fisher and Bubola 2020; Hall 1986; Lord 1981; Lorenz et al. 2016; National Center for Health Statistics 2020; or Zeitlin, Lutterman, and Russell 1977. Data on the links between social class and exposure to disaster and risk can be found in Boustan et al. 2017; the Center for Research on the Epidemiology for Disasters 2016; Hall 1986; Jansen et al. 2012; Kriner and Shen 2010; Reiman and Leighton 2016. The links between social class, mental health, and negative life events are discussed in American Psychological Association 2017; Cockerham 2020; MacLeod 2019; National Center for Health Statistics 2020; Weller 2015. Work on the links between social class, support systems, and life chances are discussed in Cockerham 2017, 2020; Finney, Kapadia, and Peters 2015; MacLeod 2019; National Center for Health Statistics 2020; Sampson 2012. The National Student Clearinghouse Research Center (2018), the National Center for Education Statistics (2021), and the National School Board Association (2021) offer information on social class and educational opportunities. For a larger review of these issues, see Ruane and Cerulo 2020.

13. The National Organization for Research at the University of Chicago has been calculating such scores for decades using a series of national surveys. For the most recent ratings, see Smith and Son 2014.

14. One drawback of self-identified class measures is the common tendency for people to most often self-identify as middle class. Our numbers reflect that tendency. However, it is worth noting that our sample breakdown is similar to figures derived from major polling firms using representative samples such as the Gallup poll. See Newport 2018.

15. The similarity in dream themes among those in the working and middle classes may result from people's tendency to conflate these two class statuses in their minds.

16. In some of these topics, our third and fourth graders are not included in the analysis, as we found that the dimensions at hand were a bit too difficult for most of the people in this age group to comprehend and answer.

17. Of course, Native Americans have experienced intense discrimination as well. But in this section, we focus on the racial categories included in our sample.

18. See Newport 2020.

19. For more on these statistics, see Bacon and Mehta 2018; CBS News/*New York Times* 2009; Dann 2017; Newport 2020; *New York Times*/CBS News Poll 2016; Pew Research Center 2017b.

20. See Ely and Driscoll (2020) for statistics on infant mortality, and Social Science Research Council (2021) and Statista Research Report (2021) for information on mortality rates.

21. See the Asthma and Allergy Foundation of America 2020; Centers for Disease Control and Prevention 2020; and National Cancer Institute 2020.

22. For more on COVID-19-related rates, see Arias, Tejada-Vera, and Ahmad 2021; Centers for Disease Control and Prevention 2021a.

23. See Beck 2021; U.S. Department of Justice 2020.

24. For more details on residential patterns and zoning policies, see Jenkins 2017; National Fair Housing Alliance 2017; Nodjimbadem 2017.

25. Green 2021. The Equity Lab currently serves 1,500 students from high-poverty schools in 35 cities. Riel (2021) writes about explicit recruitment strategies to keep charter schools predominantly White.

26. For more on educational statistics, see National Center for Education Statistics 2019a, 2019b, 2020a, 2020b.

27. For more on occupational disparities, see, e.g., Digest of Education 2020; Dowell 2020; National Center for Education Statistics 2019a, 2019b; U.S. Bureau of Labor Statistics 2021a.

28. For more on wealth disparities, see Bhutta et al. 2020; Park and Yang 2021; USAFACTS 2020.

29. For more on overall racial inequalities, see, e.g., Arias and Xu 2019; Fitzgerald 2020; PBS Newshour 2020; Ruane and Cerulo 2020: 133–150.

30. For an inclusive report on the multiracial experience in the United States, see Parker et al. 2015.

31. Our data was collected before the rise in violence against Asians that began in 2020. These events might have changed the optimism of our Asian participants.

32. For more on gender socialization in infancy, see, e.g., Eliot 2009; Kane 2009; Karraker, Vogel, and Lake 1995; Kara Smith 2005; Sweeney and Bradbard 1988. For more on gender socialization in early childhood, see, e.g., Blum, Mmari, and Moreau 2017; Eliot 2009; Kwon et al. 2013; Mascaro et al. 2017. Ruane and Cerulo (2020: 115–132) give a more extensive review.

33. See, e.g., Gunderson et al. 2012.

34. For more on gender typing in the educational system, see, e.g., Bhanot and Jovanovic 2005; Cunningham, Hoyer, and Sparks 2015; Downey and Vogt-Yuan 2005; Flaherty 2018; Gunderson et al. 2012; Ikem 2018; Mangan 2012; Miller 2017; Riegle-Crumb, Farkas, and Muller 2006; Sonnert 2009; Spencer, Porche, and Tolman 2003; Stake and Nickens 2005; U.S. Bureau of Labor Statistics 2019a, 2019b; Ziegler and Stoeger 2008.

35. For more details, see Bleiweis 2020.

36. For more details on gender differences in occupations, see U.S. Bureau of Labor Statistics 2019a, 2019b.

37. For more details on gender differences in earnings, see U.S. Bureau of Labor Statistics 2021b.

38. Ruane and Cerulo (2020: 115–132) give a good overview of gender inequality issues.

39. On gender discrepancies in health, see Dusenbery (2019). For more on the extra-health effects of COVID-19, see Wenham et al. 2020.

40. See, e.g., Horowitz and Fetterolf 2020; Jacobsen et al. 2014.

41. See, e.g., Baer and Kaufmann 2008; Greene and DeBacker 2004; Oyserman and Fryberg 2006; or Stern 2004.

Chapter 5. Dreaming through the Times of Our Lives

1. See Stanford Children's Health 2021.

2. See Klinenberg 2002; Sharkey 2013.

3. See Centers for Disease Control and Prevention 2021b.

4. See Centers for Disease Control and Prevention 2019.

5. See Suicide Prevention Resource Center 2020.

6. See Graham and Ruiz Pozuelo 2017; Rauch 2018.

7. See Semega et al. 2019.

8. See Morgan and Truman 2020.

9. See Hutchins et al. 2020.

10. BalancingEverything 2021; The Philanthropy Roundtable 2021.

11. See Bruine de Bruin 2021; Rolison et al. 2014.

12. As in the previous chapter, our third and fourth graders will not be reflected in this section's analysis as we found that the issues at hand were a bit too difficult for many of these young respondents to comprehend and answer.

13. As mentioned in earlier chapters, our third and gourth graders were not always included in some of the factors on dreaming because the concepts were too hard for them to grasp.

Chapter 6. Dreaming When Life Is Ruptured

1. For some strong examples of people who do such research, see Bertaux 2003; Maines 1993; Orbuch 1997; Polletta 1998, 2014; Somers 1994; Yamane 2000.

2. For some interesting sociological work on narrative ruptures in areas such as violence and victimization, illness, trauma, or relocation, see, e.g., Atkinson 2006; Frank 1995; Hyden 1997; O'Loughlin et al. 2014; Pemberton and Aarten 2018; Pemberton, Aarten, and Mulder 2019; Rosen 2017.

3. See National Alliance to End Homelessness 2021; World Population Review 2021.

4. See American Cancer Society 2021.

5. See National Cancer Institute 2021.

6. See National Cancer Institute 2021.

7. See Amadeo 2021; Barello 2014; Schultz 2014.

8. See Cappelli, Barankay, and Lewin 2018.

9. See Baldwin and Begnaud 2018.

10. This is not uncommon for those who are traumatized by a disaster. See, e.g., Barnes 2006; Hull, Alexander, and Klein 2002; Gill 2007; Lazarus, Jimerson, and Brock 2002.

11. Quote by Stephen Strum, prostate cancer specialist; see Cerulo 2006: 117–119. For more recent reviews of medical literature that promotes these ideas, see, e.g., Boehm et al. 2018; Conversano et al. 2010; Kim et al. 2017; Schiavon et al. 2017.

12. Ernest H. Rosenbaum and Isadora R. Rosenbaum (2021) offer some perspective on this.

13. It is worth noting that the unemployed were the least energetic of all our participants. This echoes Damaske's (2021) observations.

Chapter 7. The Importance of Studying Dreams

1. Taken from Thoreau 2020.

2. Taken from Byrnes's 2010 novel, *The Power*.

3. Quoted in Odeven 2020.

4. We refer here to Hughes' poem "Dream Deferred." This poem, it is said, was an inspiration for Lorraine Hansberry's play *A Raisin in the Sun*.

5. See, e.g., Cerulo 2006, 2020; Garud, Schlidt, and Lent 2014.

6. See, for example, Conley 2008. Also see Lareau 2003.

References

Abrams, Samuel J., Karlyn Bowman, Eleanor O'Neil, Ryan Streeter. 2019. "AEI Survey on Community and Society: Social Capital, Civic Health, and Quality of Life in the United States." American Enterprise Institute (February 5) https://www.aei.org/wp-content/uploads/2019/02/AEI-Survey-on-Community-and-Society-Social-Capital-Civic-Health-and-Quality-of-Life-in-the-United-States.pdf.

Adams, James Truslow. 1931. *The Epic of America*. New York: Little Brown.

Alacovska, Ana. 2019. "'Keep Hoping, Keep Going': Towards a Hopeful Sociology of Creative Work." *Sociological Review* 67: 5: 1118–1136.

Alkayyali, Ranam. 2019. "Shopping while Veiled: An Exploration of the Experiences of Veiled Muslim Consumers in France." In *Race in the Marketplace: Crossing Critical Boundaries*, edited by Guillaume D. Johnson, Kevin D. Thomas, Anthony Kwame Harrison, and Sonya A. Grier, 89–105. Cham: Palgrave Macmillan.

Amadeo, Kimberly. 2019. "Dow Jones Highest Closing Records." The Balance (July 28) https://www.thebalance.com/dow-jones-closing-history-top-highs-and-lows-since-1929-3306174.

———. 2021. "Unemployment Rate by Year since 1929 Compared to Inflation and GDP." The Balance. (March 16) https://www.thebalance.com/unemployment-rate-by-year-3305506.

American Cancer Society. 2021. "Cancer Treatment and Survivorship Facts and Figures 2019–2021." Atlanta: American Cancer Society. https://www.cancer.org/content/dam/cancer-org/research/cancer-facts-and-statistics/cancer-treatment-and-survivorship-facts-and-figures/cancer-treatment-and-survivorship-facts-and-figures-2019-2021.pdf.

American Psychological Association. 2017. "Stress in America: The State of Our Nation." (November 1) https://www.apa.org/news/press/releases/stress/2017/state-nation.pdf.

Amodio, David M., and Patricia G. Devine. 2006. "Stereotyping and Evaluation in Implicit Race Bias: Evidence for Independent Constructs and Unique Effects on Behavior." *Journal of Personality and Social Psychology* 91: 4: 652–666.

Archer, Louise, Jennifer DeWitt, Jonathan Osborne, Justin Dillon, Beatrice Willis, and Billy Wong. 2012. "Science Aspirations, Capital, and Family Habitus: How Families Shape Children's Engagement and Identification with Science." *American Educational Research Journal* 49: 5: 881–908.

Archer, Margaret S. 2003. *Structure, Agency, and the Internal Conversation*. Cambridge: Cambridge University Press.

———. 2007. *Making Our Way through the World: Human Reflexivity and Social Mobility*. Cambridge: Cambridge University Press.

Arias, Elizabeth, and Jiaquan Xu. 2019. "United States Life Tables, 2017." *National Vital Statistics Reports*. Vol. 68: no. 7. Hyattsville, MD: National Center for Health Statistics. https://www.cdc.gov/nchs/data/nvsr/nvsr68/nvsr68_07-508.pdf.

Arias, Elizabeth, Betzaida Tejada-Vera, and Farida Ahmad. 2021. "Provisional Life Expectancy Estimates for January through June, 2020." Centers of Disease Control. Vital Statistics Rapid Release. Report no. 010 (February) https://www.cdc.gov/nchs/data/vsrr/VSRR10-508.pdf.

Associated Press-NORC Center for Public Affairs Research. 2013. "U.S. Public Mood: Significant Differences in Optimism Broken Down by Race." NORC at the University of Chicago (August 1) http://www.norc.org/NewsEventsPublications/PressReleases/Pages/u-s-public-mood-significant-differences-in-optimism-broken-down-by-race.aspx.

Association of American Medical Colleges. 2018. "The State of Women in Academic Medicine: The Pipeline and Pathways to Leadership, 2015–2016." Association of American Medical Colleges. https://www.aamc.org/members/gwims/statistics/.

Asthma and Allergy Foundation of America. 2020. "Asthma Disparities in America: A Roadmap to Reducing Burden on Racial and Ethnic Minorities." https://www.aafa.org/media/2743/asthma-disparities-in-america-burden-on-racial-ethnic-minorities.pdf.

Atkinson, Michael. 2006. "Masks of Masculinity: (Sur)passing Narratives and Cosmetic Surgery." In *Body/Embodiment: Symbolic Interaction and the Sociology of the Body*, edited by Phillip Vannini, 247–261. London: Routledge.

ATTOM Data Solutions. 2019. "U.S. Foreclosure Activity Drops to 13-Year Low in 2018." (January 15) https://www.attomdata.com/news/most-recent/2018-year-end-foreclosure-market-report/.

Averill, James R., George Catlin, and Kyum K. Chon. 1990. *Rules of Hope*. New York: Springer-Verlag.

Averill, James R., and Louise Sundararajan. 2005. "Hope as Rhetoric: Cultural Narratives of Wishing and Coping." In *Interdisciplinary Perspectives on Hope*, edited by Jaklin A. Elliott, 127–159. New York: Nova Science Publishers.

Ayres, Ian. 1995. "Further Evidence of Discrimination in New Car Negotiations and Estimates of Its Cause." *Michigan Law Review* 94: 1: 109–147.

Back, Les. 2015. "Blind Pessimism and the Sociology of Hope." Discover Society (December 1) http://discoversociety.org/2015/12/01/blind-pessimism-and-the -sociology-of-hope/.

Bacon, Perry Jr., and Dhrumil Mehta. 2018. "The Diversity of Black Political Views." FiveThirtyEight (April 6) https://fivethirtyeight.com/features/the-diversity-of -black-political-views/.

Baer, John, and James C. Kaufman. 2008. "Gender Differences in Creativity." *Journal of Creative Behavior* 42: 2: 75–105.

BalancingEverything. 2021. "Charitable Giving Statistics." (June 21) https:// balancingeverything.com/charitable-giving-statistics/.

Baldwin, Sarah Lynch, and David Begnaud. 2018. "Hurricane Maria Caused an Estimated 2,975 Deaths in Puerto Rico, New Study Finds." CBS News (August 28) https://www.cbsnews.com/news/hurricane-maria-death-toll-puerto-rico-2975 -killed-by-storm-study-finds/.

Barello, Stephanie Hugie. 2014. "Consumer Spending and U.S. Employment from the 2007–2009 Recession through 2022." Monthly Labor Review. U.S. Bureau of Labor Statistics (October) https://www.bls.gov/opub/mlr/2014/article /consumer-spending-and-us-employment-from-the-recession-through-2022 .htm.

Barnes, Joshua. 2006. "Developing Disaster Survivor Resiliency: The Home Away from Home." *Disaster Prevention and Management: An International Journal* 15: 2: 223–232.

Beck, Allen J. 2021. "Race and Ethnicity of Violent Crime Offenders and Arrestees, 2018." U.S. Department of Justice (January) https://www.bjs.gov/content/pub /pdf/revcoa18.pdf.

Beckert, Jens. 2013. "Imagined Futures: Fictional Expectations in the Economy." *Theory and Society* 42: 3: 219–240.

———. 2016. *Imagined Futures: Fictional Expectations and Capitalist Dynamics.* Cambridge, MA: Harvard University Press.

Behr, Goethe. 2020. "Was Trump's Pre-Covid Economy Stronger Than Obama's?" Election Central (October 20) https://www.uspresidentialelectionnews.com /2020/10/was-trumps-pre-covid-economy-stronger-than-obamas/.

Bennett, Mark W., and Victoria C. Plaut. 2017. "Looking Criminal and the Presumption of Dangerousness: Afrocentric Facial Features, Skin Tone, and Criminal Justice." *UC Davis Law Rev.* 51: 2: 745–803.

Benson, Michaela, and Karen O'Reilly. 2016. *Lifestyle Migration: Expectations, Aspirations and Experiences.* New York: Routledge.

Benzein, Eva, and B-I. Saveman. 1998. "One Step Towards the Understanding of Hope: A Concept Analysis." *International Journal of Nursing Studies* 35: 6: 322–329.

Benzein, Eva, Astrid Norberg, and Britt-Inger Saveman. 2001. "The Meaning of the Lived Experience of Hope in Patients with Cancer in Palliative Home Care." *Palliative Medicine* 15: 2: 117–126.

Berman, Russell. 2015. "As White Americans Give Up on the American Dream, Blacks and Hispanics Embrace It." *Atlantic* (September 4) https://www.theatlantic.com/politics/archive/2015/09/the-surprising-optimism-of-african-americans-and-latinos/401054/.

Bertaux, Daniel. 2003. "The Usefulness of Life Stories for a Realist and Meaningful Sociology." In *Biographical Research in Eastern Europe: Altered Lives and Broken Biographies,* edited by Robert Miller and Robin Humphrey and Elena Zdravomyslova, 39–51. London: Ashgate.

Bhanot, Ruchi, and Jasna Jovanovic. 2005. "Do Parents' Academic Gender Stereotypes Influence Whether They Intrude on Their Children's Homework?" *Sex Roles* 52: 9–10: 597–607.

Bhutta, Neil, Andrew Chang, Lisa Dettling, and Joanne Hsu, with assistance from Julia Hewitt. 2020. "Disparities in Wealth by Race and Ethnicity in the 2019 Survey of Consumer Finances." Board of Governors of the Federal Reserve (September 28) https://www.federalreserve.gov/econres/notes/feds-notes/disparities-in-wealth-by-race-and-ethnicity-in-the-2019-survey-of-consumer-finances-20200928.htm.

Bishop, Peter. 2000. "The Death of Shangri-la: The Utopian Imagination and the Dialectics of Hope." http://pinnigerclinic.com/events/BISHOPThe__utopian_imagination.pdf.

———. 2011. "Hope in the Contact Zone: A Resource for Cultural Dialogue and Reconciliation." *International Journal of the Humanities* 9: 6: 205–218.

Bleiweis, Robin. 2020. "Quick Facts about the Gender Wage Gap." Center for American Progress (March 24) https://www.americanprogress.org/article/quick-facts-gender-wage-gap/.

Bloch, Ernst. 1995. *The Principle of Hope.* Vols. 1–3. Translated by Neville Plaice, Stephen Plaice, and Paul Knight. Cambridge, MA: MIT Press.

Blum, Robert W., Kristin Mmari, and Caroline Moreau. 2017. "It Begins at 10: How Gender Expectations Shape Early Adolescence around the World." *Journal of Adolescent Health* 61: 4S: S3–S4.

Boehm, Julia K., Ying Chen, Hayami Koga, Maya B. Mathur, Loryana L. Vie, and Laura D. Kubzansky. 2018. "Is Optimism Associated with Healthier Cardiovascular-Related Behavior? Meta-analyses of Three Health Behaviors." *Circulation Research* 122: 8: 1119–1134.

Bor, Jacob, Gregory H. Cohen, and Sandro Galea. 2017. "Population Health in an Era of Rising Income Inequality: USA, 1980–2015." *Lancet* 389: 10077: 1475–1490.

Bourdieu, Pierre. 1984. *Distinction: A Social Critique of the Judgement of Taste.* London: Routledge.

———. 1986. "The Forms of Capital." In *Handbook of Theory and Research for the Sociology of Education,* edited by John G. Richardson, 241–258. New York: Greenwood.

———. 1990. *The Logic of Practice.* London: Polity Press.

Boustan, Leah Platt, Maria Lucia Yanguas, Matthew Kahn, and Paul W. Rhode. 2017. "Natural Disasters by Location: Rich Leave and Poor Get Poorer." *Scientific American* (July 2) https://www.scientificamerican.com/article/natural-disasters-by-location-rich-leave-and-poor-get-poorer/.

Braunstein, Ruth. 2019. "Beyond the Dogmatic Believer: Religious Conviction across the American Political Divide." In *Religion, Humility, and Democracy in a Divided America,* edited by Ruth Braunstein, 1–22. Political Power and Social Theory 36. Bingley: Emerald Publishing.

Brenan, Megan. 2019. "Americans Most Satisfied with Nation's Military, Security." Gallup (January 28) https://news.gallup.com/poll/246254/americans-satisfied-nation-military-security.aspx.

Brewster, Zachary W., Michael Lynn, and Shelytia Cocroft. 2014. "Consumer Racial Profiling in U.S. Restaurants: Exploring Subtle Forms of Service Discrimination against Black Diners." *Sociological Forum* 29: 2: 476–495.

Bruine de Bruin, Wandi. 2021. "Age Differences in COVID-19 Risk Perceptions and Mental Health: Evidence from a National U.S. Survey Conducted in March 2020." *Journal of Gerontology and Behavioral Psychological Science and Social Science* 76: 2: e24–e29. https://www.ncbi.nlm.nih.gov/pmc/articles/PMC7542924/.

Brunstein, Joachim C., and Heinz Heckhausen. 2018. "Achievement Motivation." In *Motivation and Action,* edited by Jutta Heckhausen and Heinz Heckhausen, 221–304. New York: Springer.

Byrne, Rhonda. 2006. *The Secret.* New York: Atria Books.

———. 2010. *The Power.* New York: Atria Books.

Cannon, Carl M., and Tom Bevan. 2019. "The American Dream: Not Dead—Yet." Real Clear Politics (March 6) https://www.realclearpolitics.com/articles/2019/03/06/the_american_dream_not_dead_--_yet_139659.html#!.

Cappelli, Peter, Iwan Barankay, and David Lewin. 2018. "How the Great Recession Changed American Workers." *Wharton Business Daily* (September 10) https://knowledge.wharton.upenn.edu/article/great-recession-american-dream/.

Carr, Patrick J., and Maria J. Kefalas. 2009. *Hollowing Out the Middle: The Rural Brain Drain and What It Means for America.* Boston: Beacon Press.

Cassirer, Naomi, and Barbara Reskin. 2000. "High Hopes, Organizational Position, Employment Experiences, and Women's and Men's Promotion Aspirations." *Work and Occupations* 27: 4: 438–463.

CBS News/*New York Times*. 2009. "Poll: Blacks See Improved Race Relations." (April 27) https://www.cbsnews.com/news/poll-blacks-see-improved-race-relations/.

Center for Research on the Epidemiology for Disasters (CRED). 2016. "Poverty and Death: Disaster Mortality 1996–2015." The United Nations Office for Disaster Risk Reduction. https://www.unisdr.org/files/50589_creddisastermortalityallfinalpdf.pdf.

Centers for Disease Control and Prevention. 2019. "Coronary Heart Disease, Myocardial Infarction, and Stroke—A Public Health Issue." (July 30) https://www.cdc.gov/aging/publications/coronary-heart-disease-brief.html.

———. 2020. "Trends in Incidence of Type 1 and Type 2 Diabetes among Youths—Selected Counties and Indian Reservations, United States, 2002–2015." (February 14) https://www.cdc.gov/mmwr/volumes/69/wr/mm6906a3.htm.

———. 2021a. "Risk for COVID-19 Infection, Hospitalization, and Death by Race/Ethnicity." (April 23) https://www.cdc.gov/coronavirus/2019-ncov/COVID-data/investigations-discovery/hospitalization-death-by-race-ethnicity.html.

———. 2021b. "Risk for COVID-19 Infection, Hospitalization, and Death by Age Group." (September 9) https://www.cdc.gov/coronavirus/2019-ncov/COVID-data/investigations-discovery/hospitalization-death-by-age.html.

Cerulo, Karen A. 2006. *Never Saw It Coming: Cultural Challenges to Envisioning the Worst.* Chicago: The University of Chicago Press.

———. 2018. "Scents and Sensibility: Olfaction, Sense-Making, and Meaning Attribution." *American Sociological Review* 83: 2: 361–389.

———. 2019. "Embodied Cognition: Sociology's Role in Bridging Mind, Brain and Body." In *Oxford Handbook of Cognitive Sociology*, edited by Wayne Brekhus and Gabriel Ignatow, 81–100. New York: Oxford University Press.

———. 2020. "No Time for Blind Optimism." *Sociology Lens* (April 9) https://www.sociologylens.net/topics/collective-behaviour-and-social-movements/no-time-for-blind-optimism/30330.

Cerulo, Karen A., and Janet M. Ruane. 2021. "Future Imaginings: Public Culture, Personal Culture, Social Location and the Shaping of Dreams." *Sociological Forum* V36: S1: 1345–1370.

Cerulo, Karen A., Vanina Leschziner, and Hana Shepherd. 2021. "Rethinking Culture and Cognition." *Annual Review of Sociology* 47: 65–87.

Chaiken, Sgelley, and Yaacov Trope. 1999. *Dual-Process Theories in Social Psychology.* New York: Guilford.

Chen, Alice, Emily Oster, and Heidi Williams. 2016. "Why Is Infant Mortality Higher in the United States Than in Europe?" *American Economic Journal: Economic Policy* 8: 2: 89–124.

Cherry, James D., and Ulrich Heininger. 2017. "Measles, Morbidity, and Mortality in the Developed World Are Greater Than the Public Perceives." *Open Forum Infectious Diseases* 4: S1: 574–576. https://doi.org/10.1093/ofid/ofx163.1502.

Chetty, Raj, David Grusky, Maximilian Hell, Nathaniel Hendren, Robert Manduca, and Jimmy Narang. 2017. "The Fading American Dream: Trends in Absolute Income Mobility since 1940." *Science* 356: 6336: 398–406.

Chetty, Raj, Michael Stepner, Sarah Abraham, Shelby Lin, Benjamin Scuderi, Nicholas Turner, Augustin Bergeron, and David Cutler. 2016. "The Association between Income and Life Expectancy in the United States, 2001–2014." *Journal of the American Medical Association* 315: 16: 1750–1776.

Chua, Amy. 2019. *Political Tribes: Group Instinct and the Fate of Nations.* New York: Penguin Books.

Cockerham, William. 2017. *Medical Sociology.* 17th ed. New York: Routledge.

———. 2020. *Sociology of Mental Disorder.* 11th ed. New York: Routledge.

Conley, Dalton. 2008. "Reading Class between the Lines: A Reflection of Why We Should Stick to Folk Concepts of Social Class." In *Social Class: How Does It Work?*, edited by Annette Lareau and Dalton Conley, 366–374. New York: Russell Sage.

Conversano, Ciro, Alessandro Rotondo, Elena Lensi, Olivia Della Vista, Francesca Arpone, and Mario Antonio Reda. 2010. "Optimism and Its Impact on Mental and Physical Well-Being." *Clinical Practice and Epidemiology in Mental Health: CP & EMH* 6: 25–29.

Cook, Thomas D., Mary B. Church, Subira Ajanaku, William R. Shadish Jr., Jeong-Ran Kim, and Robert Cohen. 1996. "The Development of Occupational Aspirations and Expectations among Inner-City Boys." *Child Development* 67: 6: 3368–3385.

Corn, Benjamin W., David B. Feldman, and Isaiah Wexler. 2020. "The Science of Hope." *Lancet Oncology* 21: 9: 452–459.

Correll, Shelley J. 2004. "Constraints into Preferences: Gender, Status, and Emerging Career Aspirations." *American Sociological Review* 69: 1: 93–113.

Cox, Karen. 2002. "The Hopes of the Dying: Examining Patients' Experience of Participation in Early Phase Cancer Clinical Trials." *Nursing Times Research* 7: 1: 60–73.

Covington, Martin V. 2000. "Goal Theory, Motivation, and School Achievement: An Integrative Review." *Annual Review of Psychology* 51: 171–200.

Crapanzano, Vincent. 2003. "Reflections on Hope as a Category of Social and Psychological Analysis." *Cultural Anthropology* 18: 1: 3–32.

Crivello, Gina. 2015. "'There's No Future Here': The Time and Place of Children's Migration Aspirations in Peru." *Geoforum* 62: 1: 38–46.

Cullen, James. 2003. *The American Dream: A Short History of an Idea That Shaped a Nation*. New York: Oxford University Press.

Cunningham, Brittany, Kathleen Hoyer, and Dinah Sparks. 2015. "Gender Differences in Science, Technology, Engineering, and Mathematics (STEM): Interest, Credits Earned, and NAEP Performance in the 12th Grade." Stats in Brief: U.S. Department of Education NCES 2015-075 (February) https://nces.ed.gov /pubs2015/2015075.pdf.

Damaske, Sarah. 2021. *The Tolls of Uncertainty: How Privilege and the Guilt Gap Shape Unemployment in America*. Princeton, NJ: Princeton University Press.

Dann, Carrie. 2017. "NBC/WSJ Poll: Americans Pessimistic on Race Relations." NBC News (September 21) https://www.nbcnews.com/politics/first-read/nbc -wsj-poll-americans-pessimistic-race-relations-n803446.

Decock, Lieven, and Igor Douven. 2014. "What Is Graded Membership?" *Noûs* 48: 4: 653–682.

DeLuca, Stefanie, Susan Clampet-Lundquist, and Kathryn Edin. 2016. *Coming of Age in the Other America*. New York: Russell Sage Foundation.

Desmond, Matthew. 2016. *Evicted: Poverty and Profit in the American City*. New York: Crown.

Desroche, Henri. 1979. *The Sociology of Hope*. Translated by Carol Martin-Sperry. London: Routledge and Kegan Paul Ltd.

Dewey, John. 1981. *The Philosophy of John Dewey*. Edited by John J. McDermott. Chicago: The University of Chicago Press.

Digest of Education. 2020. "Median Annual Earnings of Full-Time Year-Round Workers 25 to 34 Years Old and Full-Time Year-Round Workers as a Percentage of the Labor Force, by Sex, Race/Ethnicity, and Educational Attainment: Selected Years, 1995 through 2019." National Center for Education Statistics (October) https://nces.ed.gov/programs/digest/d20/tables/dt20_502.30.asp.

Dowell, Earlene K. P. 2020. "Job Sprawl Results in Unemployment for Low-Income Urban Residents." United States Census Bureau (March 4) https://www.census .gov/library/stories/2020/03/spatial-mismatch-when-workers-can-not-get-to -jobs-in-suburbs.html.

Downey, Douglas B., and Anastasia Vogt-Yuan. 2005. "Sex Differences in School Performance during High School: Puzzling Patterns and Possible Explanations." *Sociological Quarterly* 46: 2: 299–321.

Dusenbery, Maya. 2019. *Doing Harm: The Truth about How Bad Medicine and Lazy Science Leave Women Dismissed, Misdiagnosed, and Sick*. New York: HarperOne.

Eccles, Jacquelynne S., and Allan Wigfield. 2002. "Motivational Beliefs, Values, and Goals." *Annual Review of Psychology* 53: 1: 109–132.

Economist. 2019. "Black Drivers in America Face Discrimination by the Police." (March 15) https://www.economist.com/graphic-detail/2019/03/15/black-drivers-in-america-face-discrimination-by-the-police.

Edelman, Peter. 2019. *Not a Crime to Be Poor: The Criminalization of Poverty in America.* New York: The New Press.

Edin, Kathryn, and Rebecca Joyce Kissane. 2010. "Poverty and the American Family: A Decade in Review." *Journal of Marriage and Family* 72: 3: 460–479.

Edin, Kathryn, and H. Luke Shaefer. 2015. *$2.00 a Day: Living on Almost Nothing in America.* Boston: Houghton Mifflin Harcourt.

Edwards, Clarence. 2016. "Race and the Police." National Police Foundation. https://www.policefoundation.org/onpolicing/race-and-the-police/.

Ehrenreich, Barbara. 2001. *Nickle and Dimed: On (Not) Getting by in America.* New York: Metropolitan Books.

———. 2006. *Bait and Switch: The (Futile) Pursuit of the American Dream.* New York: Metropolitan Books.

———. 2009. *Bright-Sided: How the Relentless Promotion of Positive Thinking Has Undermined America.* New York: Metropolitan Books.

Eliot, Lise. 2009. *Pink Brain, Blue Brain: How Small Differences Grow into Troublesome Gaps—And What We Can Do About It.* Boston: Houghton Mifflin Harcourt.

Ely, Danielle, and Anne K. Driscoll. 2020 "Infant Mortality in the United States, 2018: Data from the Period Linked Birth/Infant Death File." *National Vital Statistics Report* 69: 7: (July 16) https://www.cdc.gov/nchs/data/nvsr/nvsr69/NVSR-69-7-508.pdf.

English, Devin, Lisa Bowleg, Ana Maria del Río-González, Jeanne M. Tschann, Robert P. Agans, and David J. Malebranche. 2017. "Measuring Black Men's Police-Based Discrimination Experiences: Development and Validation of the Police and Law Enforcement (PLE) Scale." *Cultural Diversity and Ethnic Minority Psychology* 23: 2: 185–199. https://doi.org/10.1037/cdp0000137.

Estola, Eila. 2003. "Hope as Work: Student Teachers Constructing Their Narrative Identities." *Scandinavian Journal of Educational Research* 47: 2: 181–203.

Evans, Jonathan. 1984. "Heuristic and Analytic Processes in Reasoning." *British Journal of Psychology* 75: 4: 451–468.

Finney, Nissa, Dharmi Kapadia, and Simon Peters. 2015. "How Are Poverty, Ethnicity and Social Networks Related?" Joseph Roundtree Foundation. (March 30) https://www.jrf.org.uk/report/how-are-poverty-ethnicity-and-social-networks-related.

Fisher, Max, and Emma Bubola. 2020. "As Coronavirus Deepens Inequality, Inequality Worsens Its Spread." *New York Times* (March 15) https://www.nytimes.com/2020/03/15/world/europe/coronavirus-inequality.html.

Fitzgerald, Kathleen J. 2020. *Recognizing Race and Ethnicity: Power, Privilege, and Inequality.* New York: Routledge.

Flaherty, Colleen. 2018. "When a Field's Reputation Precedes It." *Inside Higher Education* (January 25) https://www.insidehighered.com/news/2018/01/25/study-finds-given-disciplines-perceived-gender-bias-not-math-biggest-predictor?utm_source=Inside+Higher+Ed&utm_campaign=64dbf47234-DNU20180111&utm_medium=email&utm_term=0_1fcbc04421-64dbf47234-198471393&mc_cid=64dbf47234&mc_eid=1dbcd5e25a.

Flouri, Eirini, Dimitrios Tsivrikos, Reece Akhtar, and Emily Midouhas. 2015. "Neighbourhood, School and Family Determinants of Children's Aspirations in Primary School." *Journal of Vocational Behavior* 87: 1: 71–79.

Fontenot, Kayla, Jessica Semega, and Melissa Kollar. 2018. "Income and Poverty in the United States, 2017." Washington, DC: United State Census Bureau. https://www.census.gov/library/publications/2018/demo/p60-263.html.

Frank Arthur W. 1995. *The Wounded Storyteller: Body, Illness and Ethics.* Chicago: The University of Chicago Press.

Fryer, Roland G., Jr. 2019. "An Empirical Analysis of Racial Differences in Police Use of Force." *Journal of Political Economy* 127: 3: 1210–1261.

Gallup. 2019. "Economy." https://news.gallup.com/poll/1609/consumer-views-economy.aspx.

Garfield, Gail. 2007. "Hurricane Katrina: The Making of Unworthy Disaster Victims." *Journal of African American Studies* 10: 4: 55–74.

Garud, Raghu, Henri A. Schildt, and Theresa K. Lant. 2014. "Entrepreneurial Storytelling, Future Expectations, and the Paradox of Legitimacy." *Organization Science* 25: 5: 1479–1492.

Gengler, Amanda M. 2015. "'He's Doing Fine': Hope, Work and Emotional Threat Management among Families of Seriously Ill Children." *Symbolic Interaction* 38: 4: 611–630.

Giddens, Anthony. 1984. *The Constitution of Society: Outline of the Theory of Structuration.* Berkeley: University of California Press.

———. 1991. *Modernity and Self Identity: Self and Society in the Late Modern Age.* Stanford: Stanford University Press.

Gill, Duane A. 2007. "Secondary Trauma or Secondary Disaster? Insights from Hurricane Katrina." *Sociological Spectrum* 27: 6: 613–632.

Goldberg, Susan, and Michael Lewis. 1969. "Play Behavior in the Year-Old Infant: Early Sex Differences." *Child Development* 1: 1: 21–31.

Gouveia, Susana O., and Valerie Clarke. 2001. "Optimistic Bias for Negative and Positive Events." *Health Education* 101: 5: 228–234.

Graham, Carol. 2018. "Why Are Black Poor Americans More Optimistic Than White Ones?" Brookings (January 30) https://www.brookings.edu/articles/why-are-black-poor-americans-more-optimistic-than-white-ones/.

Graham, Carol, and Julia Ruiz Pozuelo. 2017. "Happiness, Stress, and Age: How the U Curve Varies across People and Places." *Journal of Population Economics* 30: 1: 225–264.

Greene, Barbara A., and Teresa K. DeBacker. 2004. "Gender and Orientations toward the Future: Links to Motivation." *Educational Psychology Review* 16: 2: 91–120.

Green, Erica. 2021. "A College Program for Disadvantaged Teens Could Shake Up Elite Admissions." *New York Times* (February 18) https://www.nytimes.com/2021/02/18/us/politics/college-admissions-poor-students.html.

Greenwald, Anthony G., and Linda Hamilton Krieger. 2006. "Implicit Bias: Scientific Foundations." *California Law Review* 94: 4: 945–967.

Groopman, Jerome. 2005. *The Anatomy of Hope: How People Prevail in the Face of Illness*. New York: Random House.

Gunderson, Elizabeth A., Gerardo Ramirez, Susan C. Levine, and Sian L. Beilock. 2012. "The Role of Parents and Teachers in the Development of Gender-Related Math Attitudes." *Sex Roles* 66: 3–4: 153–166.

Hall, Wayne. 1986. "Social Class and Survival on the *S.S. Titanic*." *Social Science and Medicine* 22: 6: 687–690.

Heath, Anthony F., Catherine Rothon, and Elina Kilpi. 2008. "The Second Generation in Western Europe: Education, Unemployment and Occupational Attainment." *Annual Review of Sociology* 34: 211–235.

Heiserman, Nicholas, and Brent Simpson. 2017. "Higher Inequality Increases the Gap in the Perceived Merit of the Rich and Poor." *Social Psychology Quarterly* 80: 3: 243–253.

Henderson, Geraldine Rosa, Anne-Marie Hakstian, and Jerome D. Williams. 2016. *Consumer Equality: Race and the American Marketplace*. Santa Barbara, CA: Praeger.

Herbrand, Cathy, and Rebecca Dimond. 2018. "Mitochondrial Donation, Patient Engagement and Narratives of Hope." *Sociology of Health and Illness* 40: 4: 623–638.

Hill, Nancy E., and Ming-Te Wang. 2015. "From Middle School to College: Developing Aspirations, Promoting Engagement, and Indirect Pathways from Parenting to Post High School Enrollment." *Developmental Psychology* 51: 2: 224–235.

Hill, Terrence D., and Andrew Jorgenson. 2018. "Bring Out Your Dead! A Study of Income Inequality and Life Expectancy in the United States, 2000–2010." *Health and Place* 49: 1: 1–6.

Hochschild, Arlie Russell. 2018. *Strangers in Their Own Land: Anger and Mourning on the American Right*. New York: The New Press.

Hochschild, Jennifer L. 1995. *Facing Up to the American Dream: Race, Class, and the Soul of a Nation*. Princeton, NJ: Princeton University Press.

Horowitz, Juliana Menasce, and Janell Fetterolf. 2020. "Worldwide Optimism about Future of Gender Equality, Even as Many See Advantages for Men." Pew Research Center (April 30) https://www.pewresearch.org/global/2020/04/30/worldwide-optimism-about-future-of-gender-equality-even-as-many-see-advantages-for-men/.

Hull, Alastair M., David A. Alexander, and Susan Klein. 2002. "Survivors of the Piper Alpha Oil Platform Disaster: Long-Term Follow-up Study." *British Journal of Psychiatry* 181: 5: 433–438.

Hutchins, Helena, Brent Wolff, Rebecca Leeb, Jean Y. Ko, Erika Odom, Joe Wiley, Allison Friedman, and Rebecca H. Bitsko. 2020. "COVID-19 Mitigation Behaviors by Age Group—United States, April–June 2020." *Morbidity and Mortality Weekly Report* 69: 43: 1584–1590. https://pubmed.ncbi.nlm.nih.gov/33119562/.

Huttman, Elizabeth. 1991. "A Research Note on Dreams and Aspirations of Black Families." *Journal of Comparative Family Studies* 22: 2: 147–158.

Hyden, Lars-Christer. 1997. "Illness and Narrative." *Sociology of Health and Illness* 19: 1: 48–69.

Ikem, Chinelo Nkechi. 2018. "The Importance of Female Role Models in the Classroom." *Pacific Standard* (February 5) https://psmag.com/education/the-importance-of-female-role-models-in-the-classroom.

Inglehart, Ronald, and Pippa Norris. 2017. "Trump and the Populist Authoritarian Parties: The Silent Revolution in Reverse." *Perspectives on Politics* 15: 2: 443–454.

Insurance Information Institute. 2020. "Facts + Statistics: Wildfires." https://www.iii.org/fact-statistic/facts-statistics-wildfires.

Investing.com. 2019. "U.S. CB Consumer Confidence." (July 30) https://www.investing.com/economic-calendar/cb-consumer-confidence-48.

Ion, Irina Elena, Radu Lupu, and Elena Nicolae. 2020. "Academic Achievement and Professional Aspirations: Between the Impacts of Family, Self-Efficacy and School Counselling." *Journal of Family Studies* (April): 1–24. https://doi.org/10.1080/13229400.2020.1746685.

Jacobsen, Ben, John B. Lee, Wessel Marquering, and Cherry Y. Zhang. 2014. "Gender Differences in Optimism and Asset Allocation." *Journal of Economic Behavior and Organization* 107: 3: 630–651.

Jang, Sung Tae. 2020. "The Schooling Experiences and Aspirations of Students Belonging to Intersecting Marginalisations Based on Race or Ethnicity, Sexuality, and Socioeconomic Status." *Race Ethnicity and Education*. https://doi.org/10.1080/13613324.2020.1842350.

Jansen, Pauline W., Marina Verlinden, Anke Dommisse-van Berkel, Cathelijne Mieloo, Jan van der Ende, René Veenstra, Frank C. Veaconrhulst, Wilma Jansen, and Henning Tiemeier. 2012. "Prevalence of Bullying and Victimization among Children in Early Elementary School: Do Family and School Neighbourhood Socioeconomic Status Matter?" *BMC Public Health* 12: 1: 494.

Jenkins, Brittan. 2017. "How Historic Racial Injustices Still Impact Housing Today." Zillow. (October 16) https://www.zillow.com/blog/historic-racial-injustices -housing-221898/.

Jillson, Cal. 2004. *Pursuing the American Dream: Opportunity and Exclusion over Four Years.* Lawrence: University of Kansas Press.

Joint Center for Housing Studies at Harvard University. 2019. "The State of the Nation's Housing." Joint Center for Housing Studies at Harvard University. https:// www.jchs.harvard.edu/state-nations-housing-2019.

Jones, Jeffrey M. 2018. "Key U.S. Economic Assessments Strong, Stable." Gallup (November 16) https://news.gallup.com/poll/244805/key-economic-assessments -strong-stable.aspx.

Jung, Eunjoo, and Yue Zhang. 2016. "Parental Involvement, Children's Aspirations, and Achievement in New Immigrant Families." *Journal of Educational Research* 109: 4: 333–350.

Kahn, Kimberly Barsamian, J. Katherine Lee, Brian Renauer, Kris R. Henning, and Greg Stewart. 2017. "The Effects of Perceived Phenotypic Racial Stereotypicality and Social Identity Threat on Racial Minorities' Attitudes about Police." *Journal of Social Psychology* 157: 4: 416–428.

Kane, Emily W. 2009. "'I Wanted a Soul Mate': Gendered Anticipation and Frameworks of Accountability in Parents' Preferences for Sons and Daughters." *Symbolic Interaction* 32: 4: 327–389

Kao, Grace, and Jennifer S. Thompson. 2003. "Racial and Ethnic Stratification in Educational Achievement and Attainment." *Annual Review of Sociology* 29: 417–442.

Karraker, Katherine Hildebrandt, Dena Ann Vogel, and Margaret Ann Lake. 1995. "Parents' Gender-Stereotyped Perceptions of Newborns: The Eye of the Beholder Revisited." *Sex Roles* 33: 9–10: 687–701.

Khattab, Nabil. 2015. "Students' Aspirations, Expectations and School Achievement: What Really Matters?" *British Educational Research Journal* 41: 5: 731–748.

———. 2018. "Ethnicity and Higher Education: The Role of Aspirations, Expectations and Beliefs." *Ethnicities* 18: 4: 457–470.

Kim, Eric S., Kaitlin A. Hagan, Francine Grodstein, Dawn L. DeMeo, Immaculata De Vivo, and Laura D. Kubzansky. 2017. "Optimism and Cause-Specific Mortality: A Prospective Cohort Study." *American Journal of Epidemiology* 185: 1: 21–29.

Kim, Marlene. 1998. "The Working Poor: Lousy Jobs or Lazy Workers?" *Journal of Economic Issues* 32: 1: 65–78.

Kim, Yeeun, Sog Yee Mok, and Tina Seidel. 2020. "Parental Influences on Immigrant Students' Achievement-Related Motivation and Achievement: A Meta-analysis." *Educational Research Review* 30: (June): 1–59.

Kimmel, Michael. 2017. *Angry White Men: American Masculinity at the End of an Era.* Hachette, UK: Public Affairs.

Klinenberg, Eric. 2002. *Heat Wave: A Social Autopsy of Disaster in Chicago.* Chicago: The University of Chicago Press.

Kozol, Jonathan. 2012. *Savage Inequalities: Children in America's Schools.* New York: Broadway Books.

Kriner, Douglas L., and Francis X. Shen. 2010. "America's 'Casualty Gap.'" *Los Angeles Times* (May 28) https://www.latimes.com/archives/la-xpm-2010-may-28-la-oe -0528-shen-warcosts-20100528-story.html.

Kwon, Kyong-Ah, Gary Bingham, Joellen Lewsader, Hyun-Joo Jeon, and James Elicker. 2013. "Structured Tasks versus Free Play: The Influence of Social Context on Parenting Quality, Toddler's Engagement with Parents and Play Behaviors, and Parent-Toddler Language Use." *Child and Youth Care Forum* 42: 3: 207–224. http://www.deepdyve.com/lp/springer-journals/structured-task-versus-free -play-the-influence-of-social-context-on-zkocACotoE.

Lamont, Michele. 2000. "Meaning-Making in Cultural Sociology: Broadening Our Agenda." *Contemporary Sociology* 29: 4: 602–607.

Lareau, Annette. 2003. *Unequal Childhood: Class, Race and Family Life.* Berkeley: University of California Press.

Lazarus, Emma. 2002. "The New Colossus." Poetry Foundation. https://www .poetryfoundation.org/poems/46550/the-new-colossus.

Lazarus, Philip J., Shane R. Jimerson, and Stephen E. Brock. 2002. "Natural Disasters." In *Best Practices in School Crisis Prevention and Intervention,* edited by Stephen E. Brock, Philip J. Lazarus, and Shane R. Jimerson, 435–450. Bethesda, MD: NASP Publishers.

Leahy, Stephen. 2017. "Hidden Costs of Climate Change Running Hundreds of Billions a Year." *National Geographic* (September 27) https://www.nationalgeographic .com/news/2017/09/climate-change-costs-us-economy-billions-report/.

Levitt, Daniel, and Niko Komminda. 2018. "Is Climate Change Making Hurricanes Worse?" *Guardian* (October 10) https://www.theguardian.com/weather/ng -interactive/2018/sep/11/atlantic-hurricanes-are-storms-getting-worse.

Leschziner, Vanina. 2019. "Dual Process Models in Sociology." In *Oxford Handbook of Cognitive Sociology,* edited by Wayne Brekhus and Gabriel Ignatow, 169–191. New York: Oxford University Press.

Lewin, Kurt. 1939. *Field Theory and Experiment in Social Psychology: Concepts and Methods. American Journal of Sociology.* 44: 3: 868–897.

———. 1951. *Field Theory in Social Science*. New York: Harper and Row.

———. 1997 [1942]. *Resolving Social Conflicts and Field Theory in Social Science*. Washington, DC: American Psychological Association.

Lieberman, Mathew D. 2003. "Reflective and Reflexive Judgment Processes: A Social Cognitive Neuroscience Approach." In *Social Judgments: Implicit and Explicit Processes*, edited by Joseph P. Kipling, D. Forgas, and William Von Hippel, 47–67. Cambridge: Cambridge University Press.

Lin, Nan. 2000. "Inequality in Social Capital." *Contemporary Sociology* 29: 6: 785–795.

Lizardo, Omar. 2017. "Improving Cultural Analysis: Considering Personal Culture in Its Declarative and Nondeclarative Modes." *American Sociological Review* 82: 1: 88–115.

Lodging. 2019. "Americans to Spend Record $101.7 Billion on Summer Vacation in 2019." (July 8) https://lodgingmagazine.com/americans-to-spend-record-101-7-billion-on-summer-vacation-in-2019/.

London, Andrew S., Ellen K. Scott, Kathryn Edin, and Vicki Hunter. 2004. "Welfare Reform, Work-Family Tradeoffs, and Child Well-Being." *Family Relations* 53: 2: 148–158.

Lord, Walter. 1981. *A Night to Remember*. New York: Penguin.

Lorenz, John M., Cande V. Ananth, Richard A. Polin, and Mary E. D'Alton. 2016. "Infant Mortality in the United States." *Journal of Perinatology* 36: 10: 797–801.

MacLeod, Jay. 2019. *Ain't No Makin' It: Leveled Aspirations in a Low-Income Neighborhood*. New York: Routledge.

Maines, David R. 1993. "Narrative's Moment and Sociology's Phenomena: Toward a Narrative Sociology." *Sociological Quarterly* 34: 1: 17–38.

Maltin, Tim. 2011. *101 Things You Thought You Knew About the Titanic . . . But Didn't!* London: Penguin Group.

Mangan, Katherine. 2012. "Despite Efforts to Close Gender Gaps, Some Disciplines Remain Lopsided." *Chronicle of Higher Education* (October 29) http://chronicle.com/article/In-Terms-of-Gender/135304/.

Manove, Emily E., Sarah R. Lowe, Jessica Bonumwezi, Justin Preston, Mary C. Waters, and Jean E. Rhodes. 2019. "Posttraumatic Growth in Low-Income Black Mothers Who Survived Hurricane Katrina." *American Journal of Orthopsychiatry* 89: 2: 144–158.

Marcoulatos, Iordanis. 2010. "Merleau-Ponty and Bourdieu on Embodied Significance." *Journal for the Theory of Social Behaviour* 31: 1: 1–27.

Martin, John Levi. 2010. "Life's a Beach but You're an Ant, and Other Unwelcome News for the Sociology of Culture." *Poetics* 38: 2: 229–244.

Mascaro, Jennifer S., Kelly E. Rentscher, Patrick D. Hackett, Matthias R. Mehl, and James K. Rilling. 2017. "Child Gender Influences Paternal Behavior, Language, and Brain Function." *Behavioral Neuroscience* 131: 3: 262.

McAdams, Dan P. 2013. "The Psychological Self as Actor, Agent, and Author." *Perspectives on Psychological Science* 8: 3: 272–295.

McConnell, Allen R., and Jill M. Leibold. 2001. "Relations among the Implicit Association Test, Discriminatory Behavior, and Explicit Measures of Racial Attitudes." *Journal of Experimental Social Psychology* 37: 5: 435–442.

McDonald, Steve, and Jacob C. Day. 2010. "Race, Gender, and the Invisible Hand of Social Capital." *Sociology Compass* 4: 7: 532–543.

Mead, George Herbert. 1932. *The Philosophy of the Present*. Chicago: The University of Chicago Press.

Meece, Judith, and Charlotte Agger. 2018. "Achievement Motivation in Education." In *Oxford Research Encyclopedia of Education*. New York: Oxford University Press. https://oxfordre.com/view/10.1093/acrefore/9780190264093.001.0001/acrefore -9780190264093-e-7.

Merleau-Ponty, Maurice. 2013 [1945]. *The Phenomenology of Perception*. Translated by D. A. Landes. New York: Routledge.

Miceli, Maria, and Cristiano Castelfranchi. 2010. "Hope: The Power of Wish and Possibility." *Theory and Psychology* 20: 2: 251–276.

Miller, Claire Cain. 2017. "Why Men Don't Want the Jobs Done Mostly by Women." *New York Times* (January 4) https://www.nytimes.com/2017/01/04/upshot/why -men-dont-want-the-jobs-done-mostly-by-women.html?action=click&content Collection=U.S.&module=Trending&version=Full&region=Marginalia&pgtype =article&_r=0.

Mische, Ann. 2009. "Projects and Possibilities: Researching Futures in Action." *Sociological Forum* 24: 3: 694–704.

Mische, Ann, and Philippa Pattison. 2000. "Composing a Civic Arena: Publics, Projects and Social Settings." *Poetics* 27: 2–3: 163–194.

Mohr, John W., Christopher A. Bail, Margaret Frye, Jennifer C. Lena, Omar Lizardo, Terrence E. McDonnell, Ann Mische, Iddo Tavory, and Frederick F. Wherry. 2020. *Measuring Culture*. New York: Columbia University Press.

Morgan, Rachel E., and Jennifer Truman. 2020. "Criminal Victimization 2019." Bureau of Justice Statistics. (September) https://www.bjs.gov/content/pub/pdf /cv19.pdf.

Murray, Mark. 2018. "NBC News/WSJ Poll: Economic Satisfaction under Trump Isn't Helping His Party's 2018 Chances." NBC News (June 7) https://www .nbcnews.com/politics/first-read/poll-economic-satisfaction-under-trump-isn -t-helping-his-party-n880721.

National Alliance to End Homelessness 2021. "State of Homelessness: 2021 Edition." https://endhomelessness.org/homelessness-in-america/homelessness-statistics /state-of-homelessness-2021/.

National Cancer Institute. 2020. "Cancer Disparities." (November 17) https://www
.cancer.gov/about-cancer/understanding/disparities.

———. 2021. "Financial Toxicity and Cancer Treatment (PDQ®)—Health Care
Professional Version." (June 22) https://www.cancer.gov/about-cancer/managing
-care/track-care-costs/financial-toxicity-hp-pdq.

National Center for Education Statistics. 2019a. "Postsecondary Graduation Rates."
(February) http://nces.ed.gov/programs/raceindicators/indicator_red.asp.

———. 2019b. *Status and Trends in the Education of Racial and Ethnic Groups.* https://
nces.ed.gov/programs/raceindicators/highlights.asp.

———. 2020a. "Digest of Education Statistics." (October) https://nces.ed.gov/programs
/digest/2020menu_tables.asp.

———. 2020b. *The Condition of Education.* https://nces.ed.gov/pubsearch/pubsinfo
.asp?pubid=2020144.

———. 2021. "Report on the Condition of Education." (May) https://nces.ed.gov
/pubs2021/2021144.pdf.

National Center for Health Statistics. 2020. *Health, United States, 2019.* Hyattsville,
MD: National Center for Health Statistics. https://www.cdc.gov/nchs/data/hus
/hus19-508.pdf.

National Fair Housing Alliance. 2017. "The Case for Fair Housing: 2017 Fair Housing
Trends Report." https://nationalfairhousing.org/wp-content/uploads/2017/07
/TRENDS-REPORT-2017-FINAL.pdf.

National School Board Association. 2021. "Homeless Students in Public Schools
across America: Down but Not Out." (July 27) https://www.nsba.org/Perspectives
/2021/homeless-students.

National Student Clearinghouse Research Center. 2018. "High School Benchmarks
2018." https://nscresearchcenter.org/hsbenchmarks2018/.

Neal, Zachary P. 2018. "A Sign of the Times? Weak and Strong Polarization in the U.S.
Congress, 1973–2016." *Social Networks* 60: 1: 103–112. https://doi.org/10.1016/j
.socnet.2018.07.007.

Newport, Frank. 2018. "Looking into What Americans Mean by Working Class."
Gallup (August 3) https://news.gallup.com/opinion/polling-matters/239195
/looking-americans-mean-working-class.aspx.

———. 2020. "American Attitudes and Race." Gallup (June 17) https://news.gallup
.com/opinion/polling-matters/312590/american-attitudes-race.aspx.

New York Times/CBS News Poll. 2016. "The *New York Times*/CBS News Poll on U.S.
Race Relations." (May 4) https://www.nytimes.com/interactive/2015/05/05/us
/05poll-doc.html.

Nodjimbadem, Katie. 2017. "The Racial Segregation of American Cities Was Anything
but Accidental." *Smithsonian Magazine* (May 30) https://www.smithsonianmag

.com/history/how-federal-government-intentionally-racially-segregated-american-cities-180963494/.

Norman, Jim. 2018. "Optimism about Availability of Good Jobs Hits New Heights." Gallup (May 21) https://news.gallup.com/poll/234587/optimism-availability-good-jobs-hits-new-heights.aspx.

NurseJournal. 2021. "Covid-19 Vaccine: Obstacles among Minority Communities." (June 4) https://nursejournal.org/articles/covid19-vaccine-obstacles-among-minority-communities/.

O'Loughlin, Michael, Marilyn Charles, Jay Crosby, Secil Arac-Orhun, and Montana Queler. 2014. "Closing the Gap: Narrating the Prose of Severe Psychic Suffering." *Psychoanalysis, Culture & Society* 19: 1: 98–106.

Orbuch, Terri L. 1997. "People's Accounts Count: The Sociology of Accounts." *Annual Review of Sociology* 23: 1: 455–478.

O'Sullivan, Owen P. 2015. "The Neural Basis of Always Looking on the Bright Side." *Dialogues in Philosophy, Mental and Neuro Sciences* 8: 1: 11–15.

Oyserman, Daphna, and Stephanie Fryberg. 2006. "The Possible Selves of Diverse Adolescents: Content and Function across Gender, Race and National Origin." *Possible Selves: Theory, Research, and Applications* 2: 4: 17–39.

Padavic, Irene, and Barbara Reskin. 2002. *Women and Men at Work.* 2nd ed. Thousand Oaks, CA: Pine Forge Press.

Park, Kiwoong, and Tse-Chuan Yang. 2021. "The Wealth-Health Relationship by Race/Ethnicity: Evidence from a Longitudinal Perspective." *Sociological Forum* 36: 4: 916–938.

Parker, Kim. 2015. "Despite Progress, Women Still Bear Heavier Load Than Men in Balancing Work and Family." Pew Research Center (March 10) http://www.pewresearch.org/fact-tank/2015/03/10/women-still-bear-heavier-load-than-men-balancing-work-family/.

Parker, Kim, Juliana Menasce, Rich Morin Horowitz, and Mark Hugo Lopez. 2015. "Multiracial in America: Proud, Diverse and Growing in Numbers." Pew Research Center (June 11) https://www.pewresearch.org/social-trends/2015/06/11/multiracial-in-america/.

Patterson, Orlando. 2014. "Making Sense of Culture." *Annual Review of Sociology* 40: 1–30.

PBS Newshour. 2020. "With Mass Protests over Systemic Racism, People Trade 1 Health Risk for Another." (June 8) https://www.pbs.org/newshour/show/with-mass-protests-over-systemic-racism-people-trade-1-health-risk-for-another.

Pemberton, Antony, and Pauline G. M. Aarten. 2018. "Narrative in the Study of Victimological Processes in Terrorism and Political Violence: An Initial Exploration." *Studies in Conflict and Terrorism* 41: 7: 541–556.

Pemberton, Antony, Pauline G. M. Aarten, and Eva Mulder. 2019. "Stories as Property: Narrative Ownership as a Key Concept in Victims' Experiences with Criminal Justice." *Criminology and Criminal Justice* 19: 4: 404–420.

Petersen, Alan. 2015. *Hope in Health: The Socio-Politics of Optimism*. Basingstoke: Palgrave Macmillan.

Petersen, Alan, and Iain Wilkinson. 2014. "Editorial Introduction: The Sociology of Hope in Contexts of Health, Medicine, and Healthcare." *Health* 19: 2: 113–118. https://journals.sagepub.com/doi/pdf/10.1177/1363459314555378.

Pettman, Ralph. 2008. "On Hoping." In *Intending the World: A Phenomenology of International Affairs*, 184–208. Carlton: Melbourne University Press.

Pew Research Center. 2017a. "The Partisan Divide on Political Values Grows Even Wider." (October 5) https://www.people-press.org/2017/10/05/the-partisan-divide-on-political-values-grows-even-wider/.

———. 2017b. "Most Americans Say Trump's Election Has Led to Worse Race Relations in the U.S." (December 19) http://www.people-press.org/2017/12/19/most-americans-say-trumps-election-has-led-to-worse-race-relations-in-the-u-s/.

———. 2018. "Positive Views of Economy Surge, Driven by Major Shifts among Republicans." (March 22) https://www.people-press.org/2018/03/22/positive-views-of-economy-surge-driven-by-major-shifts-among-republicans/.

The Philanthropy Roundtable 2021. "Statistics on U.S. Generosity." https://www.philanthropyroundtable.org/almanac/statistics/u.s.-generosity.

Pittman, Cassi. 2017. "'Shopping While Black': Black Consumers' Management of Racial Stigma and Racial Profiling in Retail Settings." *Journal of Consumer Culture* 20: 1: 3–22.

Polletta, Francesca. 1998. "Contending Stories: Narrative in Social Movements." *Qualitative Sociology* 21: 4: 419–446.

———. 2014. "'It Was Like a Fever . . .': Narrative and Identity in Social Protest." *Social Problems* 45: 2: 137–159.

Portes, Alejandro, Samuel A. McLeod Jr., and Robert N. Parker. 1978. "Immigrant Aspirations." *Sociology of Education* 51: 4: 241–260.

Putnam, Robert D. 2016. *Our Kids: The American Dream in Crisis*. New York: Simon and Schuster.

Rainey, Leslie Martin, and L. DiAnne Borders. 1997. "Influential Factors in Career Orientation and Career Aspiration of Early Adolescent Girls." *Journal of Counseling Psychology* 44: 2: 160–172.

Rampersad, Arnold (ed.). 1994. *The Collected Poems of Langston Hughes*. New York: Alfred A. Knopf.

Rauch, Jonathan. 2018. *The Happiness Curve: Why Life Gets Better after Midlife*. London: Bloomsbury Publishing.

Reed, Steve, and Malik Crawford. 2014. "How Does Consumer Spending Change during Boom, Recession, and Recovery?" Washington, DC: United States Department of Labor. (June) https://www.bls.gov/opub/btn/volume-3/how-does-consumer-spending-change-during-boom-recession-and-recovery.htm.

Reiman, Jeffrey, and Paul Leighton. 2016. *The Rich Get Richer and the Poor Get Prison: Ideology, Class, and Criminal Justice*. New York: Routledge.

Reimann, Martin, Gergana Y. Nenkov, Deborah MacInnis, and Maureen Morrin. 2014. "The Role of Hope in Financial Risk Seeking." *Journal of Experimental Psychology: Applied* 20: 4: 349–364.

Riegle-Crumb, Catherine, Chelsea Moore, and Aida Ramos-Wada. 2011. "Who Wants to Have a Career in Science or Math? Exploring Adolescents' Future Aspirations by Gender and Race/Ethnicity." *Science Education* 95: 3: 458–476.

Riegle-Crumb, Catherine, George Farkas, and Chandra Muller. 2006. "The Role of Gender and Friendship in Advanced Course Taking." *Sociology of Education* 79: 3: 206–228.

Riel, Virginia. 2021. "Siting Schools, Choosing Students? Protecting White Habitus through Charter School Recruitment." *Sociological Forum* 36: 4: 1028–1048.

Rolison, Jonathan J., Yaniv Hanoch, Stacey Wood, and Pi-Ju Liu. 2014. "Risk-Taking Differences across the Adult Life Span: A Question of Age and Domain." *Journals of Gerontology: Series B* 69: 6: 870–880. https://doi.org/10.1093/geronb/gbt081.

Rosch, Eleanor. 1973. "On the Internal Structure of Perception and Semantic Categories." In *Cognitive Development and the Acquisition of Language*, edited by Timothy E. Moore, 111–144. New York: Academic Press.

Rosen, Bernard C., and Roy D'Andrade. 1959. "The Psychosocial Origins of Achievement Motivation." *Sociometry* 22: 3: 185–218.

Rosen, Eva. 2017. "Horizontal Immobility: How Narratives of Neighborhood Violence Shape Housing Decisions." *American Sociological Review* 82: 2: 270–296.

Rosenbaum, Ernest H., and Isadora R. Rosenbaum. 2021. "The Will to Live." Stanford Medicine. https://med.stanford.edu/survivingcancer/cancers-existential-questions/cancer-will-to-live.html.

Ruane, Janet M., and Karen A. Cerulo. 2020. *Second Thoughts: Sociology Challenges Conventional Wisdom*. Thousand Oaks, CA: Sage.

Rzepa, Andrew, and Julie Ray. 2020. "World Risk Poll Reveals Global Threat from Climate Change." Gallup (October 6) https://news.gallup.com/opinion/gallup/321635/world-risk-poll-reveals-global-threat-climate-change.aspx.

Saez, Emmanuel, and Gabriel Zucman. 2016. "Wealth Inequality in the United States since 1913: Evidence from Capitalized Income Tax Data." *Quarterly Journal of Economics* 131: 2: 519–578.

Sampson, Robert J. 2012. "Neighborhood Inequality, Violence, and the Social Infrastructure of the American City." In *Research on Schools, Neighborhoods, and Communities: Toward Civic Responsibility*, edited by William F. Tate, 11–28. Lanham, MD: Rowman & Littlefield.

Samuel, Lawrence R. 2012. *The American Dream*. Syracuse, NY: Syracuse University Press.

Schiavon, Cecilia C., Eduarda Marchetti, Léia G. Gurgel, Fernanda M. Busnello, and Caroline T. Reppold. 2017. "Optimism and Hope in Chronic Disease: A Systematic Review." *Frontiers in Psychology* 7: 2022.

Schultz, Colin. 2014. "The Average American Household Lost a Third of Its Net Worth During the Recession." *Smithsonian Magazine* (July 29) https://www .smithsonianmag.com/smart-news/average-american-household-lost-third -their-net-worth-during-recession-180952191/.

Schutz, Alfred. 1967. *The Phenomenology of the Social World*. Translated by G. Walsh and F. Lehnert. Evanston, IL: Northwestern University Press.

Scioli, Anthony, Erica R. Scioli-Salter, Keith Sykes, Christina Anderson, and Michael Fedele. 2016. "The Positive Contributions of Hope to Maintaining and Restoring Health: An Integrative, Mixed-Method Approach." *Journal of Positive Psychology* 11: 2: 135–148.

Semega, Jessica, Melissa Kollar, John Creamer, and Abinash Mohanty Melissa Kollar, John Creamer, and Abinash Mohanty. 2019. "Income and Poverty in the United States: 2018." United States Census Bureau. Report Number P60–266 (September 10) https://www.census.gov/library/publications/2019/demo/p60-266.html.

Sewell, William H., and Vimal P. Shah. 1968. "Social Class, Parental Encouragement, and Educational Aspirations." *American Journal of Sociology* 73: 5: 559–572.

Sharkey, Patrick. 2013. "Survival and Death in New Orleans: An Empirical Look at the Human Impact of Katrina." In *From Slavery to 9/11: Readings in the Sociology and Social Psychology of Extreme Situations*, edited by Sidney Langer, 482–501. Boston: Pearson.

Sharot, Tali. 2011. "The Optimism Bias." *Current Biology* 21: 23: 941–945.

Shepherd, Hana R. 2011. "The Cultural Context of Cognition: What the Implicit Association Test Tells Us About How Culture Works." *Sociological Forum* 26: 1: 121–143.

———. 2019. "Methods for Studying the Contextual Nature of Implicit Cognition." In *The Oxford Handbook of Cultural Sociology*, edited by Wayne Brekhus and Gabriel Ignatow, 367–387. New York: Oxford University Press.

Silva, Jennifer M. 2019. *We're Still Here: Pain and Politics in the Heart of America*. New York: Oxford University Press.

Smith, David Woodruff. 2013. "Phenomenology." *Stanford Encyclopedia of Philosophy* (December 16) https://plato.stanford.edu/entries/phenomenology/#:~:text

=Phenomenology%20is%20the%20study%20of%20structures%20of%20 consciousness,is%20an%20experience%20of%20or%20about%20some%20 object.

Smith, Eliot R., and Jamie DeCoster. 2000. "Dual-Process Models in Social and Cognitive Psychology: Conceptual Integration and Links to Underlying Memory Systems." *Personality and Social Psychology Review* 4: 2: 108–131.

Smith, Kara. 2005. "Prebirth Gender Talk: A Case Study in Prenatal Socialization." *Women and Language* 28: 1: 49–53.

Smith, Samantha. 2017. "Most Think the 'American Dream' Is within Reach for Them." Pew Research Center (October 31) https://www.pewresearch.org/fact -tank/2017/10/31/most-think-the-american-dream-is-within-reach-for-them/.

Smith, Tom William, and Jaesok Son. 2014. *Measuring Occupational Prestige on the 2012 General Social Survey*. Chicago: NORC at the University of Chicago.

Snyder, C. R., Lori M. Irving, and John R. Anderson. 1991. "Hope and Health." *Handbook of Social and Clinical Psychology: The Health Perspective* 162: 285–305.

Social Science Research Council. 2021. "Quick Facts: Overall Wellbeing." Measure of America. https://measureofamerica.org/the-measure-of-america-2010-2011 -book/quick-facts/#:~:text=Asian%20Americans%20enjoy%20the%20lon- gest%20life%20expectancy%20of,today.%20They%20live%2C%20on%20aver- age%20to%2083.5%20years.

Somers, Margaret R. 1994. "The Narrative Constitution of Identity: A Relational and Network Approach." *Theory and Society* 23: 5: 605–649.

Sonnert, G. 2009. "Parents Who Influence Their Children to Become Scientists: Effects of Gender and Parental Education." *Social Studies of Science* 39: 6: 927–941.

Spencer, Renee, Michelle Porche, and Deborah Tolman. 2003. "We've Come a Long Way—Maybe: New Challenges for Gender Equity in Education." *Teachers College Record* 105: 9: 1774–1807.

Spencer, Steven J., Christine Logel, and Paul G. Davies. 2016. "Stereotype Threat." *Annual Review of Psychology* 67: 415–437.

Stake, Jayne E., and Shannon D. Nickens. 2005. "Adolescent Girls' and Boys' Science Peer Relationships and Perceptions of the Possible Self as Scientist." *Sex Roles* 52: 1–2: 1–11.

Stanford Children's Health. 2021. "Cognitive Development in the Teen Years." https:// www.stanfordchildrens.org/en/topic/default?id=cognitive-development-90 -P01594.

Statista. 2019a. "Number of Existing Homes Sold in the United States from 2005 to 2020 (in Million Units)." (July 19) https://www.statista.com/statistics/226144 /us-existing-home-sales/.

————. 2019b. "Sales Price of New Single-Family Homes in the United States from 2000 to 2018 (in Thousand U.S. Dollars)." (July 1) https://www.statista.com /statistics/346940/sales-price-of-new-single-family-homes-usa/.

————.2021. "Life Expectancy at Birth in the United States in 2018 by Race, Hispanic Origin and Sex." (February 22) https://www.statista.com/statistics/260410/life -expectancy-at-birth-in-the-us-by-race-hispanic-origin-and-sex/.

Stern, Susannah R. 2004. "Expressions of Identity Online: Prominent Features and Gender Differences in Adolescents' World Wide Web Home Pages." *Journal of Broadcasting and Electronic Media* 48: 2: 218–243.

Stiglitz, Joseph E. 2018. "The American Economy Is Rigged and What We Can Do about It." *Scientific American* (November 1) https://www.scientificamerican.com /article/the-american-economy-is-rigged/.

Strayhorn, Terrell L. 2009. "Different Folks, Different Hopes: The Educational Aspirations of Black Males in Urban, Suburban, and Rural High Schools." *Urban Education* 44: 6: 710–731.

Suárez-Orozco, Carola, and Marcelo M. Suárez-Orozco. 1995. *Transformations: Immigration, Family Life, and Achievement Motivation among Latino Adolescents.* Stanford, CA: Stanford University Press.

Suicide Prevention Resource Center. 2020. "Suicide by Age." https://www.sprc.org /scope/age.

Swedberg, Richard. 2009. "The Sociological Study of Hope and the Economy: Introductory Remarks." In *Speaking of Hope: Towards a New Horizon in the Social Sciences,* 31–79. Tokyo: University of Tokyo Press.

Sweeney, Joanne, and Marilyn R. Bradbard. 1988. "Mothers' and Fathers' Changing Perceptions of Their Male and Female Infants over the Course of Pregnancy." *Journal of Genetic Psychology* 149: 3: 393–404.

Swidler, Ann. 1986. "Culture in Action: Symbols and Strategies." *American Sociological Review* 51: 2: 273–286.

————. 2001. *Talk of Love: How Culture Matters.* Chicago: The University of Chicago Press.

Taussig, Karen-Sue, Klaus Hoeyer, and Stefan Helmreich. 2013. "The Anthropology of Potentiality in Biomedicine." *Current Anthropology* 54: S7: S3–S14.

Tavory, Iddo, and Nina Eliasoph. 2013. "Coordinating Futures: Toward a Theory of Anticipation." *American Journal of Sociology* 118: 4: 908–942.

Thoreau, Henry David. 2020. *A Week on the Concord and Merrimack Rivers.* Henry David Thoreau online. https://www.thoreau-online.org/a-week-on-the-concord -and-merrimack-rivers-page6.html.

Turner, de Sales. 2005. "Hope Seen through the Eyes of 10 Australian Young People." *Journal of Advanced Nursing* 52: 5: 508–515.

Turner, de Sales, and Linda Stokes. 2006. "Hope Promoting Strategies of Registered Nurses." *Journal of Advanced Nursing* 56: 4: 363–372.

Turner, Erlanger A., Megan Chandler, and Robert W. Heffer. 2009. "The Influence of Parenting Styles, Achievement Motivation, and Self-Efficacy on Academic Performance in College Students." *Journal of College Student Development* 50: 3: 337–346.

Ullman, Michael T. 2012. "The Declarative/Procedural Model." In *The Routledge Encyclopedia of Second Language Acquisition*, edited by Peter Robinson, 160–164. New York: Routledge.

USAFACTS. 2020. "Homeownership Rates Show That Black Americans Are Currently the Least Likely Group to Own Homes." (October 16) https://usafacts.org/articles/homeownership-rates-by-race/.

U.S. Bureau of Labor Statistics. 2019a. "Highlights of Women's Earnings in 2018." (November) https://www.bls.gov/opub/reports/womens-earnings/2018/home.htm.

———. 2019b. *Women in the Labor Force: A Databook.* https://www.bls.gov/opub/reports/womens-databook/2019/home.htm.

———. 2021a. "Median Usual Weekly Earnings for Full Time Wage and Salary Workers by Race and Hispanic of Latino Ethnicity." (July 16) https://www.bls.gov/charts/usual-weekly-earnings/usual-weekly-earnings-over-time-by-race.htm.

———. 2021b. "Median Weekly Earnings of Full-Time Wage and Salary Workers by Detailed Occupation and Sex." (January 22) https://www.bls.gov/cps/cpsaat39.htm.

U.S. Census Bureau. 2019. "2019 Capital Spending Report Visualizations." (May 23) https://www.census.gov/library/visualizations/2017/econ/2019-csr.html.

———. 2021a. "Business and Industry. Time Series/Trend Charts." (December 20) https://www.census.gov/econ/currentdata/dbsearch?program=RESCONST&startYear=2010&endYear=2017&categories=APERMITS&dataType=TOTAL&geoLevel=US&adjusted=1&submit=GET+DATA&releaseScheduleId=.

———. 2021b. "Business Formation Statistics, Second Quarter, 2019." Release Number: CB19-105 (July 17.) https://www.census.gov/econ/bfs/pdf/historic/bfs_2019q2.pdf.

U.S. Department of Justice. 2020. "Bureau of Justice Statistics Releases Results from 2019 National Crime Victimization Survey." (September 14) https://www.bjs.gov/content/pub/press/cv19pr.pdf.

Van Duyn, Emily. 2018. "Hidden Democracy: Political Dissent in Rural America." *Journal of Communication* 68: 5: 965–987.

Venkataramani, Atheendar, Rourke O'Brien, and Alexander Tsai. 2021. "Declining Life Expectancy in the United States: The Need for Social Policy as Health Policy." *Journal of the American Medical Association* 325: 7: 621–622.

Wacquant, Loïc. 1998. "Pierre Bourdieu." In *Key Sociological Thinkers*, edited by Rob Stones, 215–229. London: Palgrave.

———. 2004. *Body and Soul: Notebooks of an Apprentice Boxer*. New York: Oxford University Press.

———. 2015. "For a Sociology of Flesh and Blood." *Qualitative Sociology* 38: 1: 1–11.

Weinstein, James N., Yamrot Negussie, Amy Geller, and Alina Baciu. 2017. "The Root Causes of Health Inequalities." In *Communities in Action: Pathways to Health Equity*, edited by James N. Weinstein, Amy Geller, Yamrot Negussie and Alina Baciu, 99–184. Washington, DC: National Academies Press.

Weinstein, Neil D. 1980. "Unrealistic Optimism about Future Life Events." *Journal of Personality and Social Psychology* 39: 5: 806–817.

Weinstein, Neil D., and William M. Klein. 1996. "Unrealistic Optimism: Present and Future." *Journal of Social and Clinical Psychology* 15: 1: 1–8.

Weller, Chris. 2015. "Chronic Stress Is Killing People in Poverty, Women Especially: CDC Report." *Medical Daily* (June 2) https://www.medicaldaily.com/chronic-stress-killing-people-poverty-women-especially-cdc-report-336170.

Wenham, Clare, Julia Smith, Sara E. Davies, Huiyun Feng, Karen A. Grépin, Sophie Harman, Asha Herten-Crabb, and Rosemary Morgan. 2020. "Women Are Most Affected by Pandemics—Lessons from Past Outbreaks." *Nature* 583: 194–198. https://www.nature.com/articles/d41586-020-02006-z.

Wilson, William Julius. 2011. *When Work Disappears: The World of the New Urban Poor*. New York: Vintage.

Winne, Philip H., and John C. Nesbit. 2010. "The Psychology of Academic Achievement." *Annual Review of Psychology* 61: 653–678.

World Population Review. 2021. "Homeless Population by State, 2021." https://worldpopulationreview.com/state-rankings/homeless-population-by-state.

Wuthnow, Robert. 2019. *The Left Behind: Decline and Rage in Small-Town America*. Princeton, NJ: Princeton University Press.

Yamane, David. 2000. "Narrative and Religious Experience." *Sociology of Religion* 61: 2: 171–189.

Zanolli, Lauren. 2020. "'A Perfect Storm': Poverty and Race Add to COVID-19 Toll in U.S. Deep South." *Guardian* (April 12) https://www.theguardian.com/us-news/2020/apr/12/coronavirus-us-deep-south-poverty-race-perfect-storm.

Zeitlin, Maurice, Kenneth Lutterman, and James W. Russell. 1977. "Death in Vietnam: Class, Poverty, and the Risks of War." In *American Society Incorporated*, 2nd ed., edited by Maurice Zeitlin, 143–155. Chicago: Rand McNally.

Zhao, Hao, Scott E. Seibert, and G. Thomas Lumpkin. 2010. "The Relationship of Personality to Entrepreneurial Intentions and Performance: A Meta-Analytic Review." *Journal of Management* 36: 2: 381–404.

Ziegler, Albert, and Heidrun Stoeger. 2008. "Effects of Role Models from Films on Short-Term Ratings of Intent, Interest, and Self-Assessment of Ability by High School Youth: A Study of Gender-Stereotyped Academic Subjects." *Psychological Reports* 102: 2: 509–531.

Zipin, Lew, Sam Sellar, Marie Brennan, and Trevor Gale. 2015. "Educating for Futures in Marginalized Regions: A Sociological Framework for Rethinking and Researching Aspirations." *Educational Philosophy and Theory* 47: 3: 227–246.

Zuckerman, Arthur. 2020. "57 Titanic Statistics: Deaths, Passengers, & Survivors." CompareCamp (May 24) https://comparecamp.com/titanic-statistics/.

Index